Prison Architecture

Prison Architecture

Policy, Design and Experience

Edited by

Leslie Fairweather and Seán McConville

Architectural Press

OXFORD AMSTERDAM BOSTON LONDON NEW YORK PARIS
SAN DIEGO SAN FRANCISCO SINGAPORE SYDNEY TOKYO

Architectural Press
An imprint of Elsevier Science
Linacre House, Jordan Hill, Oxford OX2 8DP
200 Wheeler Road, Burlington MA 01803

First published 2000
Reprinted 2003

British Library Cataloguing in Publication Data
Fairweather, Leslie
   Prisons – Design and construction   2. Prisons – Design and
   construction – History   3. Prisons – Design and construction
   – Psychological aspects   4. Prisons – Design and construction
   – Social aspects
   I. Title   II. McConville, Seán
   725.6

ISBN 0 7506 4212 2

Library of Congress Cataloguing in Publication Data
Prison architecture: policy, design, and experience/edited by Leslie Fairweather and
Seán McConville.
   p. cm.
   Includes bibliographical references and index.
   ISBN 0 7506 4212 2
   I. Prisons – Design and construction – Great Britain.   I. Fairweather, Leslie.
   II. McConville, Seán

HV8829.GB P75
725'.6'0941–dc21   00–038090

For information on all Architectural Press publications
visit our website at www.architecturalpress.com

Composition by Scribe Design, Gillingham, Kent, UK

Transferred to digital printing 2005

Printed and bound by Antony Rowe Ltd, Eastbourne

Contents

Plates

Illustrations and acknowledgements

Contributors

Elaine Bailey is a chartered civil and structural engineer. She spent 17 years as a consultant in the construction industry before taking an MBA at Imperial College. She joined the Prison Service as Head of Construction Unit where she guided the Service through the biggest and fastest building programme that it had ever undertaken. Elaine was promoted to Director of Security in the Prison Service before leaving to become Managing Director of Premier Prison Services Ltd.

Sir Andrew Derbyshire is President, formerly Chairman of the RMJM group – a multi-disciplinary practice of about 500 architects, engineers and planners working in six countries. He has extensive knowledge of the architecture of incarceration which includes experience of innovative prison design both as a Director of RMJM and member of the PSA Board 1975–9.

Ian Dunbar CB was one time governor in the English Prison Service, and has been a member of the Prisons Board for nine years, first as Regional Director South West, then as Director of Inmate Administration. He has been a member of Control Review Committee since 1984 and author of *Sense of Direction* 1985. He is now retired.

Leslie Fairweather is a Chartered Architect with a lifelong interest in prisons as consultant, writer and broadcaster. Formerly architect in general practice; Editor of The Architects' Journal; MD and Chairman of MBC Architectural Press and Building Publications.

Michael Gander (Special Projects Director, Premier Prison Services Ltd.) has had 25 years' experience in the Prison Service including ten as in-charge Prison Governor. He was Governor of HM Prison Norwich from 1990–93 and was temporarily seconded to the governing strength of HM Prison Manchester during the major riot. From 1988–90 he was Operational Adviser (P4 Division) with responsibility for female imprisonment policy and the case management of all female long term and life sentenced prisoners.

Wm. Scott Higgins (Chief of Design and Construction, Federal Bureau of Prisons) has spent 30 years with the Bureau, holding architect and management positions in the Washington Central Office and the Dallas regional office. He has, since 1983, been responsible for the design and construction of all new institutions for the Federal Prison System.

Jean François Jodry is a French architect with a private practice specializing in urban development and housing. In 1997 he was the consultant architect for the Evaluation Committee (13 000 places programme).

James Kessler is a recognized specialist in criminal justice architecture. As a Senior Principal at Hellmuth, Obata + Kassabaum Inc., one of the largest architectural practices in the world, he serves as Director of the Washington DC Criminal Justice Focus Group. A graduate of Yale University School of Architecture, James Kessler's design work has been published extensively and he frequently speaks to the community and professional organizations in support of innovative and responsive correctional design.

Seán McConville is Professor of Criminal Justice at Queen Mary & Westfield College, University of London. His interests include historical, contemporary and comparative studies of penal policy and administration. He has taught and researched on both sides of the Atlantic, and has advised various government and parliamentary bodies.

Professor Norval Morris is an Emeritus Professor at the University of Chicago School of Law. He has taught and researched in Britain, the United States and Australia and has held many consultancies and posts of responsibility in connection with criminal justice in the U.S.

General Sir David Ramsbotham (HM Chief Inspector of Prisons) became an officer in the Royal Green Jackets in 1958, and subsequently served in a wide variety of posts, at home and abroad. He retired from his final post as Adjutant General in 1993. On 1 December 1995 he was appointed HM Chief Inspector of Prisons, and elected a Council member of the International Institute of Strategic Studies (IISS) in September 1996.

Stephen Shaw was secretary of the Prison Reform Trust, 1981–99. He previously worked as a researcher in the Home Office Research Unit for many years, and in 1999 was appointed as Prisons Ombudsman.

Sir Richard Tilt was Head of the Prison Service for England and Wales and was the first Head to have been a serving governor. During his time in the Prison Service he served at prisons throughout the country. He retired in 1999.

Peter van Hulten (Ministry of Justice, The Hague) studied architecture at Eindhoven University of Technology. After several years with architecture agencies and as an urban developer, he joined the government buildings agency as an architect in 1982. He has designed several buildings and advised on a variety of subjects. Currently, he is a consultant to the government buildings agency.

Richard Wener is an environmental psychologist specializing in the study of the behavioural and social needs of people in built environments. He is currently head of the Department of Humanities and Social Sciences at Polytechnic University, in Brooklyn, New York. Professor Wener has conducted dozens of post occupancy evaluations of jails and prisons in the United States. His research has focused on factors involved in the success of the so-called 'new generation' facilities – particularly in reducing violent behaviour.

Michel Zulberty (Ministère de la Justice, Paris) is a Chief Engineer of bridges and buildings. He joined the Ministère de la Justice in 1996 and is Assistant Director in charge of implementing the multi-annual programme on the construction of courtrooms and prisons.

Foreword

Lord Hurd of Westwell CH CBE
chair of the Prison Reform Trust

I know of no-one who visits prisons who does not find the experience a daunting one. No matter what the status of the visitor (and, as Home Secretary, I suppose I was more likely to benefit from red carpet treatment than most), there is something inherent in the very deprivation of liberty which causes one to breathe more comfortably when once again outside the prison gate.

This is true whatever the type of prison and whatever its design. Yet the designs are far from accidental, albeit many prisons now represent the accretions of more than a century of penal history. The forbidding silhouettes of jails like Dartmoor or Armley or the old Strangeways were intended to denote power and to exercise a deterrent effect. In contrast, the beguiling red brick of Holloway suggests a degree of normality, as well as allowing the conversion for non-punitive purposes which its proponents ultimately intended. More recent designs – especially of top-security prisons – present a bleak face to the world: slabs of grey concrete so high that the passer-by can see nothing of what happens within.

Good prison design allows good relationships to develop between staff and prisoners, provides space and opportunity for a full range of activities, and offers decent working and living conditions. The Victorian radial prison designs had much to recommend them. Both staff and prisoners could feel safe because of the good sightlines, and the taxpayer benefited because fewer staff were required. If not quite a Panopticon in the way Jeremy Bentham intended, standing on the centre of a prison like Wandsworth you can indeed see into the far reaches of every wing.

In contrast, the prison designs of much of the post-war period, like post-war public architecture in general, have proved shoddy, expensive and just a little inhuman. It comes as a shock to realize that when Risley was built in the 1960s, no attempt was made to provide integral sanitation. The hotel corridor approach is claustrophobic and difficult to staff. Yet because prisons are enduring institutions (Jebb and Du Cane would have no difficulty recognizing Brixton and Wormwood Scrubs even today), the effects of bad designs echo down the generations.

For all these reasons, one might expect the issue of prison architecture – and the philosophies which it reflects – to have been the subject of much academic, professional and lay debate. In recent years, this seems not to have been the case. As Home Secretary in the 1980s, I do not recall ever being asked to adjudicate on matters of design. Nor was it a subject raised in official reports or in presentations by the pressure groups. Indeed, there had been very little public debate until the Symposium on Penal Ideas and Prison Architecture, which I attended, and on which the essays in this volume are based.

I hope publication of this book will encourage a wider debate – not just among prison practitioners and architects, but among the interested public as well. My guess is that most people would be surprised to learn of the enormous variation which exists between jails in terms of their size and capacity, and in the way they look. Think of the fortress at The Verne, Latchmere House in Richmond Park, an inner-city pile like Walton, or a top-security prison like Full Sutton, never mind the innovative design features in the new jails being constructed by the private sector. On casual inspection, they seem to have few features in common – save a perimeter wall.

But prisons are public buildings, and the public is entitled to have its say about them. How large should they be? Where should they be situated? What access should the community have to their facilities? What messages should their design promote: inclusiveness (prisons as part of their community) or exclusiveness (prisons apart from their community)? Is it possible for designs to encompass both ideas (since prisons should be good neighbours, even if their function is to separate out offenders from the community at large)?

Public interest in prison matters should be encouraged, not rebuffed. Besides which, we all know that fashions amongst experts – penal experts and architects no less than any other profession – can chop and change. After the War the judgement was that old equalled bad (because the very worst physical conditions tended to concentrate in the older local prisons) while new equalled good (because there were newer buildings in the so-called training estate). During my time as Home Secretary this was beginning to change. With the renewed interest in galleried designs, and the successful refurbishment and modernization of the Victorian legacy, it is now clear that the 'old–bad, new–good' division was simplistic and wrong-headed.

Since taking over as chair of the Prison Reform Trust, I have visited a dozen or so prisons – of all functions, shapes and sizes. Perhaps I gain a more accurate view of an establishment's performance now than I did as Secretary of State as I am no longer offered the red carpet. In general terms there is no question that the Prison Service is in markedly better shape. (Sadly, its performance against key performance indicators – and the improvement which it represents – has not yet entered public consciousness. Nor, for that matter, has it come to the notice of Parliamentarians, who remain woefully ignorant of most penal matters.)

Some of that improvement in performance has resulted from changes in prison architecture. This is most obviously true in respect of escapes. For every ten who got out at the beginning of the 1990s, only one makes it now – an astonishing statistic. No doubt staff have become more vigilant in the aftermath of the Woodcock and Learmont reports, but the principal reasons are pretty obvious; higher walls, more zoning with fences, and closed circuit TV surveillance.

But while architecture can permit or prevent good penal practice, it is not the whole story. Prisons are living institutions. People can make them work or they can make them fail. Security is more than high walls, barbed wire and sniffer dogs. All prisons can be run in an oppressive manner. Equally, the best governors and staff will make a go of things no matter what the physical conditions or restrictions of the site.

Prison design is not the be-all and end-all. But as a topic for research, analysis and debate, it has been neglected for too long.

Douglas Hurd

Preface

This book arises from a symposium on penal ideas and prison architecture, held in London in April 1998. The symposium brought together architects, academics, prison administrators and staff, private sector providers and penal reformers; we also benefited from the views and experiences of a former prisoner. Participants came from several Continental countries, the United States, Australia, Ireland and the United Kingdom – altogether a wide range of views, experiences and knowledge.

A similar meeting was held in 1976, and it is instructive to reflect on the change in circumstances in the intervening period. In the 1970s prison populations were generally static or declining, and there was little prison building or refurbishment. There persisted a belief that prison numbers would fall as social, environmental and educational programmes finally took hold. For a variety of reasons governments wished to hear this message (waning even then), one consequence of which was that prison building could be given a low priority in expenditure. Penal reformers shared in this thinking, and were likely to see poor prison conditions as yet another reason for reducing the use of imprisonment rather than campaigning for the improvement of existing buildings and for new construction. In the eyes of some, talk about building and updating was defeatism and a repudiation of positive social policy.

Many developed nations today face a rise in prison populations, unparalleled in numbers and rapidity of growth, and have committed huge sums to construction and operation. This dramatic turnaround arises to some extent from changing patterns of crime and the impact of the trade in illegal drugs. There has also been a shift in public and political attitudes towards imprisonment, and a considerable rethinking of the nature of sentencing and penal policy. New methods of prison construction, financing and operation have emerged in response to this historic growth in the penal estate.

It is quite remarkable that the outcome of these levels of expenditure has had so little study, especially since the consequences of certain designs, construction and management methods will be with us for many years to come. This is not to argue that prison building has been undertaken carelessly or negligently (though there has been some of that), but is rather a concern that a number of uncertainties and imponderables have not been sufficiently addressed. In particular, there has been little systematic examination of the relationships between the government departments that commission prison work, and the architects, operators and users.

Some problems are obvious. The rapid (and seemingly continuing) growth in prison numbers puts enormous pressures on administrators to provide, rapidly and economically, as many new spaces as possible. This process tends to be impatient of design debates, looks for ready-made solutions, and must raise questions about the design component of the process. Given the monopolistic position of governments as purchasers of prisons and prison services, can a healthy and productive balance be established between client and architect? What steps must each side take to strike this balance, if indeed they think it desirable? And what of the briefing process: even now, do architects receive sufficient information on prison life and management priorities, as well as the broader penal context? Are architects encouraged to present alternative design possibilities, and if not, are their professional capacities being properly used? Are users – prisoners and institutional staff – sufficiently involved? And what of local and regional issues – environment, materials and traditions of design?

Since the 1980s we have seen a steady expansion of private sector involvement in prison construction and operation, from finance and construction to management. Given the imperatives of commercial competition, is there a degree of confidentiality that inevitably and necessarily inhibits exchanges of information on vital topics? Might this blockage offset some of the advantages arising from competition in this sector?

At the heart of many discussions is a fascinating but perhaps unanswerable question about the penal aesthetic. The Pharoesque slabs of stone and gothic revival walls and gateways of the nineteenth century sought to express the prevailing penal sentiment of the times: crime would be suppressed – crushed – and the wrongdoer thoroughly and ineluctably punished by an omnipotent state. What is the image for our times? Do we seek a type of institutional normality – the prison blending into the high street, the shopping complex or health services? Do we want plainness and austerity to express our condemnation of crime and disapproval of the criminal, and contrast his or her lot with the variety, colour and affluence of our consumer society? Do we want to communicate these sentiments as homilies to the public and establish them as a part of the daily life of the offender under punishment? Is there a belief that architecture – design, embellishment, functionality and quality of finish – can have a moral influence? Can it awaken the sensibilities of the atrophied, bring order to those whose experience of the world seems chaotic? We can design for safety, economy and ease of operation, but with what certainty do we venture into design and construction as moral influence? Is this a speculation too far? Or, as we contemplate the years and whole lives of captivity, is it a question that cannot ethically be avoided? Can societies that treat home improvement as such a central part of their culture, leisure and consumption answer such questions in the negative?

The essays that follow address these and other questions in a variety of ways. Not all symposium contributions have been reproduced. Some were informal, and others were withdrawn from publication or were incomplete. We have attempted to convey the rich discussions of the symposium by summarizing and synthesizing certain sets of contributions, and we have also included in their original form (sometimes modified by discussion and comment) the majority of the papers that were offered. We are conscious that some of what was said has not been published, and that there were probably issues that should have been explored but were missed. In recognizing the limitations of the symposium, and of this book, we reaffirm our belief in the need for the greatest possible exchange of information in this field, and for systematic, expert and continuing evaluations of all aspects of the commissioning, design, user experience and the feedback process. Fiscal prudence and healthy politics require nothing less.

Without the generous and steadfast support of the Nuffield Foundation it would not have been possible to hold the symposium or to publish this book. We are deeply grateful to the Foundation, and to Sharon Witherspoon, Assistant Director (Social and Innovation). We also had much valued assistance from Professor Paul Paulus of the University of Texas at Arlington, Peter Lord of Austin-Smith:Lord, Architects and Designers, Ian Mutton and Brian Reynolds from HM Prison Service Construction Unit, Michael Warnock, Computer and Prison Service consultant, and Allan Brodie of the Royal Commission on the Historical Monuments of England. Linda Cox was the symposium co-ordinator, and dealt with the inevitable myriad of details (and a few minor crises) with enthusiasm, *sang froid* and friendliness; for this and for her labours on the book we are considerably in her debt. The conference staff of Queen Mary and Westfield College, University of London, responded positively and promptly to all our requests, and helped to make the symposium run as smoothly as it did.

Leslie Fairweather
Seán McConville

1 The architectural realization of penal ideas

Seán McConville

Prison construction is booming across the industrialized world. Since the late 1970s, around 1000 new prisons and jails have been built in the United States. Rates of incarceration had been fairly stable there for most of this century, but doubled in the 1980s and again in the 1990s. There are now around two million American adults incarcerated, a number that is currently being added to at a rate of between 50 000 and 80 000 annually. With an incarceration ratio of 645 per 100 000 of the general population, the United States now imprisons a higher portion of its population than any other Western nation. The gross numbers are in themselves astonishing; 17 states have smaller populations than America's penal estate. Even at state level the figures are formidable. By itself, California has the largest prison system in the Western world, having grown from around 20 000 in 1977 to 94 000 in 1990 and 159 000 in 1998. Despite an enormous construction programme, the state's prisons remain grossly overcrowded[1] and its Department of Corrections estimates that over the next decade $6.1 billion more will be required simply to keep overcrowding at current levels.[2]

The expansion in Europe has not been as great or dramatic, but it has been substantial in many countries.[3] In 1974, England and Wales had an average daily prison population of some 37 000; by 1990 this had grown to 45 000 and by mid-1999 to 65 000.[4] Between 1993 and 1997 there was an increase of almost 40 per cent. There has been a building programme to match. In 1978, less than a quarter of prison accommodation in England and Wales was twentieth century and purpose-built, and 40 per cent of prisoners were sleeping two or three to a cell.[5] Twenty years later there were 136 prisons, and in addition to the many new institutions there has been, since the mid-1980s, a major programme of refurbishment and

---

1 At the end of 1997 California's prisons were operating at 206 per cent of capacity (Bureau of Justice Statistics (1998). *Prisoners in 1997*, p. 9. US Department of Justice).

2 Various statistics on US prison construction have been brought together in an interesting essay by Eric Schlosser (Schlosser, E. (1998). The prison–industrial complex (*The Atlantic Monthly*, December, 51–7). Individual sets of statistics are to be found in the continuing series published by the US Department of Justice, Bureau of Justice Statistics.

3 See Chapters 12 and 13.

4 This number does not include some 2000 offenders subject to a home detention scheme using electronic monitoring. Those persons remain formally in Prison Service custody, though not in prison.

5 The Expenditure Committee (1978). *Fifteenth Report from the Expenditure Committee*, HCP-1, pp. xvi–xvii. HMSO. Those cells, it should be noted, did not have integral sanitation.

extension of existing stock. However, the pressure on accommodation is inexorable. The 1997 rate of incarceration in England and Wales – 120 per 100 000 of general population – is now the second highest in Western Europe, although still modest in comparison to Russia (687) and the USA (645).[6] Home Office projections envisage a prison population of between 64 400 and 92 600 in 2004–5.[7]

Yet for all this enormous expenditure, the nature of the connection between rates of imprisonment and crime rates is far from certain. Much crime is unreported, undetected, unprosecuted and unpunished, and when, through victim surveys, one looks at this hidden crime (the so-called 'dark figure'), one sees a declining or static picture. The most recent American criminal victimization survey reported rates of property and violent crime which were the lowest since victim surveys started in 1973;[8] the equivalent British survey shows no movement in overall crime figures.[9] The uncertainties of reporting, together with police, prosecutorial and sentencing policies, all control the volume and characteristics of those who pass from the offence to prison, and determine how long they will remain there; there is no 'natural' connection between crime and punishment.

The criminal law deals with a wide and heterogeneous range of activities – from reckless or dangerous industrial, environmental and road traffic matters to treason; from rape and murder to the smallest of thefts; common assault to large-scale fraud; and drug-dealing to animal cruelty. Despite this variety in crimes and dispositions, most of those who make their way to prison are young men with prior criminal convictions. Women, the elderly and the handicapped remain a small proportion of the prison population, but they have particular needs and often require special services and accommodation.[10] There is a tendency to overlook these groups, both in prison management policies and regimes and in design and construction, but there can be little doubt that they will grow in size and proportion, and their special needs will become more pressing.[11]

The vast bulk of prisoners have committed offences of violence or theft, although these categories have been substantially augmented in the last two decades by drugs and drug-related offences. In 1996, the

---

6　Research and Statistics Directorate (1998). *Research Finding No: 76*. Home Office.

7　Research and Statistics Directorate (1998). *The Prison Population in 1997*, p. 11. Home Office.

8　Bureau of Justice Statistics (1998). *Criminal Victimization 1997*. US Department of Justice.

9　Research and Statistics Directorate (1998). *The 1998 British Crime Survey*. Home Office.

10　Because of the increasing proportion of long sentences, there is an accumulation of older prisoners in the system. Between 1990 and 1996, the proportion of persons aged 35–39 years in American prisons increased by 66 per cent, 40–44 year olds by 75 per cent and 45–54 year olds by 71 per cent. (Bureau of Justice Statistics (1998). *Prisoners in 1997*, p. 10. US Department of Justice). In 1988, 40 per cent of persons convicted of felony in state courts in the United States were aged 30 years or older; by 1996 this proportion had risen to 50 per cent (Bureau of Justice Statistics (1999). *Felony Sentences in State Courts*, p. 10. US Department of Justice). The number of life sentence prisoners in England and Wales is now in excess of 4000, which is greater than the total for the whole of the rest of Western Europe. Between 80 and 90 lifers are released each year, but another 300 are sentenced (Prison Reform Trust (1998). *Prisoners' Views of the Lifer System: Policy vs Reality*. Prison Reform Trust).

11　Largely because of the 'war on drugs', the rate of incarceration of women has increased sharply. Between 1990 and 1996, incarceration rates for women in the US increased by 65 per cent (as compared to a 43 per cent increase for men) (Bureau of Justice Statistics (1998). *Prisoners in 1997*, p. 10. US Department of Justice).

offences of state prisoners in America were as follows: violence, 47 per cent; property, 23 per cent; drugs, 23 per cent; and public order and other, 7 per cent.[12] In federal prisons the figures are much more skewed to drug offences because of the different jurisdictional powers, and in 1996 violent offenders comprised 12.4 per cent of federal prisoners; property offenders, 8.4 per cent; drugs, 59.6 per cent; public order, 18.6 per cent; and other or unknown, 1.0 per cent.[13] In English prisons, 21 per cent of male prisoners had committed sexual or violent offences, 40 per cent property offences, 14 per cent drug offences and 11 per cent 'other' offences. No less than one-third of female prisoners had been sentenced for drug offences.[14]

Penal policy

Given the heterogeneity of offences and the multipurpose nature of prisons and jails, it is always misleading to discuss penal philosophy as though some kind of coherent and unified policy determined the disposal of all offenders. The careless or dangerous motorist is likely to be the subject of a deterrent sentence; a compulsive sex-offender may draw a reformatory or, more likely, an incapacitory one. A judge will want to keep the professional armed robber out of action for a lengthy period, both as retribution and as a deterrent to the offender and like-minded confederates. Indeed, to assert one sentencing priority in all circumstances would produce injustices and lead to a failure of public confidence in criminal justice. There have always been gaps between the rhetoric, high philosophy and academic and judicial debates about sentencing, the sentencing conducted in the courts, and what goes on in prisons; this is no bad thing, but it can deceive the outsider who does not know the system.

Since the mid-1960s, the ostensible penal consensus has moved from reform to retribution to incapacitation, all with surprising ease and, considering the moral, humanitarian and practical issues at stake, with surprisingly little research. The switch away from reformatory punishment exemplifies this process. It came in response to a set of rather undiscriminating empirical findings and a strange political alliance. Evaluation studies – measuring the effect of different types of prison programmes in terms of the subsequent offending behaviour of those who passed through them – suggested that the claims which were being made for various types of reformatory treatment could not be supported. Given the heterogeneity of offenders, the vast scope of their impulses to crime and the range of penal regimes and conditions, a general statement about the lack of success is hardly surprising. One approach might have been to redesign and refine programmes, better to match them with types of offenders. This was probably beyond the management skills of the penal managers of the time, and what actually happened was that it was proclaimed with increasing unanimity and fervour that 'nothing works'. This generalization met with a ready response from both the liberal and conservative ends of the political spectrum, while its sound-bite quality gave the notion considerable momentum.

12 Bureau of Justice Statistics (1998). *Prisoners in 1997*, p. 11. US Department of Justice.
13 Bureau of Justice Statistics (1998). *Prisoners in 1997*, p. 12. US Department of Justice.
14 Research and Statistics Directorate (1998). *Research Finding No: 76*. Home Office.

Liberals had long been concerned about unsubstantiated reformatory claims and the sloppy evasions of some penal administrators, who had acquired great discretionary powers. An offender sentenced to a one- to five-year term, for example, would be released when enough favourable reports had been obtained from the prison authorities to secure a positive decision from the parole board. In England, after 1968, discretionary release on parole could come after one-third of the sentence was served and was equally dependent on officials' recommendations. The English notion was that freedom should come at an optimum point, supposedly when the prisoner would be least likely to reoffend. Apart from the lack of evidence to support such a theory this amounted to resentencing, usually without the benefit of due process; it violated the separation of functions and powers basic to legality and democracy, and almost from the outset the scheme was criticized in England.[15] Release turned on prison behaviour as interpreted and reported by staff, and in any event of no demonstrable predictive value; a good prisoner might not make a particularly good citizen and vice versa. Great weight was given to such non-juridical factors as the state of the offender's marriage and the availability of accommodation and employment after release, and critics condemned the whole process for caprice, uncertainty and substantial injustice. There were calls for sentencing to be limited solely to the harm done by offenders and to their culpability; supposedly predictive characteristics, positive and negative, together with all factors not immediately relevant to the criminal process, should be excluded from sentencing.

Many conservatives were equally unhappy with the assumptions implicit in the penal process. Criminal justice (and much of civil society), they argued, is based upon the notion of free will, for without that there can be no choice, no culpability and therefore no justification for punishment; the very notion of moral capacity depends upon free choice. Emphasizing reformation as a prime objective of sentencing allowed the concept of individual responsibility to be diluted, since it suggested a deficiency – social or psychological – which had to be rectified, and this in turn implied that it was not the individual but his or her circumstances that were culpable. Ultimately, this doctrine suggested that all criminals, by Erewhonian logic, should be considered mentally ill. Even short of this extremity, social, cultural and psychological determinism was seen as an attack on the moral structure of society. The treatment philosophy had a malign political influence by allowing criminals to represent themselves as victims of circumstance, rather than as responsible persons who had made wrong and bad choices. By contrast, retribution unambiguously upheld individual responsibility, and made it clear that the purpose of the criminal process and penal system was to identify wrongdoers and to punish them to the extent of the harm that they had caused. Some who took this view also argued that repeated offending should attract cumulatively severe sentences, since persistent criminality aggravated culpability by showing contempt for society and the legal process.

Some liberal thinkers also rejected deterrence, arguing that it was simply a sub-set of reformation, achieved by severe and harsh rather than positive means. Those who have favoured deterrence in penal

---

15 For early criticisms of the operation of the English parole system, see Hood, R.
(1974). *Tolerance and the Tariff*. NACRO.

policy and administration have always emphasized behaviour rather than motivation. They have had little concern whether an offender refrained from further criminality because of a change of heart, or because of the unpleasant and painful memory of punishment (or knowledge of others' punishment). At the heart of deterrence theory is a belief that, in making decisions about crime, the offender at some point more or less rationally balances the rewards of crime against the risks and pains of being caught and punished. Certain liberal and religious thinkers objected to such a theory of humanity, particularly when applied to exemplary deterrence; others maintained that there was little distinction between reformatory treatment of a vigorous and unpleasant kind (and incarceration can scarcely fail to be either) and a regime which was in all its details explicitly, positively and intentionally deterrent. On grounds of principle they were therefore unlikely to lament the removal of deterrence from the penal agenda.

Conservatives were equally divided about the place of deterrence in criminal and penal policy. Some argued that it strengthened law-abiding reflexes in society – in the words of the nineteenth-century English jurist, James Fitzjames Stephen:

Some men, probably, abstain from murder because they fear that if they committed murder they would be hanged. Hundreds of thousands abstain from it because they regard it with horror. One great reason why they regard it with horror is that murderers are hanged with the hearty approbation of all reasonable men.

Deterrence and the notion of choice that it embodies appealed to those who could envisage choices being influenced by the apparatus of order. That choice might be governed by the apprehension of arrest, trial and painful punishment rather than by an ethical reflection upon right and wrong hardly mattered; the latter would perhaps have been more welcome, but it was the outcome that was critical. This simplicity in objective lent itself to empirical testing, which showed that deterrence was apparently no more successful in producing positive outcomes than reformatory treatment. These evaluations were no more sophisticated when applied to deterrence than they had been with reformatory penal measures.[16] The general message, which was nevertheless widely received, was: don't waste time with deterrent programmes, since the offender is incapable or unwilling to make choices, even when confronted with probably adverse consequences.

Of the principal penal objectives retribution and incapacitation are left, and these are notions that appeal to many in both liberal and conservative camps. The difficulty for retributivists is to construct a rational and defensible matrix that will produce a suitable sentence and regime for each crime and offender. Sentences and forms of punishment can be pulled out of the air (or, rather, the traditions of sentencing); it is much

---

16 A difficulty with many types of evaluation study is that they measure overall outcomes. This is particularly true with retrospective analyses, where it is usually impossible to match types of offenders to types of regime. Bearing in mind the diversity of offenders, this is a crucial component of any evaluation. More recent attempts to design reformatory or deterrent programmes have been careful to specify the type of offender for whom the regime is intended, together with his or her critical characteristics. This, together with a statement of what would constitute a positive outcome, enables more sensitive evaluation to be conducted.

more difficult – or impossible – to argue that these scales have a rational basis. It might be argued that they resemble a bizarre and hopeless kind of algebra in which random and changing values have to be determined without the benefit of quadratic equations. There must be a significant degree of arbitrariness in the assignment of punishment x for aggravated rape, y for large-scale fraud, and z for drug-dealing. Without a general logic, scales of retribution are open to ideological manipulation and are constantly vulnerable to the pressures arising from exceptional and outrageous crime, the volatility of public opinion, and the opportunism of politicians. The many changes in the sentencing 'tariff' over the years, and the great variation between countries (and sometimes regions and localities), underline this point.

The politics of punishment

In the United States, the modern politicization of penal policy has been traced to Richard Nixon's 1968 presidential campaign. When the heat of that battle died, however, penal policy largely continued to be conducted on a bipartisan basis. In 1970, Congress repealed almost all mandatory sentences for drug offences. State prison populations were falling, despite increases in the US general population, and the Federal Bureau of Prisons was planning to close some of its large and outdated prisons. The use of drugs as an effective campaign issue in 1973 by Nelson Rockefeller, the liberal Republican governor of New York, who demanded mandatory life sentences for all drug dealers, fatefully changed the context and tempo of criminal policy debates. Rockefeller had simultaneously sensed, hoped to benefit from and contributed to a swing in public attitudes towards drug addicts and their suppliers. The issue moved decisively from public health to the penal arena. Concurrently, social protection in the form of long mandatory sentences began to mingle with and gradually replace retribution as a leading factor in penal thinking. The cocaine epidemic that hit America's metropolitan areas in the 1980s moved beyond rational policy responses into the rhetoric and attitudes of war.

A similar if less extreme shift occurred in the United Kingdom a decade later. British penal policy (apart from extremists on both sides) had been almost entirely bipartisan. However, in the struggle between political parties there comes a moment when tactical needs overwhelm any desire for or tendency towards consensus, and the sense of what constitutes an acceptable and honourable competitive agenda is substantially modified. Such a point was reached in British politics in 1993 when Michael Howard succeeded Kenneth Clarke as Home Secretary. The latter occupied a middle position in his party, and had adopted an aggressive but still generally bipartisan approach to criminal policy. Apparently through a combination of conviction and ministerial ambition, Michael Howard decided to make criminal justice policy (for which his office was largely responsible) a spearhead in his party's electoral strategy.[17]

---

17 For a penetrating account of penal policy in England in the 1990s, see Dunbar, I. and Langdon, A. (1998). *Tough Justice: Sentencing and Penal Policies in the 1990s*, Ch. 7–10. Blackstone Press Ltd.

Michael Howard's central statement on criminal justice policy was that 'prison works'. Although he acknowledged that imprisonment could serve a variety of functions, what he primarily meant was that locked-up offenders could not commit crime.[18] From this it followed that longer periods of incarceration were better than shorter ones, and that it would be in the public interest for more rather than fewer offenders to be imprisoned. Both by exhortation (urging the judges and magistrates to make more use of imprisonment) and changes in the law, Howard set out to increase the prison population. His success in this task may easily be measured. The proportion of those sent to prison for indictable offences in the Crown Courts increased from 44 per cent in 1992 to 60 per cent in 1997. In magistrates' courts, the proportion doubled from 5 to 10 per cent.[19] This was the country's most radical change in criminal justice policy in more than a century and a half, and because it was made in the context of competitive party politics was bound to provoke a reaction from the other side.

Howard's counterpart in the Labour Party was Tony Blair, then Shadow Home Secretary. As with most of his colleagues, the experience of 15 years out of power had bred in him a determination to do what was necessary to put his party in office again. Labour, with its traditional insistence that social amelioration was a prime response to crime, was portrayed as overlooking individual choice and responsibility. Blair's response was the slogan 'Tough on crime and tough on the causes of crime'. In electoral terms this formulation proved very effective, and continued to be the basis of policy when Labour came to government in May 1997. Both components of the statement have since been addressed. Minimum and mandatory sentences have been introduced. There has not, however, been the same commitment to incapacitation at the heart of penal policy. Rather, certain types of offenders who are said to cause the greatest public concern have been selected for exceptional treatment – recidivists, sexual and drug offenders. The bark of this legislation is a great deal fiercer than its bite. However, even though the rate of increase of the prison population has slowed, the introduction of preventive imprisonment for a limited group of offenders will, over the years, cause an accumulation of long-term prisoners, the prime reason for whose incarceration is incapacitation.

Jails and local prisons

Jails are often omitted from discussions of penal policy, despite their core contribution to the administration of criminal justice. This indifference may arise partly from their limited range of functions. Jail policy and management are perhaps unattractive topics of academic, judicial and political debate, since they involve practical rather than philosophical issues. In the United States, sentences of a year or less are served in a jail; in England and Wales, short-term prisoners are kept in a local prison on a limited regime.[20] Jails and local prisons also hold untried and unsentenced persons.

18 *Independent on Sunday*, 7 October 1993.
19 Research and Statistics Directorate (1998). *The Prison Population in 1997*, p. 31. Home Office.
20 Jails ceased to exist as separate institutions in England and Wales in 1865, when the Prison Act 1865 (28 & 29 Vict., c.21) removed the distinction between them and houses of correction. A further consolidation occurred in 1948, when penal servitude was abolished. For the purposes of this discussion jail is taken to include the jail functions of English local prisons.

The needs of these short-term prisoners and the administrative structures necessary for their management differ in several respects from those required for medium- and long-term sentenced prisoners. Although the average daily population of short-term prisoners, convicted and unconvicted, is relatively small, the turnover is considerable. In the USA there are around ten million new receptions a year into jail. The English figures are not strictly comparable, but are still substantial.

A jail order can have one of several objectives – short sentences for relatively minor offences; to await trial, extradition, deportation or removal to a long-term prison; to force the payment of a fine or certain forms of civil debt, or punishment in lieu; a sanction for breach of the conditions of a non-custodial punishment; and punishment for failure to comply with an order of the court or (rarely) to purge contempt or to guarantee the appearance of a material witness. For administrators, the prime objective is to sort these prisoners out on first reception, to classify and separate them appropriately, and to keep them in safe and orderly custody, producing them as required. In some areas, jails are now major vectors of tuberculosis and other serious illnesses. The person newly admitted to jail is especially prone to suicide and at risk of attacking staff or other prisoners, or of being a victim. To minimize such risks requires services well beyond simple custody, including initial mental and physical health assessment, treatment and surveillance, personal and legal counselling, and an effective system of classification. The daily production of prisoners for personal or legal visits, or for court appearances, is a major logistical exercise. Well-designed reception blocks and all the other facilities for processing large numbers of persons are critical.

Receiving large numbers of prisoners from police and court custody, sometimes in unexpected surges, involves many difficult and risky tasks. Without prior knowledge of these prisoners, in many cases, and frequently with insufficient documentation, complicated judgements must be made about their needs, vulnerabilities and risks – and all within tight time constraints, with triage conducted by basic grade staff. These processes can reduce safety margins for staff and inmates alike. Physical security is only one answer, but it is an important one. The building must be adequate and appropriate to the level of risk, in order to avoid unnecessary financial and human costs, and its divisions must be swiftly accessible for the containment of disorder, fire or medical emergency. There must be several sub-divisions to accommodate the different categories that cannot properly be held together – men and women, adults and young adults, remanded and sentenced prisoners, those with short and long sentences, serious and less serious offenders, civil and criminal, the mentally and physically ill, the vulnerable, and those requiring high security. For all these divisions to function properly there must be a strong management system able to work under pressure and to cope with the crises that so frequently occur.

The architectural contribution

(a) Penal expression

Architecture has many components, including the mathematical, technical, aesthetic and ethical. The last two are of particular interest for our discussion. Since ancient times we have believed in the beneficial effects of beauty. Generations may differ in their definition of the beautiful, and at any given time there will be a wide range of views on the subject. There is, nevertheless, broad agreement on the requirement for proportion, harmony of parts, originality, clarity of expression, relationship with setting and quality of finish. One of the difficulties that became evident at the symposium from which this book originated is that propositions about the effects of aesthetic properties cannot be tested. We need to know about attitude, character, predisposition and sensibility before the experience of, for example, living in a beautiful place or building; and we need to be able to measure these attributes after the experience. We may test the short-term effects of simple, easily isolated stimuli, but longer-term and more general effects may elude us. When we add to the picture all the complicated differences in people's biographies and endowments, the separation of cause and effect is extraordinarily difficult; it becomes all but impossible when we are wrestling with an experience as diffuse as beauty or ugliness in a building or setting. Yet, like the concept of free will, we insist on the beneficent effects of beauty and the need to avoid ugliness, because in doing so we reaffirm one of the core values of our civilization.

Beauty cannot speak to all, and a building or setting of outstanding quality may fail to have an effect on a surprisingly large section of the population. Everyday preoccupations may mean that one lives amidst noble and harmonious buildings, but fails properly to notice or be moved by them (although they may, of course, have subliminal effects). But imagine an existence in which there are few countervailing interests, domestic preoccupations or shared joys and worries – what we call private life – what are the effects and consequences of the aesthetic experience, good or bad, in such circumstances? Does the absence of distractions and compensations intensify the effect of space and building? We cannot with any certainty answer this question, but it must worry us when we contemplate the necessarily restricted and sometimes bleak and arid nature of prison life.

The example of what has sometimes been an architecturally similar institution may be instructive. The medieval monastery or convent sought to eliminate the private and all material distractions to encourage and enrich the spiritual life. A plain cell and minimal possessions encouraged meditation on the transcendent, while intricate and elaborate rituals involving precious objects, the enactment of mysteries and the communion of prayer, response and music asserted the triumph of the spiritual over the temporal, the balance of individual and collective. And from the solitude of the plain cell the monk or nun came to this communal life in a setting of magnificent and soaring architecture, embellished with the finest of crafts of present and past times. Imagine the opposite of this. Not a glorious and sacramental vocation, but a carnal nature in toils; a cell whose plainness emphasizes exclusion and loss; communal activities conducted in drudgery in a setting that exuded social stigma and lack of trust in the shameful here and now – no craftsmen, no embellishment, nothing but penal functionalism. If that void is further filled by ugliness in personal relations and self-perception, what is the likely consequence?

The millennia of our Western civilization, and the even more numerous millennia of some Eastern civilizations, have reinforced the belief that exposure to beauty improves us and ugliness will tend to degrade. In the *Symposium* Diotina observes (with the approval of Socrates) that 'the deformed is always inharmonious with the divine, and the beautiful harmonious'.[21] It should follow that we should strive for beauty in our prisons – perhaps above all, for here we have fellow beings manifestly in need of restoration or improvement. However, no sooner do we formulate the words than their political absurdity echoes back: beautify prisons. Beauty, harmony and comity are rare qualities, prizes to be toiled for, a sober-minded citizen might expostulate; they must be reserved for those who abide by the law and embrace and serve our society.

Should the punishment and repression of crime lead us to a penal aesthetic? Should ugliness, vulgarity – or mere indifference – be a part of punishment? Few would go that far. Tasteless (or intentionally repulsive) food, coarse and ugly garments, exhausting and intentionally unproductive work, utterly featureless and comfortless cells, sleep-denying beds and rest-denying stools have all in the past been carefully blended into the regimen of punishment. These ingredients in the penal mixing bowl have been rejected, since they were seen not to work in the reduction of crime, and because they held up a mirror to the broader society which made it seem ugly and mean. We may comfort ourselves, perhaps, as we contemplate our modern hygienic and climate-controlled human warehouses, that we do not face a similar indictment. No act of petty vindictiveness on our part is required – simply the routine grinding of politics, administration, and public expenditure priorities, and adherence to the rules of public health and safety. Decisions are taken impersonally, by a dispassionate system, and we shall never have to face the ridiculous question of whether prisons should aim for a degree of transforming beauty or contrive to be places of ugliness and justly deserved aggressive discomfort.

All buildings are a combination of function and expression, and perhaps none more so than those where state business is conducted. The large castle and fortress-like prisons of the early nineteenth century showed the might of the state in a traditional style, emphasizing continuity alongside the modernity that replaced the makeshift, adapted or dilapidated structures of earlier times; it was almost as though the weight of stone would crush the malefactor and suppress crime. A different form of omniscience and omnipotence was emphasized in the new separate-system prisons such as Pentonville in London and the Eastern State Penitentiary in Philadelphia. In their cells, seen but not seeing, the prisoners' isolation and shallow personalities were turned terribly against them in a setting that could have been an ossuary for the living. The back-to-back interior cellhouses, arranged in tiers and enveloped in enormous blocks, emphasized twentieth-century America's industrialized response to crime and offending, with open-barred cells denying the inmate any individuality in the face of pervasive authority. Impersonality and uniformity were both functional and expressive in dealing with such large congregations of prisoners, from timetabled and synchronized movement to a common stock of clothing: here was equality before the law, the prison in mass society. The advance of psychology and social studies, rising standards of living and general affluence shifted the spotlight from the individual to the wider context of crime.

---

21   *Symposium*, p. 206, c–e (Jowett translation). For the ancient Greeks, beauty was to be found in the symmetry and proportions of the cosmos. Its discovery and contemplation was the framework within which to conduct both spiritual and civic life. (For an interesting paper exploring this aspect of Greek civilization, see Gammel, I. (1999). The philosophy of beauty: from Plato to modernity, and back again? Unpublished paper, Clare Hall, Cambridge.)

Prisons might compensate for defective upbringings and spoiled natures, and return the offenders to citizenship. Education, domesticity and therapy found expression in cottage-style prisons for women. More recently, a hospital or campus look refined, normalized and modernized this reformatory work being undertaken behind the walls – which were not supposed to be walls.

(b) Function

Framing incarceration in a civilized society is the fact that prisoners retain all their human and most of their civic rights, and that these can be abridged only to a certain point by custodial imperatives. Food, clothing, services and accommodation must meet regulatory, legal, constitutional and international treaty requirements. Having removed the individual's ability to provide for him or herself, and for personal security, the authorities assume these obligations to the fullest extent. All of this would seem self-evident, were it not for frequent and notorious lapses, both in the history and current practice of imprisonment. A tendency on the part of politicians and the public (and until recently, prison reform groups) to give a low priority to prison design and construction, and a residual notion that squalor and danger contribute to the deterrent and retributive properties of imprisonment, mean that prison and jail conditions will probably never cease to pose problems for public administration, and will feature in recurrent cycles of scandal, reformation and neglect.

For the principal element of the prison population, adult males, style has rarely obscured function. Efficiency, economy, security and control dictate uniformity in design and provision. Cells are identical, as is all that goes in them, from furniture and equipment, layout, lighting, heating and the rate of ventilation, to clothes and bedding. The amount, volume and nature of personal possessions are specified, down to the size and permitted contents of any display board. To avoid the ravages and costs of vandalism, carelessness or ignorance, buildings, equipment and decoration have been kept simple and durable. At its most extreme, this could mean tear-proof garments, a raised platform bed, a stainless steel sanitary unit and mirror, paper plates and papier-mâché utensils. The meals of food-throwers would be served in one-course mashed-together sausage form. Practitioners of the 'dirty protest' (excrement smearing) would be accommodated in well-drained wash-down units, with double doors or outside screens.

For the mainstream population, as the pace of incarceration has increased, standardization has become more central in prison architecture and design, allowing swift and economic construction and ease of management. Eating, sleeping, exercise, work and recreation are delivered in a functional, machine-like way – certainly to acceptable minimum standards, yet often remotely and with little human intervention, comfort or acknowledgement of the individual. In some modern prisons the inmates must have a sense of being the raw material of machines – but there is, of course, no product other than their durance.

Prisons are never without risk, to prisoners, staff or members of the public. Through neglect, ignorance or ill design, some verge on or become dangerous. Male prisoners, as all the sociological studies show, attempt to re-empower themselves and overcome the pains and deprivations of captivity by covert and illegal activities. These usually involve the extortion of their weaker comrades, trafficking with staff and inducing visitors to smuggle contraband goods (nowadays mainly drugs). To the extent that the prison regime permits promiscuous freedom of movement and association and is lax in surveillance and intelligence gathering, inmates will establish a counter-authority. Not a crack, cranny, hesitation or uncertainty will go unnoticed; not the slightest opportunity to undermine authority will be neglected: there is no power vacuum in prison.

Regime and management are prime defences against the malign counterculture of the prisoners. An administration that ignores human relations will soon find itself facing anarchy or presiding over an oubliette. However, while physical control and security are never enough in themselves, if they are sufficiently flawed management may become impossible. There are obvious rules, such as providing sufficient barriers against escape and the loss of internal control, the provision of clear lines of sight and the secure compartmentalization of the various sectors of the prison. It is elementary that access to staff offices and vantage points must be restricted or denied, and there must be no path to the roofs. Prisons are residential institutions where the inmates may have little control over their own movements, so it is particularly important that there should be effective means of containing fire and flood. The list might easily be extended, and the design and technology to achieve these various objectives almost endlessly discussed. These are very special buildings, overlapping in function with others, no doubt, but in totality – *sui generis*.

No matter how diverse the functions a building must serve, appropriate design and technology can be provided and a body of construction expertise developed.[22] The relationship between regime and building and technology – which is constantly shifting – complicates the picture. A prison run at a low level of custody will permit a considerable amount of freedom of movement and fairly large congregations of prisoners; qualification for assignment will include a low level of anticipated risk. Such an institution will require extensive workshops and recreation rooms and grounds, together with ample open-plan visiting rooms where prisoners may be given a certain amount of conversational and social privacy.

At the other end of the continuum, a maximum (or super-maximum) security prison will have few spaces outside of cells and their immediate vicinity where prisoners may move or (in very small numbers) mix with each other. Food and many other services will be delivered to cells. Remote communication, electronic security and a high degree of inmate and staff–inmate separation will be emphasized. Between these extremes of minimum and maximum security, however, there will be many levels of security and control, with a constantly shifting relationship between the possibilities and restrictions of the building and its technology and the requirements of management. This emphasizes the need to design flexible buildings, which in turn raises questions of expense in construction and running costs; it hardly makes sense to over-design and incur heavy costs for features that may never be used. Equally, a decision not to build to a higher security specification may be costly should there be a shift in the type of inmate entering the system. A prison designed for

---

22 The issue of user feedback and the briefing of architects and designers is discussed in Chapters 5 and 6. In any field of construction, the flow of information between the two sides may be problematic. Prisons, where the status of 'user' is uncertain, pose special difficulties.

maximum security but used for a lesser level of custody will incur unnecessarily high construction and running costs; a medium security prison used for maximum security prisoners will require expensive and almost certainly not wholly effective adaptation.

(c) The economic context

Regardless of the traditions and values of management, or even the desires of policymakers, are there other forces that will shape prison design and technology? The picture is unclear, but there are some significant trends. In all labour-intensive industries and services there has been a hugely significant introduction of cost-saving technology in the last two decades. Industries as diverse as banking and steel-making have shed and continue to shed large numbers of workers in order to improve, or in some cases simply maintain, their efficiency, competitiveness and profitability. This is a global process from which no modern economy can escape, while within countries political shifts and fiscal pressures have ensured that it is not confined to the private sector. Public or private standardized tasks involving large numbers of transactions most easily lend themselves to labour-replacement technology.

Until comparatively recent times, the micro-economies of prisons were heavily influenced by the doctrine of less eligibility – i.e. that the condition of the prisoner should remain inferior ('less eligible') to the condition of the poorest free man. Formulated by the utilitarians at the turn of the nineteenth century as a means of safeguarding the deterrent properties of the prison, the doctrine had the secondary but attractive consequence of restricting expenditure on prisoners' maintenance. Such issues are now rarely debated, and there is a general acceptance that prisoners should live at a restricted but reasonable standard, reflecting national wealth and wellbeing. Constitutional and convention obligations, and court judgments, prevent any retreat from this. Therefore, if savings are to be found in running costs they cannot come from reductions in prisoners' food, clothing, maintenance and care provisions. This is not to say that there can never be such savings; only that they are likely to be both marginal and elusive.

When capital replaces labour in any setting, the calculation is that the initial investment will, over time, pay the dividend of reduced labour costs. Prisons are particularly labour-intensive, involving a high ratio of staff to inmates and 24-hour coverage. The latter means that for every member of custodial staff on duty, there must be between 2.7 and 3.0 full-time established posts to allow for the proper coverage of three shifts together with sickness and training leave and holidays. If technology can reduce staff–inmate ratios (currently three custodial staff to two prisoners in England and a rather less generous ratio across the United States),[23] medium- and long-term savings on running costs will be considerable. Bearing in mind that in the United States (and to a lesser but still emphatic extent in Britain) the phenomenon of mass incarceration has been accompanied by fiscal restraint and tax reduction, the attractiveness – and inevitability – of high technology prisons becomes pronounced.

The application of this technology becomes attractive only from medium security levels upwards, since low security prisons by definition cater only for persons who can be trusted not to attempt escape or

---

23 Council of Europe (1998). *Penological Information Bulletin*, 21 December, p. 88.

to misbehave. Medium- to maximum security prisoners are defined as being likely to attempt to escape (although they have varying abilities to do so) and to pose progressively greater control problems as one passes upward through the security categories. The restrictions on their freedom of movement and association intensify, and only a limited number of choices are offered to them in their daily life. As noted, the sociological and psychological literature suggests that (excluding completely separate confinement) the tighter the custody, the greater the prisoner's compensatory and necessarily illicit counter-organization and culture. It is this dynamic of restriction and subversion that requires ever more intensive staffing and therefore greatly increased running costs. These are the circumstances where labour replacement becomes attractive, if not imperative.

Labour replacement involves a sharp reduction in face-to-face encounters between staff and inmates. Two-way cell communications, closed-circuit television, electronic door controls and remote surveillance from a control centre allow one or two staff to exercise control over 200–300 prisoners without difficulty. Refusals to return to cells and disturbances either in the cells or among the very limited numbers of inmates allowed to congregate in the common areas may be countered by summoning pre-designated staff from other parts of the prison and (in some US jurisdictions) by the use of immobilizing gas or firearms from the control centre or other secure access points. For prisoners under close custody, lockup is for 23 hours a day or more, with exercise taken in subdivided exercise pens. As the prisoner drops down the security and control categories more freedom of movement and association is permitted, but staff may still remain largely separated from prisoners, with design and technology used to ensure an appropriate level of control.

Apart from the cost–benefit considerations of such systems, a number of other calculations must be made. While staff enjoy a high level of physical protection from inmates, the lack of routine contact has certain managerial disadvantages – including an increased tendency on both sides to stereotype, with the concomitant decrease in intelligence gathering. In the past, prisons have relied on a combination of physical security and human relations and intelligence gathering to provide security and control. Balance between these is important, and too great a dependence on the physical component may weaken the system. (Although it is possible to envisage a regime of total imprisonment, this is unlikely to be legally acceptable, and any system short of that remains vulnerable when handling particularly difficult prisoners unless very generous staffing levels are maintained.)

If the rationale behind close custody enforced by design and remote control includes a declaration of the ineluctable power of the state, the so-called new generation high technology prisons must be deemed successful. If other objectives, including reform and retribution, are included, the balance of advantages and disadvantages becomes more difficult to read. As noted elsewhere,[24] the psychological effects of imprisonment are many and complex, and response to the built environment is only part of a much larger picture. For the vast majority of people, confinement in psychologically bleak circumstances with little positive social contact cannot be anything but brutalizing and dehuman-

24 See Chapter 3.

izing, and may engender despair, anger and long-lasting aggressive and destructive urges – none of which can be said to be in the interests of the broader community.

Conclusion

Two centuries ago, John Wesley observed of a prison keeper:

The first case must be to find a good man for a gaoler; one that is honest, active and humane. Such was Abel Dagge ... I regretted his death and revere his memory.

Even under the best conditions this is difficult work – fairly and humanely handling disturbed and sometimes extremely unpleasant, unpredictable or dangerous people. Prisons can and do brutalize staff, and the pressures to withdraw into defensive social arrangements and psychologically supportive compacts with other staff must be managerially counterproductive and against the ethos of civilized public administration. If design and technology almost completely separate prisoners from staff, one must wonder to what extent either group can treat the other as human beings. While the immediate consequences of this dehumanization may be restrained by physical barriers and appropriate organization, they cannot be totally eliminated; all but a tiny group of prisoners must at some point return to the community, while prison staff return to it daily.

These difficulties seem to come together in the context of mass incarceration, political momentum and the imperatives of fiscal restraint. Architecture and design offer many possibilities to contain construction and running costs, and humane, positive, labour-intensive regimes thus may become harder to defend. Changing public, political and legal standards should (although it is by no means certain) ensure that the squalid and haphazard prison conditions of the past do not return. However, this may be little reward if we instead provide conditions that are hygienic, nutritionally and environmentally sufficient, but socially bleak and psychologically brutalizing, with the whole enterprise being conducted in an ethical vacuum.

Architecture distinguishes itself from mere building and design by holding and promulgating theories of the nature of man, how people may live together, and the aspirations they might have. Like other humane enterprises, it cannot properly be conducted in bad faith – by pretending that our common humanity may be circumvented. While some currents in penological thought suggest that we can overlook the moral capacities of prisoners and staff, surely the whole ethos of architecture – its integrity as a tool in the refinement and development of civilization – cannot allow it to proceed without placing the human element at the centre of its endeavours. Yet architecture must always be more than a body of ideas; it also means groups of practitioners who attract clients and meet their needs. Without a strong and well-articulated body of penal and organizational ideas, policy may fade into mere responsiveness and design into a form of accountancy. Competition and the marketplace may in this, as in other fields, lead to critical decisions being made by default rather than principle and intent.

2 English prison design

Ian Dunbar and Leslie Fairweather

Introduction

An overview of the period since 1945 reveals many fluctuations in philosophy and public mood. Initially this was a time of slow swings punctuated by dramatic crises; then, from the middle 1990s, the changes suddenly became very rapid indeed. Overshadowing everything was the large expansion of the prison estate from 39 prisons in 1945 to 136 in 1999. The growth was not so much gradual as sporadic, usually unplanned, and in response to severe crises caused by overcrowding.

The period just after the Second World War started with penal certainties and hope – a belief that reform was achievable. However, gradually hope evaporated to be replaced by cynicism and despair, with one governor even referring to his prison as a 'penal dustbin', another as a 'human warehouse'. By the end of the century there was a more realistic expectation as to what could be achieved by imprisonment, but that aspiration was constantly being thwarted because of the huge upsurge in the prison population.

The problems of overcrowding stemmed initially from judges being encouraged to give prisoners longer sentences for their own good. Latterly this has developed into judges being encouraged, even more robustly, to give longer sentences for other people's good. Partly as a result of these considerably longer sentences, the hopes of rehabilitation were replaced by the despair of incapacitation. The belief that 'treatment works' was gradually transformed through a long period of 'nothing works', to 'prison works' and, latterly, to the more pragmatic policy of doing 'what works'. Concern about crime and prisons had not originally been political, but later it became highly politicized. Approaches to regimes had been relaxed, albeit with long periods dominated by a concentration on security. Today there is an even greater concentration on security.

Earlier stability was spasmodically and violently interrupted by disturbances by prisoners and industrial action by staff. Following the last of the major riots at the beginning of the 1990s, the report by Lord Justice Woolf[1] appeared to herald a period of change for the better. It raised expectations that prisons could be run more satisfactorily by minimizing their harmful influences. However, these gains were largely negated by continuing overcrowding and publicly-led demands for

---

1 Woolf, A. and Tumim, S. (1991). *Prison Disturbances April 1990*, Cm 1456. HMSO.

policy changes. In particular, the extensive nationalization of the post-war years was gradually replaced by contracting out, and this change in the prison service affected the building of new prisons.

What signalled the most profound change of the twentieth century was a challenge in the early 1990s to the assumption, held for many years, that prisons should be used only as a last resort. They were finally to be used almost as the first choice of sanction.[2]

So far as design is concerned, philosophy and buildings have rarely synchronized because of stop/go policies and the long lead-in time for designing and building prisons. Design has largely been backward looking, and related more to expediency and cost than to the latest penal ideas and philosophies. The contribution of prison architecture over most of the past 50 years, with a very few exceptions, has largely been negative. The period began with a vast inheritance of rundown and overcrowded nineteenth century radial prisons, and ended with the more hopeful management-inspired 'new generation' designs from America. In between were many doomed experiments aimed to deal with constantly rising populations. Every shape known to geometry was tried: radials, cruciforms, telephone poles, rectangles, courtyards, triangles, squares, T-blocks, and finally back to radials. Buildings ranged from the huge Victorian prisons with open tiers of cells in wings radiating from a central observation point, to smaller-scale closed-corridor prisons. More recently, the new generation designs enclose a large association space with two low tiers of cells spread along three sides (*Figures 2.1–2.5*).

Each change in design has been justified by a new penal philosophy or change in policy, management or regime, but the actual connection between policy and design is often tenuous and very much more difficult to establish.

Springboard for the future – 1945–1958

Alexander Paterson (1884–1947) was a dominant influence on the inter-war years and those immediately following, when there was a gradual liberalization of prison regimes and regulations. At the same time, courts used custody far less with no obviously dire consequences. The English penal and legal system was, at that time, acknowledged to be the best in the world, with a strong and developing emphasis on reform and rehabilitation as the primary aims of penal policy.

The 1930s saw the growing influence of the Borstal system for young offenders, which had been started two decades earlier, and the development of open establishments. On 4 May 1930, a group of young offenders was marched from Feltham, Middlesex, to a virgin site at Lowdham, Nottingham, where they built an open Borstal. This was followed by similar institutions at Hollesley Bay, Suffolk, and North Sea Camp, Lincolnshire. Such was their success that an open prison for adults was opened in 1936 at New Hall Camp in Yorkshire, which can now be seen as the start of the open prison experiment.

The open prison concept radically changed the face of the English penal scene and that of other countries. It enabled flexibility where

2 Dunbar, I. and Langdon, A. (1998). Prison work. In: *Tough Justice: Sentencing and Penal Policies in the 1990s*, Ch. 10. Blackstone Press.

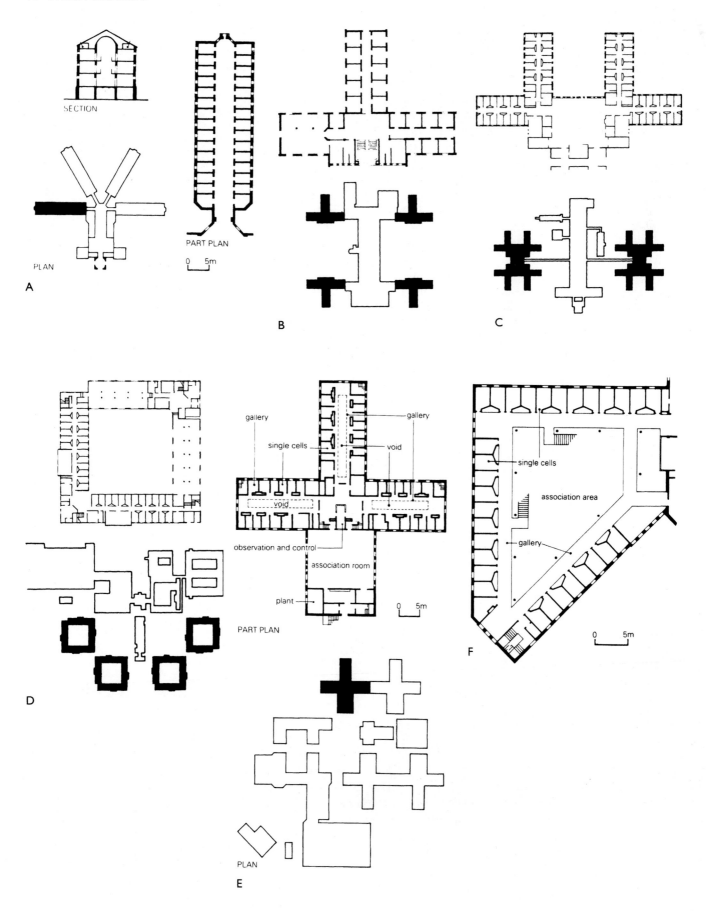

SECTION

PLAN

A

PART PLAN

0   5m

B

C

D

PART PLAN

gallery

single cells

void

observation and control

association room

plant

gallery

void

0   5m

single cells

association area

gallery

0   5m

F

PLAN

E

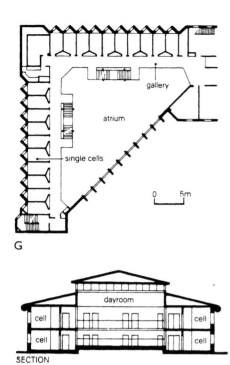

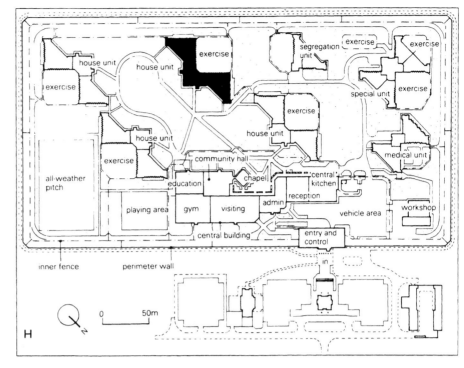

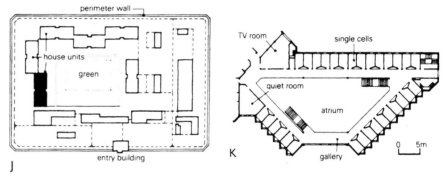

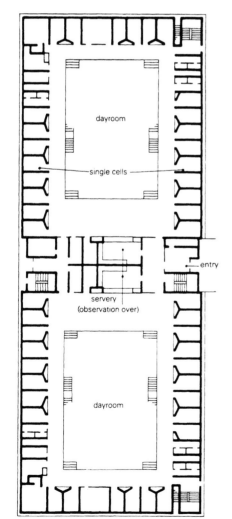

Figure 2.1

The development of prison plans from nineteenth-century radial prisons to twentieth-century new generation designs.

- A. Typical radial prison (Pentonville, 1842)
- B. Self-contained house blocks (Blundeston, 1963)
- C. Telephone-pole layout (Featherstone, 1977)
- D. Courtyard plan (Low Newton, 1978)
- E. Galleried prison (Bullingdon, 1991)
- F. New generation prison (Doncaster, 1993)
- G. New generation prison (Woodhill, Milton Keynes, 1992)
- H. Woodhill site layout (1992)
- I. Prison Design Briefing System (PDBS) prison, suggested plan and section (1992)
- J. PDBS prison, suggested site layout (1992)
- K. New generation prison (Lancaster Farms, 1993).

before there had been uniformity, and also increased the potential for greater contact with the outside world. Previously there had been active discouragement of any sort of community participation, which was reinforced by the symbolism of the high perimeter walls. The first separate open prison for men was inaugurated at Leyhill, Gloucestershire, in 1946. Its success began the open prison movement and ushered in the extensive use of dormitories, common because of the increasing use of old military accommodation.

Until then, there had never been any shortage of cellular accommodation; rather the reverse. In 1877, the number of prisons was reduced from 113 to 56. After 1918, a further 29 prisons were closed.[3] Indeed, up until 1952 only two new establishments had been built this century, those at Camp Hill, Isle of Wight, and Lowdham, Nottingham, where the last wing was finished in 1949.

After this period of retrenchment, the years immediately following the Second World War led for the first time to a period of expansion, from 39 to 59 prisons. Seven were in existing prison buildings, the rest were in adapted buildings of other types. No new prisons were built until 1958, when Everthorpe prison, North Humberside, was opened – the first new adult prison to be constructed in England in the twentieth century. Sadly, it was out of date before it even left the drawing board and hardly reflected the high aims of the Prison Commission, which commented with dismay:[4]

Even more remarkable than the innovations is the evidence of how little the basic design has altered in a century. Here are the familiar double blocks . . . above all, here are the usual open halls. They may not be so dauntingly tall, but the idea is the same as every prison since Pentonville, when isolation rather than training was the chief demand. Others were built when the aim was to oppress the prisoner.

Whereas prisons had formerly been monolithic, uniform and intimidating, now almost any sort of building was dragged into service and designated as a prison. Old convict prisons existed alongside converted country mansions, public buildings and hutted camps.

With the passing of the 1948 Criminal Justice Act it looked as though, with other measures in the emerging welfare state, a prison service might emerge that could make a positive contribution in keeping crime at bay and helping those in its custody. Except for persistent offenders, the Act was designed to further the existing practices for keeping offenders out of prison. The uses of fines and probation were redefined to enable this to happen. The Act enshrined the reformative aim of the Prison Service:[5]

The purposes of training and treatment of convicted prisoners shall be to establish in them the will to lead a good and useful life on discharge, and fit them to do so.

It was a time of growing penal optimism. With these measures in place it was anticipated that the rise in crime which had occurred during the war would return to the reduced figures of the inter-war years. This was

---

3 Fox, L. (1952). *The English Prison and Borstal Systems,* Ch. 7. Routledge & Kegan Paul.
4 *The Times,* 19 May 1959.
5 Rule 6 of the rules published in accordance with the Criminal Justice Act 1948.

another false hope; in fact, the opposite happened. From 1955 there was an unprecedented rise in crime and, against all expectations, the crime figures suddenly took off and have continued to rise to this day.

Out of control? – 1954–1984

The government was taken aback by the growing prison numbers and expressed its concern in the 1959 landmark White Paper *Penal Practice in a Changing Society*.[6] It acknowledged that its hope that the crime wave would recede had proved ill founded:

It is a disquieting feature of our society that in the years since the war, rising standards in material prosperity, education and social welfare have brought no decrease in the higher rate of crime reached during the war; on the contrary crime has increased and is still increasing ... Existing penal methods have of necessity been developed piecemeal and imperfectly in response to experience and to the pressure of current problems.

Arising out of the White Paper, 40 new establishments were opened; however, had it not been for the earlier success of the open prisons it is difficult to see how sufficient accommodation could have been provided in a reasonable time-scale.

New secure training prisons were to be built along with the reclaimed ex-military camps and other buildings around the country. The prison estate was now larger and more varied than ever before, but it did little to relieve the chronic overcrowding.

As an attempt, *inter alia*, to resolve the overcrowding problem, the 1967 Criminal Justice Act introduced suspended sentences and parole. However, this was not enough, and overcrowding, often acute, and attempts at short-term expediency measures have been almost unremitting features ever since. Most of the prison estate was still an inheritance of Victorian radial prisons, usually by now finding themselves either in the centre of towns or on the outskirts and rapidly being engulfed by other development. They had little room left for building outside the prison walls, and hardly any scope for improvement within.

Out of this past history of failure, a great deal was expected from the so-called 'new wave' of prisons resulting from the 1959 White Paper. The first of these was built at Blundeston, Suffolk, in 1963, and was a model or 'treatment prototype' for a further 22 prisons built to the same or a similar pattern (*Figure 2.2*; see also *Figure 3.9*). Hailed as breaking away from the Victorian punitive philosophy, cells were smaller because it was assumed that for most of the time prisoners would not be in them, but the opportunity was not taken to install integral sanitation. This had to be added, expensively, about 30 years later. It was the first prison in England with inbuilt regime facilities, incorporating workshops, education, communal dining, association areas and different chapels, and encapsulated the philosophy of providing treatment and training as the main purpose of the prison. The prison provided for the subdivision of the inmate population into separate regime and security categories with

---

6 (1959). *Penal Practice in a Changing Society*, Cmnd 645. HMSO. (A White Paper sets out government policy and the supporting analysis; a Green Paper is more tentative and invites discussion and comment.)

Figure 2.2
Blundeston prison design model, 1963. The first real departure from radial principles, with separate housing units sited around a central facilities block. (see plan in Figure 2.1B.)

smaller, more manageable groups, but it also sowed the seeds of control problems because it allowed the inmates more freedom to move around at will. This was a departure from the Victorian prisons, which were designed to keep prisoners in their cells for most of the time, only moving them under strict supervision. After disturbances in later similar prisons, more security gates were erected and movement was restricted – freedom had its price.

In terms of design, Blundeston was a major departure from the long open-tiered cell blocks of the radial prisons. The layout was more spread out and less monolithic, with smaller cell blocks at the four corners of a central nucleus of communal facilities. Workshops and playing fields completed the design, all within a secure perimeter. The new cell blocks had separate solid floors (instead of landings arranged in tiers), with hotel-style corridors from which small groups of cells opened off. They each contained only about 75 inmates rather than hundreds. The scale was more personal and less intimidating, and the small groups allowed, in theory, a more productive regime. There were small association rooms on the ground floors of each block, an experimental use of dormitories, and improved cell designs with larger windows. It was a remarkable change in attitude and design, but was still a very rigid and inflexible solution in its own way. A fresh approach was attempted, but the challenge was only partially met because it was only partially taken up. Other prisons based on the Blundeston model were similar, but with the original four-storey cell blocks reduced to three storeys. Some had similar cell arrangements but the blocks were spread out in a telephone-pole pattern; others were arranged around rather claustrophobic courtyards.

Domination of security over treatment

The old 'liberalism' of the prison service received a blow from which it never fully recovered following the notorious escape of the spy, George Blake, from Wormwood Scrubs, London, on 26 October 1966. Lord

Mountbatten's ensuing report[7] into that and other incidents introduced a security classification system which determined, from then on, the quality of life for the prisoner and also, by implication, the staff. The introduction of strict security classifications and a system of dispersing the higher-risk prisoners around the country had profound implications for regimes and prison designs. It also introduced the anomaly that high security prisoners were to have better facilities than non-sentenced prisoners on remand and those shorter-term prisoners held in local prisons.

The Mountbatten report changed the entire approach to security. The debate that followed his report centred on whether special-risk prisoners should be dispersed, or, as he suggested, whether they should be concentrated in a few super-security prisons. The need for more security was taken for granted. The Mountbatten proposal for a single high security prison to contain all maximum security prisoners was not acted upon, and, following the Radzinowicz Report in 1968, such prisoners were 'dispersed' throughout a group of high security prisons, with the intention that there should be a liberal treatment within a secure perimeter. The debate over the rival merits of 'concentration' and 'dispersal' has often resurfaced within the prison service from that time on.

This obsession with security, and the constant rise in prison population, dealt the treatment model an almost fatal blow in England. Treatment programmes were cancelled, security became stifling, and despair and confusion set in. In America a similar situation occurred at about the same time, with a reaction against long, indeterminate sentences, the introduction of a stricter 'just deserts' policy, and then the publication of the seminal paper by Robert Martinson, *What works? – Questions and Answers about Prison Reform*,[8] broadly fuelling the notion that 'nothing works'.

During the late 1970s and 1980s, the prison system went through yet another long bout of serious crises. Collapse in control was a dominant theme, which affected staff morale and encouraged the rise in union power. Buildings too experienced change and modification. Security was further increased, with more control gates and zoning of the prison to prevent prisoners enjoying free access. Dining in association in large halls was no longer acceptable, and many prisoners had to eat in their cells. Physical barriers replaced dynamic personal interaction. Staff were put into control rooms or 'bubbles', stationed behind gates or a 'cordon sanitaire'. Offices proliferated, and staff withdrew into them.

It was largely because of the industrial relations problems arising from these measures that an inquiry was instituted under Mr Justice May. His report in 1979[9] agreed that 'the rhetoric of treatment and training has had its day', and argued in favour of 'positive custody'. No one fully understood what this meant, and within the moral vacuum that ensued custodianship, security and human warehousing became the norm.

---

7   Earl Mountbatten (1966). *Report of the Inquiry into Prison Escapes and Security 1966*, Cmnd 3175. HMSO.
8   Martinson. R. (1974). What Works? – Questions and Answers about Prison Reform *The Public Interest*, pp. 22–54.
    Radzinowicz, L. (1968). *The regime for long-term prisoners in conditions of maximum security*. The Report of the Advisory Council on the Penal System. HMSO.
    King, R. and McDermott, K. (1989). *British prisons 1970–1987: the ever deepening crisis*. Br. J. Criminol., 29, 107–28.
9   Mr Justice May (1979). *Report of the Inquiry into the United Kingdom Prison Service*, Cmnd 7673. HMSO.

Lack of a building programme

By the early 1970s, hit by expenditure cuts, there was a total halt on prison building – designs were ready, but there was no cash to build them. By the time the programme got underway again about ten years later, the designs dusted off the shelf were already out of date and did not reflect the latest thinking. The problem was further compounded by the time needed to bring a programme to fruition – in those days it took about ten years from design to completion, by which time the prisons were even more outdated.

In 1982 another large building programme was set in train. This was subsequently expanded to include 21 new prisons, for completion by 1994. The older, out-of-date designs were reactivated, involving the colossal expense of partial redesign resulting from the time lag. This was especially noticeable in high security prisons, where security requirements had been considerably tightened up, and money used to improve security was taken away from improvements in lower category establishments, young offenders' and women's prisons, and from improving regimes. However, overcrowding steadily got worse, and there was still no sign of any obvious relationship between penal policies and the design of penal establishments which they should have generated.

New directions – 1984–April 1990

The period between 1984 and 1990 was an extraordinary time, when a considerable amount of effort was expended to provide a new sense of direction and more urgency in a Service that had been drifting badly. There was widespread public concern about violent crime, to which the government responded by lengthening sentences for serious violent offences. Within the Prison Service there was concern about the occurrence of disturbances, particularly in dispersal prisons. There had been nine major disturbances in these prisons in ten years.

At the start of this period, in 1984, the Control Review Committee[10] was set up to report on the problems facing the long-term prison system. Up to this point the Service had been insular in the extreme, but change was in the air, and officials visited prisons at home and abroad, including the USA, Canada, Germany and Scotland, to see how those countries were coping with similar problems.

The formation of the Committee marked an important stage in reforming prisons policy and attempting to make better use of the system and making it more flexible. One recommendation was that the 'new generation' management system and designs in use in the USA appeared to avoid many of the dangers that led the Radzinowicz and May committees to advise against a policy of concentration. The committee also recognized the importance of designing buildings for economy in the use of staff, and for the more relaxed control of prisoners. It presaged a change from staff fitting into buildings to making buildings fit for staff.

Soon after this, a Home Office Working Team visited the United States to study the new generation principles and the design solutions which arose from them. The Team had no doubts about the efficacy of the new ways of working:[11]

10 Control Review Committee (1984). *Managing the Long-term Prison System*. HMSO.
11 Home Office (1985). *New Directions in Prison Design*. HMSO.

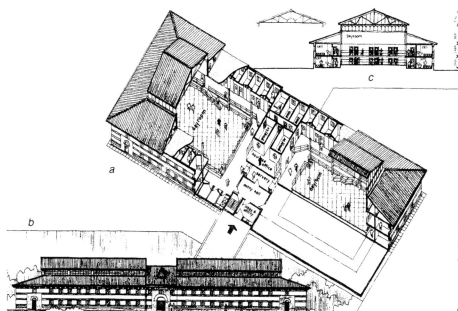

Figure 2.3
Prison Design Briefing System (PDBS) suggested design.
  a. Axonometric
  b. Elevation
  c. Section.
See also plans in Figure 2.11 and J

The 'new generation' concepts taken as a whole do in principle offer considerable advantages in terms of prison management, supervision and control and we consider that it will be important for the review that is to be undertaken of the existing Prison Briefing Guides [published in 1976] to take the 'new generation' thinking fully into account in restating the principles that should inform and direct our own future design approach . . . we are in no doubt that a comparable clear management philosophy is fundamental to the smooth and effective operation of any prison system. Unless this key point is grasped no amount of design innovation will of itself serve to fill the resultant vacuum.

At the same time, *A Sense of Direction* (published in 1985)[12] looked at the importance of activity, individualism, relationship and the implications for architecture. It highlighted the need for discrete living units to facilitate the relationships between staff and prisoners, and good facilities for regime and industrial activities.

In the following year, major disturbances accelerated this process of change. A spectacular wave of riots broke out in 40 prisons.[13] These were partially sparked off by prison officers refusing to work overtime in protest at staffing levels in local prisons and remand centres. The later introduction of 'Fresh Start', which in effect bought out overtime working for staff, caused further troubles. Official reports after that came thick and fast. The House of Commons 25th Report of the Committee of Public Accounts was severely critical of the current prison systems and buildings, and insisted that the costly mistakes of the 1960s and 1970s had to be avoided in future. In 1987 the Prison Building Board was set up, and a start was made on producing the Prison Design Briefing System (PDBS; *Figure 2.3*). This set aside the previously published design guides of 1976 and started completely from scratch.

12 Dunbar, I. (1985). *A Sense of Direction*. Home Office.
13 Hennessy, J. (1987). *Report of an Inquiry by Her Majesty's Chief Inspector of Prisons for England and Wales into the Disturbances in Prison Service Establishments in England between 29 April and 2 May 1986*. HMSO.

The following year the Prison Service revised its Statement of Purpose, about which there had been constant debate since the demise of the treatment model. It was changed to:

Her Majesty's Prison Service serves the public by keeping in custody those committed by the courts. Our duty is to look after them with humanity and help them lead law abiding lives in custody and after release.

Also during that year, design, develop and construct principles were introduced to encourage speedier private sector building of remand centres and open prisons. This would be expanded a few years later to a more comprehensive private involvement known as PFI (Private Finance Initiative), by which private prison operators would be responsible for design, construction, management and finance (DCMF).

As a precursor to more private involvement, government canvassed the possibility of contracting out court and escort duties and involving the private sector in the management of remand prisons. The private sector bandwagon was beginning to roll. In the meantime, however, more army camps were opened to cope with the steady rise in the prison population.

Change was suddenly and dramatically accelerated by serious rioting in six prisons and disturbances in others during 25 days in April 1990. The initial and most critical riot started in Strangeways prison, Manchester, and lasted from 1 to 25 April. So serious were the outbreaks that the Home Secretary ordered an inquiry into the disturbances, headed by Lord Justice Woolf and Judge Stephen Tumim. Their 600-page report was presented to Parliament in February 1991, and set off a flurry of activity.[14]

Up to this time, there had been much planning but little concrete evidence to show for it. Briefs were meticulously prepared but, instead of new prisons, house blocks were frenetically built without matching facilities for work or education. This resulted in managerial and architectural confusion, jumbled up design and many one-offs. Despite a huge investment, there was little need at the time to build very much that was new, as police cells were available for overflow use and existing prisons could be expanded to provide double cell occupancy.

The Prison Service was desperately trying to provide more and more cells, anywhere, to keep up with the constantly rising tide of prisoners being committed by the courts. There appeared to be no overriding philosophy other than the favourite principle of the day, 'humane containment'. So far as buildings were concerned, there had been no 'philosophical input' since Blundeston.

Building for growth – 1990 onwards

The Strangeways riot forced an awareness of prison conditions on the public at a time when drastic policy changes were being signalled by the Criminal Justice Act of 1991, one of whose goals was to achieve a significant reduction in the numbers of offenders in custody. The government of the time acknowledged that prisons were an expensive way of making bad people worse.[15]

14 Woolf A. and Tumim S. (1991). *Prison Disturbances April 1990*, Cm. 1456. HMSO.
15 Home Office (1990). *Crime, Justice and Protecting the Public*, Cmnd. 965. HMSO.

Figure 2.4
Typical corridor-type cell block, Bristol. The original prison opened in 1882; this block was added 1967. (© Crown Copyright. NMR photograph by James O. Davies.)

When the Act was implemented in October 1991, it presaged more hope for prisons than at any other stage since the end of the war. It was paralleled by the Woolf Report, which set out the way in which a decent and effective prison system should be run – by getting the right balance between security, control, humanity and justice. It was firmly held that fairer, better regimes led to better ordered prisons and better behaved prisoners. While recommending that urgent security and control measures should be taken, Woolf emphasized the essential balance needed between physical security and an over-oppressive atmosphere. He also recommended that prisons should be built to accommodate no more than a total of 400 prisoners, and subdivided into smaller units of between 50 and 70 inmates each.

In 1993, the Prison Service was created as an executive agency headed by a Director General. This allowed the Service to operate at one remove from central government; previously, prisons had been run by the Home Office Prison Department. In common with other agencies, it is required to publish corporate and business plans, both of which need approval by the Home Secretary.

The stage was set for a period of stability with, at last, a fall in prison population from its peak of 51 000 in 1988 to a new low of 40 600 in 1992. Even when it began climbing again in 1993, the problem was offset by the places coming on-stream from the 1982 building programme. In fact, 1993 was the only year since the 1950s in which the amount of accommodation available was greater than the prison population.[16]

However, perhaps inevitably, there was a backlash. In October 1993 new policies were announced that would again result in more people

---

16 Dunbar, I. and Langdon, A. (1998). Prison work. In: *Tough Justice: Sentencing and Penal Policies in the 1990s*, Ch. 10. Blackstone Press.

being sent to prison, and this presaged the first consciously manufactured rise ever in England. It was also the first time any government had been in a position to increase imprisonment. For the only time in 50 years, accommodation and numbers were in balance. The government announced its belief that 'prison works', and initiated a programme of six new prisons, this time to be provided by the private sector.

Another change of direction was also signalled, towards a more austere view of imprisonment. With two further setbacks – the escapes from Whitemoor prison, Cambridgeshire, in 1994 and Parkhurst, Isle of Wight, in 1995 – there was a massive reorientation towards increased security. A study was begun concerning a new super-maximum security prison for the highest security risks, and for a new specialist control prison.

The 1997 Crime (Sentences) Act introduced honesty in sentencing, and also mandatory sentences for certain offences. This 'justice model', in which the prime purpose is to punish offenders proportionately to the gravity of their crimes, can so easily lead to a 'confinement model' of imprisonment to the exclusion of all else, and this is what began to happen.

The involvement of the private sector security industry in the prison system has been the largest recent organizational change in the prison world. The big question is whether operational costs and convenience can also enhance the goals of treatment and rehabilitation while maintaining security. Also, will the gap between penal ideas and prison design widen still further? Because of their financing regime and speed of construction, private prisons are very relevant to the rate at which the prison system can be expanded; however, this also means that prison design is now almost entirely for outside contractors to decide. The private security industry has become established in the prison system in a way that was not even contemplated ten years ago.

The problem of providing more prison places quickly became even more urgent; by 1999 the prison population had risen yet again, this time to over 65 000, and was still rising. Five years before it had stood at under 42 000, giving an increase of 54 per cent. A rise as dramatic as this called for emergency measures, and the solution adopted was to purchase fast-build industrialized houseblocks, which could be set up in days. These were residential only and were not backed up by the building of workshops and other facilities, thus leading to a different sort of overcrowding. The lessons of the past had not been learned, and the Prison Service was forced to place these units, and others of more permanent designs, where they could be fitted in, with no overall integration. A prison ship towed over from America was even called into service: a 1999 Chief Inspector's report praised the regime and its operation.[17]

One of the most important recent developments in prison regimes, on which the future must be built, has been the introduction and expansion of offending behaviour programmes. Their growth throughout the English prison system has been a highly positive innovation, as focussed and targeted programmes can make a significant difference to re-offending rates.

A prison system can only function properly where there is a balance between security and a humane environment, and buildings that will facilitate positive activities with staff and prisoners. Prisons relying solely on sophisticated electronic devices and separating staff from

17 Chief Inspector of Prisons (1999). *Report on HMP The Weare*. HMSO.

Figure 2.5
Interior of Woodhill prison, 1992, showing open association area with two tiers of gallery access cells and glazed wall (left) (see also *Plate 1*).

prisoners will not be able to achieve this. Neither will buildings that intimidate rather than facilitate.

Has architecture matched aspiration?

Until the building of Blundeston, Suffolk, in 1963, which was the first real advance on radial prisons, there had been a lack of precision in what prisons were trying to achieve. This resulted in arbitrary changes in direction and a lack of appreciation of the fundamental importance of collaborative design. By breaking down the vast mass of the prison into smaller parts, Blundeston and its successors did at least show a more pioneering spirit. However, the change had more to do with control than with policy involving the treatment of inmates.

It was not until the Control Review Committee in 1984, and the subsequent reports described earlier, that the emphasis shifted from control of the prison to the needs of the prisoner. This change in emphasis implied a greater flexibility of programmes and designs to suit different individuals, while questioning the basic assumptions about what should be happening in prisons.

The final and most important influence was the official visit made to the United States, where experimental designs that arose entirely out of a new system of prison management were being built. This 'new generation' of prisons brought together inmates and officers in a much closer relationship, where prisoners were allowed a greater freedom of movement and staff could control inmates less conspicuously and foster better personal relationships in a more relaxed atmosphere. The typical design that resulted avoided long grey cell corridors, and replaced them with small groups of cells arranged in two levels around a large multi-use space where prison officers and inmates intermingled.

This was what the Prison Service had been looking for. This was the first design since the Victorian radials fully to express current penal ideas, at first unproven and even unpopular with some, but as time went on apparently achieving good results and acceptance.

The first manifestation of this new approach in England was the preparation and publication, in 1989, of a remarkable series of booklets called the Prison Design Briefing System (PDBS).[18] This was a considerable

---

18 See Chapter 6.

achievement in understanding the operational and human requirements of the new generation prisons and expressing them in design terms.

The new American prisons tended to be triangular in shape, and indeed three such English triangular prisons were built – Woodhill in Milton Keynes (*Figure 2.5* and *Plate 1*), Lancaster Farms in Lancaster (*Plate 2*), and Doncaster. The PDBS designs tended to be rectangular, but the principles of small groups, small scale, and closer involvement of staff were the same. While this was going on, there was a huge programme of upgrading the existing prisons. Although desirable in their own right, these improvements did not further new thinking in terms of new designs related to new penal ideas. With the advent of privately funded and built prisons, it is possible that the good work springing from new generation principles could come to naught. There is no imperative for private operators to use the guidance in PDBS, nor to pay more than lip service to new generation ideas or designs. Indeed, one proposed private prison has been designed in the form of a large radial. The new prisons are described and illustrated throughout this book. Here, the intention is to show the relationship, if any, of architectural solutions to penal thinking and ideas. It is difficult to think of many such examples since the Victorian radial prisons, where the design precisely matched their purpose of strict isolation, hard labour and moral introspection as a means of reform and salvation, combined with total ease of supervision and control by a minimum of staff. Nothing since had matched so precisely the stated aims until the new generation ideas were taken up with such enthusiasm; however, these may now run the risk of being prematurely abandoned.

3 Psychological effects of the prison environment

Leslie Fairweather

Introduction

This chapter examines the extent to which prison design can influence the behaviour, attitudes and feelings of the users – inmates, staff and visitors.[1]

There are no obvious design formulas and no certainty that what works in one location will work in another, or with different cultures and in other countries. Some elements are, however, common to most penal institutions, and some broad conclusions can be drawn. These include the importance of the building environment, the location and size of the institution, the operational philosophy, violence and the fear of violence, the satisfaction and perceived safety of the staff, and the relation of all of these to design and construction.

Much of our knowledge is based on experience, common sense and speculation, some is based on empirical research; all may help to produce guidelines or standards. Scientists and designers have, over the past few years, begun to visit prisons and measure the relationships between environment and behaviour and the impact of prison design on the users. There is a feeling among researchers that their results are sometimes not welcome. They do not always perceive much enthusiasm on the part of authorities to pay heed to their results and act on them.

There is still too little empirical research, and what there is may be conflicting. Often no clear relationship can be established between behaviour and design, as too many other variables exist to challenge the results. Changes in behaviour may be as much a result of management procedures and personal characteristics of inmates and staff as of their environment. Architectural design is only one of several variables, and it is not always easy to identify its effects separately. Other research is strongly suggestive but unproven. Some of these uncertainties arise from the difficulty of providing appropriate methodologies to test relationships; others undoubtedly reflect weak or uncertain design effects.

The most fundamental design change of the last 30 years has been the switch from radial layouts to direct supervision 'new generation' designs, where a greater degree of staff–inmate contact has been encouraged. This has had far-reaching psychological and security implications for both

---

1 This chapter draws on the work of several contributors to the Symposium, including Dr Brian Crabbe, Professor Paul Paulus, Richard Wener, David Waplington and Sir Peter Woodhead, plus other research papers, some of which are included in the bibliography on page 48. Interpretation and inaccuracies are mine and not the original authors' and contributors'.

inmates and staff, not all of whom are entirely comfortable with the new relationships. Indeed, some inmates at one British prison asked to be moved back to the bleaker prisons to which they were accustomed, because staff were 'too friendly' in the new ones. They preferred the certainty of the mutual antipathy that they claimed existed in the older radial or corridor prisons – they could understand and handle that better.

Staff, too, can feel threatened and retreat from direct supervision into a more remote system of control where they believe they are completely in charge and free from attack. As Richard Wener asserts in Chapter 4, violence and assaults are 'a driving concern that influence the architectural design of a correctional facility'. In the USA, new generation design has even been used to *reduce* staff–inmate contact and to allow fewer staff to control prisons – sometimes 300–400 men are controlled by a two-man team in a control room.

The *perception* of risk is almost as important an influence as the risk itself, and will vary among prison users. Too much reliance on technology to eliminate danger and reinforce control can be perilous; in the event of equipment failure, staff can feel virtually helpless. Technology should not be an end in itself, but only an aid to officers' personal control and supervision, which may be far more effective in the long run than electronic devices. Not only is technology insufficient in itself, it can be counterproductive by getting between inmates and officers and thus reducing the personal contact upon which direct supervision relies. The presence of too much CCTV and other technical devices may be an indication of bad design.

The prison experience is traumatic and stressful for most inmates, and detrimental to the physical and mental wellbeing of many. Within a wide range of physical and social conditions, however, prisoners do adapt, although not always in ways that would meet with official approval. Stress levels vary throughout, being highest during reception and the first few weeks in prison and, later, just prior to release.

The prisoners' major problem lies not so much in their physical environment as in separation from family and friends, loss of freedom, concern about life after release, maintaining their self-esteem or self-identity, and how to manage their time. Inmates respond fairly negatively towards the buildings they inhabit, but do not frequently officially complain about the standard of accommodation. It is noticeable, however, that inmates respond more positively to newer accommodation and keep it cleaner and tidier.

Complaints from prison officers and other staff are far more frequent and critical, but usually concern control and safety issues, sightlines and staff–inmate relationships. However, they too are frequently unhappy with the quality of the buildings, especially with the older establishments. It should not be forgotten that the effect of the working conditions on staff will indirectly affect the inmates. It can be very instructive to learn where inmate and staff opinions converge or diverge, and American studies of direct supervision jails have often found surprising convergence. Staff are aware that conditions that reduce inmate frustration and stress serve to make their own jobs less difficult.

Stress-related effects of confinement are, fairly obviously, more severe in highly crowded maximum security prisons than in uncrowded minimum security environments. Indeed, overcrowding is a major source of stress in most prisons, and there is a strong tendency for the more overcrowded prisons to be less effective. The combination of unpredictability and uncertainty can produce powerful stress reactions, and there is also a strong connection between predictability and crowding. One reason that crowding is stressful is the increase it causes in social unpredictability.

Can design affect behaviour? And if so, in what way? What advice can be given to architects who have to design within the limited knowledge available regarding the psychological effects of their buildings? Are there designs and conditions that should be avoided? The remainder of this chapter is a distillation of guidance aimed at helping designers to use the experience and research currently available.

Lord Justice Woolf, in his report on the British prison disturbances of 1990,[2] wrote that:

the way in which the buildings are designed, their state of repair and decoration are important to management, staff and prisoners alike. They can significantly affect the atmosphere of a prison.

However, he offers the caveat that:

poor physical conditions are not a necessary or sufficient excuse for a badly run prison or for poor relations between those who live and work within the prison. The quality and attitude of the management and staff are more important than the buildings.

What is required is a partnership between all those involved in the policy, design, staffing and administration of prisons. This is especially important when, as in Britain and the United States over the last 20 or so years, there have been extensive programmes of prison building and refurbishment. Very substantial sums of public money have been expended, and it is important that staff at all levels are encouraged to contribute their experience and suggestions. In some cases, quite large sums of money could have been saved if those who run prisons had been trusted on design issues and consulted early in the design process. Unnecessary accommodation could have been avoided or made flexible for other uses. Obvious security risks, such as bad positioning of stairs that obstruct sightlines, blind corners, or weaknesses in perimeter security, could have been designed out at an early stage.

It is the combination of everybody's skills and experience, backed up by monitoring and research, which will produce the best results. And while it may not always be possible or easy to do, it is surely sensible to seek comments and suggestions from current prisoners and those who have served their time.

Implications for designers

Architects cannot determine with precision what effect their buildings will have on the users. At best, their designs can support the rehabilitative process and offer a humane environment for staff and inmates; at worst, they should at least do no harm. They should always respect the human dignity of the prisoners, staff and visitors.

---

2 Woolf, A. and Tumim, S. (1991). *Prison Disturbances April 1990*, Cm 1456. HMSO.

Buildings affect people in a wide variety of ways. Some are deeply influenced by their surroundings, others scarcely notice them. Many are profoundly affected at the early stages of their imprisonment, only to become inured to conditions as their sentence wears on, although some long-term negative effects may lessen.

The guidance offered arises out of current research, such as it is, and experience on how physical, social and environmental conditions can be improved by understanding the psychology of those who use the prison. It does not cover every aspect of prison design, only those where research has revealed useful findings. Neither is it an academic summary of research. It is a practical guide on what can be culled for designers from published research papers.[3]

There are a number of key design factors to consider, from the major issues of location, size, layout and control, to the smaller-scale but no less important questions of living accommodation and environmental conditions.

Location of the prison

It is generally agreed that prisons should be sited within reasonable proximity to, and have close connections with, the community with which the prisoners have their closest ties. Should the institution function as a local prison ('jail' in the United States; 'maison d'arrêt' or equivalent in Europe) holding pre-trial prisoners, it is important that its location be convenient for the courts it serves and the supporting legal community of defence and prosecution lawyers and probation officers.

There should be good public transport links for ease of access for family and friends, and it should be in reasonable proximity to a town or city. Prisons isolated from other communities are not desirable, and they are also more difficult for staff. It must not be forgotten that prison officers and other staff need the support and facilities that a normal community can offer in terms of housing, shops, schools and leisure activities. An isolated community of prison staff faces a number of problems.

One of the most important factors in an inmate's successful return to freedom is to facilitate and encourage the social and emotional support that can be given by family and friends. Being within a self-contained unit as part of a larger outside community with its own facilities such as hospitals and places of worship can also provide psychological reassurance. Local communities that are willing to become involved in 'their' prison by voluntary help and by participating in sports and other activities are an added and valuable bonus. The design, zones of circulation and control of the prison should take this possibility into account, for example by providing support space outside the secure perimeter.

Overall layout

There are effectively two basic types of layout: those using indirect supervision and those with direct supervision. Prisons with indirect

---

3 See bibliography on page 48.

supervision are those where inmates and staff occupy, to some extent, their own territories. Staff may intermingle with inmates to a limited degree, but supervision and control are more remote and characterized by reliance on distant visual surveillance; officers can retreat to their own secure stations. Control may be exercised from one central point or by patrolling corridors and landings. Such prisons include radial and cruciform layouts, with variations such as courtyards and 'T' and 'L' configurations. They may have central open galleries with cells off a series of landings or enclosed corridors.

A sense of alienation is evident in many prisons of this sort, leading to the development of inmate cultures and hierarchies that officers may find it difficult to understand and control. On the staff side, there may be a tendency to stereotype and a failure to treat the prisoners as individuals. Direct supervision prisons have a much larger central association area surrounded by only one or two storeys of cells. The central space is usually triangular or rectangular, and officers roam and mingle there with the inmates. Greater staff–inmate contact has been found to lead to increased positive relationships, allowing more effective surveillance and better security. Such contacts also help to dissolve tensions and lower the social temperature.

However, they may not suit every inmate. Careful classification is needed to weed out those who, for various reasons, will not flourish in such an environment. This is usually a fairly small number - about 5 to 10 per cent of inmates. Staff, too, will need extra training to learn how to cope with and exploit the special demands made on them. Depending on the security level and mix of prisoners, extra support may have to be given to staff by means of debriefings and motivation meetings.

Such prisons are now usually termed 'new generation', and while their geometry may vary (and is sometimes quite elaborate), many, but not all, share the common management and operational philosophy of greater staff involvement with inmates. Some American prisons, however, use new generation to support almost total separation of staff and inmates, and a regime based on remote surveillance and command.

Many advantages are claimed for direct supervision prisons. Much of the research has been undertaken in Federal Bureau prisons in the United States where, after initial mistrust that the new design would place officers at the mercy of inmates, they appear to work better than was thought possible. Officers in constant contact with inmates get to know them well. They learn to recognize and respond to trouble before it escalates into violence. Compared to traditional prisons, there is less conflict among inmates and between inmates and staff. Violent incidents are drastically reduced, homosexual rape virtually disappears, and vandalism and graffiti are almost eliminated. New generation units also lend themselves more easily to subdivisions, all of which may be overseen from one control room.

However, it has also been found that while inmates and line officers have similar attitudes concerning 'acceptable' levels of vandalism, administrators are less tolerant. Attitudes towards the prison environment between officers and administrators do not always align. This is an interesting phenomenon in itself. In some cases it is because officers actually see what is going on and why, while administrators get only reports of problems. It is not uncommon, for instance, for an administrator to assume that a broken television is the result of vandalism, whereas the officer may know that the problem is simple wear and tear.

It has been shown that the new prisons are no more expensive to build. They are in some ways cheaper over time, because vandalism is less frequent and construction money can be saved by using standard materials such as porcelain sanitary fittings and ordinary lighting fixtures rather than more costly vandal-proof versions. However, some new generation prisons meet a range of needs by providing a number of living units equipped with steel WCs and washing fittings for men with a history of vandalism. While officers and inmates agree that direct supervision works better than traditional approaches, they are worried about the air quality in sealed, environmentally regulated buildings. They also complain that confining all activities to the small housing unit is very monotonous, although they admit that constant boredom is better than the constant terror pervading many older prisons. One improvement in some of the later prisons is the addition of an outdoor recreation yard for each living unit to vary the surroundings.

It is possible that the broad principle of greater staff–inmate involvement will influence the design of many new prisons, whether or not they adopt fully-fledged new generation principles and layouts. In the United States, however, there is a considerable move now to use design and technology as a way of reducing staff costs.

Visitors and outside community involvement

This section is concerned with any special design features that are directly influenced by psychological factors. Provision for normal activities, such as visits by solicitors and other officials, conform to the sorts of design found in the outside community. However, visits from relations and friends fall into a special category. There is a degree of nervousness and anticipation on the part of many visitors, plus excitement from the children. Many visitors will want to be advised by specialist staff and, even more, will need reassurance in such strange surroundings.

Visitors should never be required to wait out in the open, exposed to the weather, before being shepherded into a dingy visiting hall. There should be a visitors' centre where they can wait in the dry, where there is a play space for the children, advice available from social and welfare workers, and lavatories. The visiting hall inside the prison itself should be brightly decorated and lit, with simple comfortable furnishings and areas for children to play. Within the bounds of security, every effort should be made to provide a relaxed atmosphere for families and friends to meet with inmates (*Plate 3*). Visits should help to boost confidence in both inmates and families, and a bad visit may result in bad behaviour. Visiting booths, when required for security reasons (for example where the prisoner is violent or dangerous, or to prevent smuggling), should be designed so far as possible to reduce tension. The debate over visiting is often about whether 'contact' or 'non-contact' visiting should be allowed in all or particular cases.

Institution and group size

There is common agreement that prisons should not be too large, but differences of opinion persist regarding the optimum size. The answer, to some extent, depends on the needs of the community and what treatment activities are proposed. Overall size has an effect on the balance between the custodial measures required and the amount and type of treatment possible. If the balance swings too far towards custody and control, inmates can feel alienated from involvement with measures to assist their return to a lawful life.

There is also a considerable psychological effect on inmates and staff if the institution is too large and individuals feel swamped and intimidated by its sheer size and scale. Suggested maximum inmate numbers range from 100–600. If numbers are higher than this, it is recommended that the institution be divided into separate semi-autonomous units sharing the infrastructure of the whole. This can considerably affect the apparent size of the institution. At the lower end of the range, 100–125 beds, staff are able to recognize every resident and develop personal relationships. Although this small size may prove to be too expensive a solution as a free-standing prison, it is possible as a subdivision or specialist group.

Most recommendations are for a middle range of 300–400 beds. Above this size it is claimed that regimentation and excessive concentration on routine will be inevitable, anonymity fostered, and the institution's image tend towards rejection and oppressive security. In the UK, Lord Justice Woolf proposed a maximum of 400, while the official guidance document, the Prison Design Briefing System,[4] suggests 600. Woolf believes this is higher than the ideal. In Australia, a capacity of 500 is considered a maximum.

Despite a widespread belief, there appears to be no empirical research that prison size influences behaviour inside or after leaving prison. The English prison statistics show that prison offences, and more specifically *assaults*, are less likely in larger prisons, possibly because they are less likely to be observed. Also, size is only weakly related to effectiveness, but overcrowding does have a high negative relationship in larger prisons. This does not necessarily mean that the widespread belief is incorrect; only that it is not based on empirical evidence. However, American experience showed that prisons that had experienced riots tended to be larger than those that had not.

There is no dissension about whether the prison should be subdivided, but there is some disparity of view about the size of the sub-units. The lowest figures suggested are 12–20 inmates, with the claim that small units achieve more spontaneity, support and autonomy, and allow closer personal relationships to develop between inmates and officers. A more usual average is between 40 and 50 inmates, with 50 as the optimum. Woolf recommends 50–70, and there seems general agreement that a maximum should be 80. With the smaller numbers there are indications that vandalism and graffiti are almost non-existent, levels of violence are low, general tension is reduced and staff–inmate relationships are more positive.

Inmate living accommodation

For decades overcrowding has bedevilled most prisons, certainly the older ones, and has sometimes led to desperate conditions for inmates

---

4 Home Office (1988). *Prison Design Briefing System (PDBS)*. Home Office Library
   Publications, updated 1989, 1990, 1991.

and created huge difficulties for staff. To some extent overcrowding is a subjective variable, but there can be no doubt when it is too high in any particular prison.

While environmental conditions will be severely affected, the major impact of crowding on inmates is in their lack of privacy and the reduced ability to preserve much semblance of normal human behaviour. This fosters considerable stress and aggression. Privacy provides an emotional haven; it allows the opportunity for self-evaluation, permits limited communication and establishes a psychological distance from others. It provides personal autonomy and a sense of individuality and control over one's situation. Research indicates that lack of personal control exacerbates the effects of crowding. Privacy in institutions is related to occupancy patterns (single versus multiple rooms) and density (the number of people per unit area). The manipulation of distance or barriers in the environment is a critical mechanism in achieving privacy. A barred cell provides physical separation but little visual or auditory isolation; in a dormitory, no separation is possible. An inability to achieve socially accepted norms for bodily functions has a dehumanizing effect – an exposed toilet, for example, shows little respect for the privacy or dignity of the inmate concerned, and may further blunt or debase sensibilities.

Cells or dormitories?

Considered from a purely financial standpoint, the minimum area needed to house inmates will be the most popular and hence dormitories will win out over single cells as being the most economical in terms of space/cost per inmate. Double bunking is also effective in accommodating more prisoners in less space, and the Federal Bureau of Prisons is increasingly adopting double bunking for this reason. What should never happen, although it has been common in the past, is the addition of extra beds in a cell designed for one – especially if the cell contains exposed toilet facilities and if inmates are expected to eat there.

Some inmates do prefer the companionship of a dormitory or a shared cell to the isolation of a single bed cell, and there should be sufficient variety to cater for individual needs and preferences. The needs of security and control must in this, as in other matters, be matched to the inmate's level of risk or vulnerability.

If a prisoner wishes, he or she should be entitled to have a single cell. An extreme view is that dormitories are a disaster because they deprive people of privacy and invariably foster intimidation, bullying, extortion, blackmail, and disruption of the kind that can lead to riots. These concerns may be less in an open (minimum security) prison, where the risk level of inmates has been assessed before assignment and where, for example, short sentences are being served or selected prisoners are at the end of long sentences.

With regard to cell occupancy, an analysis of recent research has produced some useful guidelines for designers; these are detailed below.

Single cells v. doubles

Double cells or cubicles were found to have greater negative effects than single occupancy housing. However, the double cells measured provided less space per inmate than the singles, and greater space per inmate and double bunking with a compatible companion could well change the negative reactions. Indeed, some prisoners prefer double bunking.

Single cells v. small occupancy units (three to six persons)
Illness, complaints and perceived crowding increased as the number of inmates increased. In this case it was the numbers that triggered the unhappiness rather than the space per person, which was actually quite generous.

Single cells v. open dormitories
One indisputable result of recent research is that dormitories have more negative consequences than single-person units or doubles. Findings were consistent for all races, ethnic groups, security levels and lengths of time in the institution.

Open v. segmented dormitories
When dormitories with 10–20 inmates were subdivided into bays, less negative effects were found when compared to the open arrangement. Dormitories with cubicles perform much better than those without, and cubicles represent an inexpensive means of affording privacy in otherwise open dormitories.

Cubicles v. rooms
Generally, partitioning the sleeping area within a dormitory into cubicles can be almost as effective as providing a single cell in terms of reducing stress. The more the cubicle resembles a single room (higher partitions, storage, desk space), the more it duplicates the positive effects of the room. Other research results found that inmates in dormitories perceived officers more negatively than those in other housing units. There was also a direct relationship between density and anger. While the threshold is not established, it may be that inmates in multiple cells with 3.25–4.65 square metres (35–50 square feet) each become more angry than if in single cells of 6.5 square metres (70 square feet).

It has also been reported that there is more violence, sexual assaults, contraband and medical emergencies in double-bunked cells when compared with single cells, but it is not always clear whether this is attributable to the amount of space, the number of people or to both, although research suggests that the critical factor is the number of people. Certainly it indicates the need for stringent assignment policies and effective monitoring.

To sum up, the amount of space in single and double cells does not appear to be an important factor in inmates' reaction to their housing, but space may become a more serious problem in multiple occupancy cells or dormitories. While limited space in a single cell has an impact on how cramped the space feels, in multiple housing there are the additional effects of decreased interpersonal distance, reduced privacy and increased potential interference. Sharing may also increase the number of unpredictable and unwanted interactions, including threatening behaviour. It is fairly clear that spatial density assumes much greater importance in dormitories than in single occupancy housing. Many inmates rated the outside cell areas as crowded, and were much more concerned about the lack of space and crowding outside their cell than inside.

The 'safe' cell

To reduce opportunities for suicides in cells, and to provide a more humane environment, the English Prison Service has designed a 'safe' cell based on their PDBS standard cell. It will gradually be adopted for

Figure 3.1
New design of single and double cells 'moulded' from one material. These examples are from a rehabilitated wing at Belmarsh prison, completed in 1997. Single cell (left), double cell (right).

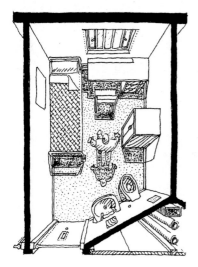

Figure 3.2
Standard single cell.
Area 6.8 m²–7.2 m²

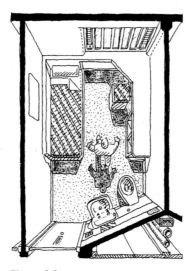

Figure 3.3
Single cell redesigned as 'safe' cell.

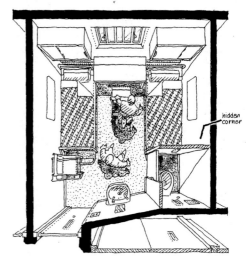

Figure 3.4
Standard double cell.
Area 9.8 m²–10.6 m²

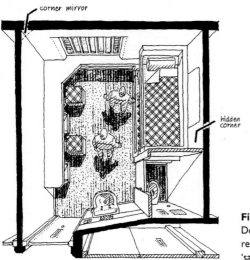

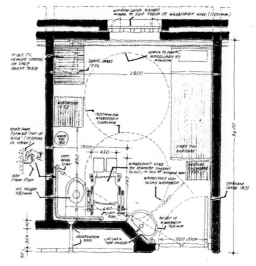

Figure 3.5
Double cell redesigned as 'safe' cell.

Figure 3.6
New cell design for disabled inmate with wheelchair.
Area 9.1 m²

new prison cells, but the design has already been used to transform existing cells to the satisfaction of inmates and staff (*Figures 3.1–3.6*). The safe cell has been designed to avoid suicide attempts, but it also provides a more ordered and stabilizing quality, and appears more supportive and calming. Every element of the cell was analysed and redesigned, with furniture and sanitary fittings formed of new materials such as Corian or Velstone to give a unifying character. These are much 'warmer' materials than stainless steel, but just as tough.

Cell certification standards have also been produced which can be consistently applied throughout the prison estate. They define areas and layouts that can be identified as 'uncrowded' or 'crowded'.

Environmental perception

There can be no justification for deliberately designing unwholesome accommodation or choosing dowdy colours, dim lighting and excessively harsh materials. This sends out quite the wrong message and inhibits the hopes of encouraging prisoners back into a society which, to them, sometimes looks as though it has given up on them. This form of institutional brutality only brutalizes society as a whole. It also has a severely detrimental effect on the working conditions of officers, and restricts the formation of any effective relationships between them and the prisoners. While many cannot analyse their reactions to their surroundings, it is at least arguable that high design quality must have, overall, a more benign influence than squalor. This in turn will affect the way people behave. Oppression and ugliness can lead to alienation and aggression. Flat, square, barren concrete yards overlooked by cells and littered with rubbish thrown from cell windows could more effectively be designed as a series of terraced, grassed and softer landscaped areas, appreciated by inmates and staff. Landscape design is as important as design within the walls, and can induce a mood of calm and repose in an atmosphere not associated with either. At the very least, prisons must be without smell or echo, well lit, warmed and ventilated, and above all healthy, both physically and mentally.

There will always be a small hard core of prisoners for whom decent standards are a sign of weakness and laxity, which they will seek to exploit and undermine. However, this is no reason for the great majority to be denied decent and more hopeful living conditions. An important element of psychological health is adequate space within which to live, work and relax. A former governor of new generation Lancaster Farms prison, which he describes as 'the most exciting prison I have ever seen', is convinced that the sense of space provided by the design is of major importance, both in keeping control and in providing the sort of conditions where officers can have a positive impact on helping the inmates.

A threatening environment will invariably encourage staff to seek the security of an office or find excuses for frequent temporary absences. It cannot be stressed too often that the safety of prisoners and staff should be a major preoccupation for designers.

Sensory deprivation

Sensory deprivation implies a severe limitation to one or more of the senses. While very little appears to be known about the effects of long-term confinement on sensory abilities, it has been suggested that monotony and boredom, caused by enforced idleness, lack of variety and sensory deprivation, can contribute to vandalism. American research indicates that inmates do not always prefer the relatively open and non-institutional prisons to more traditional facilities, which allow a wider range of movement and more access to the outdoors.

None of these sensory issues is simple and none acts singly on the individual; rather, they act in concert as part of the total setting of the prison.

Thermal comfort

Thermal comfort – or discomfort – represents a complex of psycho-physiological responses to conditions in the physical environment, including temperature, humidity and air movement. In prison, the outcome will depend on the individual's level of activity or exertion, quality of clothing and level of control over thermal conditions. Complaints from inmates and staff in prisons about thermal discomfort are very common. Irritability and aggressive behaviour undoubtedly increase with thermal discomfort, especially when it is too hot.

Even new prisons often have difficulty achieving thermal comfort, perhaps because prison buildings are frequently complex structures with spaces varying widely in volume, exterior exposure and occupant load. This increases the difficulty of mechanical system design. Some degree of inmate control should be recognized, given the considerable variability in individual responses.

Air quality is also of importance. It has been found that relative to a no-odour group, the presence of even a moderately offensive smell increased aggression.

Noise

Noise is one of the prison environment's most persistent problems, pervading even the new 'soft' prisons. Communication becomes difficult, conversations are shouted, sleep is often disturbed, and stress and discomfort are experienced. Uncontrolled noise levels spiral as everyone seeks to compensate for a background that prevents one being heard or listening to another or to radio or television.

There are two main issues: the source of noise, and the hard materials used, which exacerbate the problem. In many prisons the clang of metal on metal is common. Multiple conversations, shouted orders, and radios and televisions in the same space create an indeterminate, disorientating and very high level of sound. Unexpected or unpredictable noise can be even more disturbing than a constant high level.

In some US prisons music was piped into the cells, over which the inmates had no control. They resorted to stuffing up the speakers to reduce the annoyance. Other prisons insist that television and radio listening is conducted with earphones rather than speakers.

The second factor is the hard, reflective quality of most prison buildings. Very few soft and absorbent materials are used, possibly because they are less tough and require higher maintenance and more frequent replacement. It is recommended that acceptable daytime levels are about 70 decibels (dbA) or less, and night-time levels about 45 decibels, based on sleep interference levels. Noise levels can also be reduced by isolating or dispersing audio systems, using sound-absorbing materials such as carpet or acoustic tiles, and limiting the metal-on-metal contacts of structure, equipment or furnishings. Where inmates do not have any control over unwanted noise, they exhibit physiological reactions typically associated with stress. All studies have shown that individuals exhibit more aggression under noisy than under quiet conditions.

Light and view

While considerable research has been undertaken on the psychological effects of windowless environments, little or no research has been carried out in prisons. Results from other settings, however, suggest that windows are more than just a luxury for the incarcerated, and that lack of contact with the outside world heightens stress and depression. In restricted and monotonous situations, a view out becomes a necessity. The highest stress areas in prisons, isolation cells, are those that most commonly lack windows.

James Kessler[5] believes that natural light is the lifeblood of architecture, and has to be prioritized in terms of cost-effectiveness in city prisons where space is at a premium and not all rooms can be naturally lit. A balanced judgement has to be made on how much natural light can be provided and where. He also cautions that the height of windows is important, as views in as well as out must be considered. Does the public want to see quite so blatantly what happens inside? And do those inside want to become a public spectacle?

Standards of artificial light should be those acceptable in normal and similar situations outside prison.

Interior design

It is generally accepted that colour plays a large part in affecting behaviour, but there has been very little research in the correctional field. Such advice as there is, is fairly general and obvious, but is perhaps worth restating here (see also plate section).

Cells should be painted a light colour, but studies have shown a positive inmate response to bright colours and murals elsewhere, especially those painted by the inmates themselves. However, there can be problems with inmate-inspired painting; in large gang-infested penitentiaries in the United States, the gangs use house paints to display group colours to denote the sectors of the prison they control. The object of interior design is to make the prison more attractive, brighter, more cheerful and personalized – in general, less institutional. In concert with other factors, this positive physical appearance is considered by inmates and staff to improve morale and lessen tension.

Colour can enhance light by brightening or subduing spaces, provide sensory stimulation, give directional and other information, and optically change the proportions of a room. It can also help to differentiate parts of the prison or give identity to similar-looking cell blocks. 'Saturated' colours are thought to be inviting and reassuring, although only a moderate level of stimulation is advised. Certain hues of blue, red, black and yellow should be avoided, due to their psychological or cultural connotations. In a jail at Rockingham, North Carolina, there is an isolation cell painted from floor to ceiling in vivid yellow, broken up with purple dots of varying sizes – described as a form of 'psychedelic torture'. Similar very bright colours are used throughout the prison. The Sheriff warned potential inmates that if they went to

---

5 American prison architect. See Chapter 10.

Rockingham jail, they were not going to like it! Colour and change of materials can assist in the management of large open spaces, allowing safe movement and control without the need for corridors and additional gates. A different kind of flooring, for example, which creates a 'path' alongside a carpeted area, results in inmates using it as a natural circulation route.

Furniture has a psychological impact in terms of inmate satisfaction or frustration. It is not enough merely to use standard furniture and equipment developed for other purposes unless it is right for the special requirements of a prison. Cell furniture, especially, has to be very carefully thought out and designed to cater for *all* the requirements of living in such a confined space.

Social environment

The ability to control one's sensory environment is closely linked with control of one's social environment – who one meets or communicates with, and under what circumstances. In prison this ability is significantly reduced, and frequent and positive staff–inmate interactions are desirable from correctional and security standpoints.

The physical size, shape and location of an area affect visual surveillance, since this depends on the ability of staff to see inside certain intimate spaces. Where there are unobservable spaces, surveillance is likely to become much more formalized and obtrusive, and informal contacts will decrease. This may be directly contrary to the programme goals. When a certain physical area is identified with or controlled by an individual or group, territoriality may be a problem.

On an individual level, inmates sense an intrusion into their zone when others, especially strangers, enter it. The situation is further compounded when the territory is so clearly marked out, as in the penitentiary example quoted above. The size of the zone is much larger for violent inmates (about 2.7 square metres – 29 square feet) than for non-violent ones (about 0.7 square metres – 7 square feet).

The issue of personal territory has implications for sleeping and dayroom design, as size and layout affect distance and direction of approach. On a group level, it is common for ethnic or other groups habitually to occupy or take over certain areas. This may clarify and control contact between groups, which in turn reduces tension, although it increases ethnic or group polarization. Even a change in furniture arrangement may increase inter-group conflict, as it might result in the loss of clear territorial boundaries.

Likely centres for bullying and assault must be recognized. Communal showers can be a flashpoint, and their access may need to be controlled or restricted to one inmate at a time. Similarly, enclosed telephone boxes should be located near control points so that prisoners can use the telephone singly and safely under supervision. Closed TV rooms are potential trouble spots for bullying, and should be relatively open for supervision – consistent with acceptable noise levels.

Behaviour

One American prison study divided observable behaviour into a simple typology:

- aggressive, isolated passive (e.g. sitting, sleeping)
- isolated active (e.g. exercising alone)
- social (e.g. playing games, talking)
- traffic (e.g. movement).

That particular study was for behaviour observed during daytime hours only. It found that sleeping time accounted for about 20 per cent and isolated, low energy activities for about 80 per cent of the time. Only 2 per cent of the time was spent on active games.

In a women's prison, an easily accessible TV room replaced an outdoor yard as a natural congregating area. Consequently, TV watching increased. This and other studies seem to confirm the conclusion that questions must be asked about how the prison building and regimes can elicit more social and involved responses.

Feelings of control

There are two particular frustrations felt by inmates: lack of freedom of movement, and the inability to manipulate important aspects of their immediate environment. Easy and safe accessibility to key personal and group activities in the prison is often lacking. If inmates are kept waiting too long for action by officers, frustration sets in, leading to aggression and violence.

Another cause of frustration is the inability of prisoners to control their own personal environment, to regulate the airflow and temperature, or turn off the radio or light in their cell. This may lead to attacks on the offending source. Staff are also dissatisfied with their own inability individually to regulate temperature and fresh air.

Safety and security

Personal safety is of prime importance to inmates, staff and other prison users, and its provision is a basic duty of the prison authorities. Design that promotes safety includes:

- single occupancy rooms
- allowing inmates 24-hour access to their own room or cell plus the ability to lock the door (with staff override)
- increased visibility of all areas – no hidden bends or features such as staircases which obstruct clear views
- staff presence in inmate areas.

Where these precautions have been observed, research reports that fewer weapons were found and gang activity, tension and assault were all reduced. Frustration, leading to aggression, can also result from competition for scarce resources such as televisions and telephones. Controlling access to telephones is, of course, a prime gang activity.

Suicides have become more common in prisons since they have held higher proportions of inmates with mental health and drug abuse problems. Two-thirds of suicides in one survey took place in isolation cells.

Single cells facing on to a large dayroom space may not produce as extreme a sense of isolation. In theory, inmates in multiple cells and dormitories should be safer because others can stop and report a suicide attempt;

Figure 3.7
Original imposing and forbidding Pentonville gatehouse designed by Sir Charles Barry (1842): classical order and symmetry inspiring respect for the law. (© Crown Copyright. NMR photograph by Derek Kendall.)

Figure 3.9
Four-storey house blocks at Coldingly prison (1971) based on the Blundeston design. A very institutional, austere, and overpowering presence, with minimal landscaping.

Figure 3.8
The more modest entrance at Durham prison (1987). This building could almost be a community centre, law court or college.

however, it has been argued to the contrary, that the stresses are higher as inmates may be harassed by other inmates to the point of desperation.

Areas of special stress

One of the most stressful times for a detainee is usually on reception and intake into the prison. For novices especially this is their first contact

Figure 3.10
A more complex but smaller-scale facade at Woodhill prison (1992), which does not express the cellular nature of the building. The rear elevation, however, very much expresses its purpose with a saw-tooth arrangement of cells.

with the prison system, with all the uncertainties, anxieties and fears that this can generate. Information, the appearance of the prison, human contact, and the interiors of the spaces should all be especially reassuring in this part of the prison. Subsequent court appearances are also stressful. Visiting areas, mentioned earlier, should be designed to reduce anxiety and reassure the visitor.

Prison image and symbolism

The image of the prison will send out different messages depending on which side of the wall the observer happens to reside. Both social and psychological aspects of security need to be considered. The public needs reassurance that the due processes of the law are being carried out: prisons must not seem to be weak or excessively lenient, or their confidence will be forfeited. A new image is needed to break away from the old fortress-style exterior to something more positive and 'normal' (*Figures 3.7–3.10*; see also plate section).

Prisons are places from which inmates must not escape, and that should be expressed in the design. However, they should also be places that can be accepted, even adopted, by the community, with local people invited to participate in suitable activities.

There has to be an appropriate balance between the requirements of security and the adverse consequences of an over-oppressive atmosphere, which can lead to a hostile reaction from the inmates and a negative response from the public. American research in settings that have eliminated the symbols of incarceration and attempted to achieve a more normal and humane environment has shown that this is effective in contributing to a variety of positive results.

An avoidance of harsh institutional design, both inside and out, can reduce the stress and trauma caused to inmates by sudden removal from the outside environment. It is argued that softness serves as a cue for socially acceptable behaviour (whereas harsh institutional design invites aggressive acts against it) and that it encourages accountability and feelings of ownership within the prison community. It has been reported that in some prisons there has been a lower incidence of vandalism and graffiti due to the softer image. Not all inmates react in such a positive way, but even so the findings do show quite clearly the positive effects of a softer design approach on most inmates.

Conclusions

There is clearly a wide variety of ways in which the prison environment can affect the attitudes and behaviour of its users, but there is no certainty about which of these will trigger sudden violent or aggressive behaviour in particular individuals or groups.

Relatively little research has been carried out worldwide, and most of the published results have originated in the USA. The general tenor of findings is fairly consistent: the design of the prison environment is crucial to its operation and to the impact it has on the achievement of correctional goals for inmates, staff and public users.

However, the physical environment cannot guarantee or ensure the achievement of those goals. It can only work in conjunction with the administration, staffing, operations and activities, and with community support, to help the prison become an effective institution serving society's ends.

Bibliography

Farbstein, J. and Associates, with Wener, R. (1979). *Evaluation of Direct vs. Indirect Supervision Correctional Facilities (literature review)*. National Institute of Corrections, Federal Bureau of Prisons.

Farrington, D. P. and Nuttall, C. P. (1980). *Prison size, overcrowding, prison violence and recidivism*. J. Criminal Justice, 8, 221–31.

Paulus, P. B. and Dzindolet, M. T. (1999). *The effects of prison confinement*. In *Psychology and Social Policy* (P. Suedfeld and P. E. Tetlock, eds), pp. 327–41. Hemisphere Publishing Corporation.

Wener, R. (1990). *Jail and prison evaluations and design*. Presented at the CSTB Conference, Paris, 25–27 June.

Wener, R. (1993). *An environmental model of violence in institutional settings*. Edited version of the Division 34 Presidential Address, Annual Convention of the American Psychological Association, Toronto, 1993. Published in Division 34 Newsletter, 14 October 1994.

Wener, R., Frazier, W. and Farbstein, J. (1985). *Three generations of evaluation and design of corrective facilities*. Environ. Behav., 17(1), 71–95.

Wener, R., Frazier, W. and Farbstein, J. (1987). *Building better jails*. Psychology Today, June, pp. 40–9.

Zimring, C. M., Munyon, W. H. and Ard, L. (1988). *Reducing stress in jail*. Ekistics, 331, 332, pp. 215–29.

4 Design and the likelihood of prison assaults

Richard Wener

Assaults by inmates on each other or on staff are a central fact of life in prisons and jails. It is not that assaults are necessarily commonplace occurrences – in many facilities they are quite rare. However, whatever the frequency of assaults, their likelihood and prevention is almost always a driving concern that influences the architectural design of a correctional facility as well as its regime. It often plays as much of a role as do considerations of programmes and rehabilitation, and such attention is not without good reason. The minimal requirement of any correctional administration is to protect the safety of staff, inmates and the general public. Only after such concerns are satisfied can attention be turned to broader issues of rehabilitation, education, and the like.

Most observers agree that correctional architecture can affect violent behaviour, although this objective is typically discussed only in vague and general terms. Older, linear facilities often addressed assault by providing physical barriers (bars, walls) between groups of inmates, and between inmates and staff. In newer institutions, planners pay attention to removing 'blind spots' where inmates can hide and assaults can occur out of the sight of staff.

Rarely is there discussion of the more subtle role design can play in influencing the likelihood of an inmate acting in a violent manner – ways in which architecture can actually increase or reduce the tendency to be assaultive. More often, violent behaviour is ascribed to personality or dispositional factors. Dispositional models note that since the criminal justice system filters out less violent people at every stage of the judicial process, it is no surprise that those who remain in the system frequently exhibit violent behaviour. Since prisons are violent places because they are the places where violent people reside, it seems that the main role design can play is to keep these violent people apart, or make their actions visible.

This way of thinking has been challenged by the success of the so-called new generation jails and prisons. These use a regime that has been called 'direct supervision', because it places the officer in direct and continual contact with the inmates. In 25 years of operation (the 'new' generation is not so new anymore), these facilities have had an impressive record of success (largely in the USA but increasingly elsewhere as well). Facilities built and operated along these lines have been remarkably free of violent behaviour, as verified by many anecdotal commentaries and a number of formal evaluation studies. It has not been uncommon to receive reports that the entire character of a regime changes for the better upon moving into a new generation facility. In some cases, assault rates have dropped by 50, 60 or even 90 per cent.

New generation designs have also proven to be quite robust in that they have been able to operate reasonably well even when design and operational parameters have been modified and stretched well beyond original intentions. Facilities designed with single-bed cells have survived large-scale double bunking without major outbreaks of violence – which is not to say that crowding is without consequences. Some of the earliest new generation facilities that included many 'soft' elements (carpeting, soft furniture, bright colours) have been followed by designs with none of those qualities, with no obvious drop in the quality of operation. Designs based on inmate–staff ratios of 35–40 : 1 have survived, as have those with 70 : 1 ratios.

None of these factors alone (privacy, staff–inmate ratio, 'soft' design) seems to be the 'magic bullet' that explains the success of this model, even though all may be involved. As the new generation model is modified, stretched and transferred across countries and continents, it may be more critical than ever to try to identify as clearly as possible the crucial elements that make this kind of setting work, so that they can be adopted and adapted as best possible. I shall try to address that question directly by presenting a conceptual model that describes the way design works within the complex social and organizational system of a correctional facility to affect the behaviour of both staff and inmates, with a particular focus on assaultive behaviour. This model is based on my own experience conducting design evaluation research, and on experiences borrowed from the broad correctional literature. I call this a 'contextual model' of the impacts of design on assaultive behaviour, because it tries to place design into the context of the broader fabric of the whole operation of the facility.

We should note at the outset that this model of design and assaultive behaviour makes several basic assumptions. First, it assumes that violence in an institution is influenced by environmental, organizational, interpersonal and intrapersonal factors. These inevitably interact with one another, in the sense that no behaviour occurs in isolation and is always best understood as part of its broader context. Secondly, it is not a deterministic model. It assumes that changes in the environment or in an organization's style do not usually cause or eliminate violent acts *per se*, but rather may set in motion a series of events that affect the likelihood of violent acts occurring. Last, it accepts that there are some kinds of violent behaviour that are unique and have unique causes, and do not fall under the discussion here – such as planned 'hits', terrorism, and other activities related to outside circumstances. I also do not attempt to account for general disturbances (riots), even though factors in this model may be related to their instigation.

This conceptual model has three parts: context, perception, and resulting behaviour. It proposes that the facility context in which behaviour occurs (including facility design, organization or regime, and staff/inmate social systems) will influence the way inmates perceive their situation (in particular, how safe they feel, how much they feel in competition for scarce resources, and how likely they are to suffer the consequences of actions), and that these perceptions lead to behaviours that directly and indirectly affect the likelihood of violent action.

While the full model is graphically described in *Figure 4.1*, in this Chapter I will focus on architectural issues – most particularly, how they affect perceived safety and how that can lead to violent behaviour. In many ways this model suggests that perceived safety is at the heart of institutional violence. That is, when inmates feel that they are at risk of

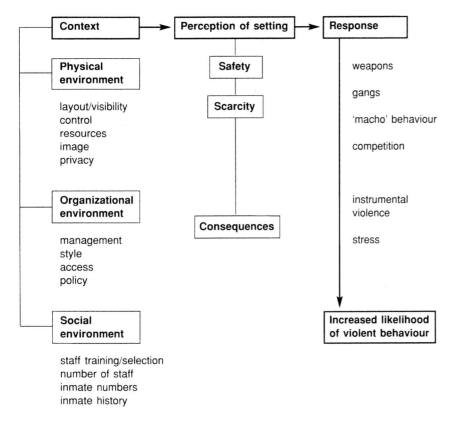

Figure 4.1 Violence model.

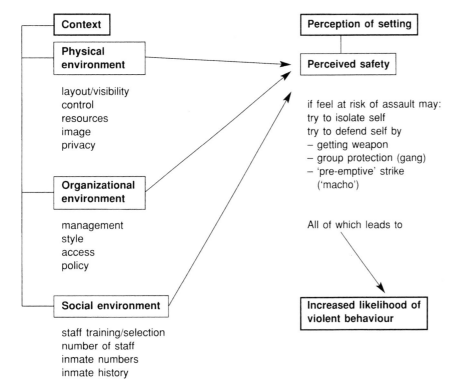

Figure 4.2 Relationship of context to perceived safety and violence.

assault, a series of events is set in motion that significantly increases the likelihood of assaultive behaviour occurring. Conversely, when inmates feel relatively safe and secure, the likelihood of such behaviour is very much lessened.

This model suggests that a number of contextual factors affect perceived safety, which then leads to behaviours that increase or reduce violence (*Figure 4.2*). Context can affect perceived safety in a number of ways. The regime determines policies and rules about inmate schedules, behaviours and consequences that have an important impact. For example, how much emphasis (and supervision) is given to making sure officers focus their attention on inmate safety? What is facility policy about the response to an assault in progress (should officers intervene immediately, or wait for backup)? What is the schedule, shift pattern and staffing level of officers? What kinds of programmes are provided to keep inmates busy, or to provide conflict resolution skills?

Social factors – of both staff and inmates – are also important. What are the level, quality and training of staff? How many inmates are in each cell or living unit? How are inmates classified and how are classifications mixed or separated? Obviously, at the extreme, a facility with poorly trained staff who are inadequate in number, insufficiently supervised by management and who are dealing with unpredictable inmates (e.g. the criminally insane) will provide a situation that is much more violence-prone than one in which none of these are true.

Within this context, architecture plays a role in a number of ways. First, on a global level, design influences the impressions that facility users – staff and inmates – get as to expected or appropriate behaviours. Social psychology argues that expectations powerfully affect behaviour. Some important expectations come from the instant impressions the user receives from visual images – the layout, lighting, colours and so forth. In the same way that upon entering a restaurant we immediately judge whether to speak in a hushed voice according to the dimness of the light and plushness of the furnishings, an inmate entering a correctional space gains an immediate impression of expected behaviour, which may verify or contradict prior expectations.

For example, in a traditional jail the 'cages' with bars, graffiti-stained walls, hard materials and a detached aspect of staff sends a clear message: 'this is a scary place – even the staff need the protection of separation by bars. I'd better be careful or tough here!'. By contrast, the soft colours and materials, open layout and more casual contact between staff and inmates in a new generation institution carry a very different message – that this is not at all like jails pictured in the cinema, and that civil and reasoned behaviour is expected and is the norm.

Design affects perceived safety in other more direct ways. Open settings provide good visual access and exposure, reducing the amount of space that is out of sight and hearing of the staff. This is more than the provision of good visibility of inmate behaviour that can be obtained in other design and management types which are very unlike new generation institutions, such as panopticon or 'podular indirect' designs. As officers are helped to become closer and more connected to inmate activities, and know what is going on in all areas of the living unit, inmates are more likely to feel that staff will know and respond if they are attacked.

Privacy – in particular, environmental support for exerting control over social interactions – can play an important role in affecting the inmates' sense of security. A door to a cell or bedroom that can be opened or closed gives inmates the ability to shut off or remove themselves from potentially difficult situations. If, for example, another person is agitated and threatening, an inmate may be able to avoid confrontation simply by going into his or her room. The ability to increase or reduce access to others in this and in more subtle ways can alleviate the tensions that lead to violent confrontations.

Design also affects violent behaviour in other ways, although there is not space here to discuss these in detail. For example, design can increase the amount of and access to critical resources. Conflict over scarce and important resources is often the source of, or at least the trigger point for, conflicts among inmates. It is not uncommon, for example, for verbal and then physical arguments to start over such things as access to telephones or which channel to watch on television. In the early Federal Bureau of Prisons' Metropolitan Correctional Centers, conflicts were reduced simply by providing four televisions rather than two, and two or three telephones instead of one.

The entire context of a correctional setting, including its architectural design, can influence the degree to which inmates feel safe from violent assault. When the setting creates a sense of insecurity – when inmates do not feel protected by the system in general, and by the staff in particular – a chain of events is set in motion that makes violence much more likely. Inmates who are afraid of being attacked have a limited number of options for self-preservation and protection. They might, as one option, choose to isolate themselves. However, while such options are used on occasions by administration as protective custody, policies do not allow such hiding or barricading in a room.

Other options open to inmates are even more problematic and counterproductive for the system as a whole. They may try to protect themselves by obtaining a weapon, and evidence from many sources suggests that this is often the case. Most inmate weapons that are found in institutions are defensive in nature, and they are usually not hard to get. Many prison managers acknowledge that weapons can be made or smuggled in, even at relatively secure facilities. The presence of weapons, then, is a sign that inmates feel insufficiently protected by the officers and the regime, and feel the need to defend themselves.

Another option fearful inmates may choose is to associate themselves with others for the protection afforded by numbers. They may feel that they are less likely to be assaulted if the assailant fears the response of a group. In the USA, these kinds of associations tend to form along the lines of racial and ethnic groupings. Their existence increases the chance that any localized incident will spread and set off a wider confrontation.

Sometimes inmates take a more proactive, if more dangerous, approach and attempt to scare off any potential assailant by acting 'crazy' or 'macho'. They often do this by assaulting an officer or another inmate without provocation. The act tries to send a message that says, 'I am tough (and maybe a little crazy), so you had better stay away from me'.

All of these responses have negative consequences for the facility. As more inmates have weapons, as they are set against one another in protective groups or strike out more often to show how tough they are, the objective reality becomes more dangerous and threatening for all. Officers may typically respond to this heightened tension by distancing themselves, physically and psychologically, from inmates. They will be less likely to 'hang around' and converse with inmates, and will spend more time with colleagues, putting themselves even more out of touch with inmate concerns, problems and conditions. In a dangerous spiral of action and reaction, other inmates may respond to this increased staff distance by feeling a greater need to protect themselves, and so are more likely to obtain weapons, seek protective groups, and so forth, which raises the tension one more notch. It is not hard to see how this can lead to a very dangerous environment.

The success of new generation prisons and jails also becomes clearer in this light. It is not just the carpeting, colours or the private rooms that make them work better. It is the combination of staff presence, attitudes and policies along with the design features that create the successful atmosphere. The omnipresent staff, whose ability to know what is going on is supported by an open setting, are clearly and visibly able to maintain inmate safety. The inmates have other options – other places to go, other things to do – to control their own social interactions. The easy access to critical resources (privacy, telephone, television, bathrooms) reduces the likelihood of competition leading to conflict and fights. This is all within an environment that clearly brings a message supporting 'normalized' behaviour. The success shows itself in the small number of weapons usually found and in the low levels of tension often reported at these institutions, and in the ability of inmates to interact rather than separate along racial and ethnic group divisions.

Since this is a contextual model, without simple, unidirectional causality, all elements can influence all other elements. For example, while policy and design can affect perceived safety, the reverse is also true. Tension and fear can cause administrations to change rules and procedures, and add locks, cameras and the like. What is important in this perspective is the understanding that setting has an explicit role in determining the level of violence, and can play a part in creating a safer environment and one more conducive to successful programmes.

Plate 1
Interior of cell unit at Woodhill prison, Milton Keynes. This is one of only three triangular cell block prisons in England. (See p. 30).

Plate 2
Exterior of another UK triangular prison, Lancaster Farms. Large windows to the enclosed association space are to the left and right. (See p. 30).

Plate 3
More human scale and colourful visiting centre at Belmarsh prison, Thamesmead, London. (© Crown Copyright. NMR photograph by James O. Davies.) (See p. 36).

Plate 4
Imposing entrance front to Wake County Public Safety Center, Raleigh, North Carolina. The jail tower is to the rear of the site. (See page 92).

Plate 5
Calm interior of Mecklenburg Work Release Center, for those who can accept more responsibility while awaiting a return to the outside community. (See p. 96).

Plate 6 Slab blocks of Mecklenburg County Jail designed to respond to its urban context. (See p. 96).

Plate 7
Interior of prison at Epinal, France, showing softening effect of indoor landscaping. (See p. 112).

Plate 8
'The Street' at Epinal prison, which links all the prison cell units and facilities. This is a new concept in French prisons. (See p. 112).

Plate 9
A break with tradition at Epinal, with an exterior facade quite unlike other prison buildings. (See p. 112).

Plate 10
Interior junction of cell wings at Zutphen prison in The Netherlands, forming an airy and well-lit hub. (See p. 119).

5 Architects and the prison experience

Sir Andrew Derbyshire

The English Prison Service in recent years seems to have abandoned any thought that the architecture of prisons is worthy of consideration as a major strategic issue. It appears to reject any belief that architects can make a significant contribution either to penal philosophy or to solving the architectural problems that flow from new ideas. Architects are regarded as subservient to the building process, which is itself seen as less important than extracting private capital to take the load off the Treasury by getting prisons built and run as cheaply as possible.

It was not always so. In the 1980s, great efforts were made through the Property Services Agency (PSA) to introduce greater rationalism into prison design through the Prison Design Briefing System (PDBS), to learn from the past, and to make progress through development projects such as Woodhill prison in Milton Keynes, Buckinghamshire (1992), where new ideas in prison design were tried out in practice. Alas, that all died when the PSA was sold off to the highest bidder. Since then, design policy has fallen into the hands of administrators who are inclined to respond to the short-term demands of ministers and who lose sight of the bigger strategic issues.

Alternative approaches to design

These matters are handled very differently in other countries. In the United States, for example, there has been a stable line of management for many years in the Federal Bureau of Prisons, which means that feedback and learning from experience is an integral part of the penal system. There is a long history of interaction between design and management. This encouraged the evolution of new generation prisons with their triangular dayrooms surrounded by eight cells on each of the three sides, developed to achieve flexibility between direct and indirect supervision according to the status of the prisoners, the degree of overcrowding and the political climate of the times.

Since many of the federal prisons are located in city centres, the architects take great care to establish an attractive public interface, balancing the need for the building to look approachable with the necessary symbols of incarceration, and acknowledging the demands of civic pride in sensitive urban design. Many American prison architects are confident about their role in the Prison Service and the respect with which their views are treated, although even they acknowledge that architecture is marginal in the sense that a prison is only as good as its management.

The administrators, for their part, agree that the right prison environment can reduce tension and that the architecture should emphasize that prisoners are to be treated like human beings.

In France, design innovation is organized through architectural competitions responding to standard briefs for different kinds of prison. Programmes are administered centrally using a series of standard designs emerging from the competitions. The basis of the architectural strategy is the 25-cell unit with direct supervision. A central objective is to maximize socialization through communal education programmes. At the same time, prisoners are given more privacy, for example by installing a shower in each cell. Improving staff accommodation and working conditions is also a high priority.

The programme emphasizes rigid control, although variations are allowed for different regional and climatic conditions. There is no doubt, however, about the central importance attached to design. The competitions are judged as much on architectural quality as on value for money.

The situation in The Netherlands reflects the high regard that the Dutch have for architecture as an important element in the culture of government. This is personified in the longstanding appointment of a distinguished professional as the chief government architect in the Department of Housing and Building, which is responsible for the prison building programme. A carefully chosen cadre of private architects is encouraged to design first-class buildings that both enhance the neighbourhoods in which they are placed and, thanks to the obligatory 1 per cent for art (embodied in all Dutch government building programmes), have produced some witty and enjoyable contributions to the prison scene by artists.

However, this apparently humanistic approach chimes oddly with some of the designs. These demonstrate an extreme version of indirect supervision based on one-way windows and surveillance cameras – a technique that would appear to do little to alleviate the unavoidable feelings of alienation already suffered by the prisoners. On the other hand, the Dutch have great faith in the virtues of community prisons of modest size embedded in the locality from which the prisoners are drawn. This obviously makes family contact easier during imprisonment and, it is claimed, makes earlier release possible because of the voluntary supervision imposed on the parolee by his or her own people.

In the United Kingdom, hopes for a more enlightened prison regime seem permanently blighted by lack of money and overcrowding, although the administrators are very confident about their abilities in crisis management. Their attention is focussed on coping successfully with the immediate problem rather than looking ahead to a long-term solution. Managing an unpredictable flood of numbers seems more important than developing a strategy for improving the quality of service. In such a climate, it is not surprising that architects are marginalized as servants of the builder.

The new generation of prisons promoted originally by the PSA and the Prison Department has been dismissed as too expensive, although no evidence has been presented of even a rudimentary cost–benefit study. They have, by contrast, been warmly praised by the prison staff and the local communities, and are evidently appreciated by the prisoners.

In spite of this, the old regime of dialogue and development has been replaced by the Private Finance Initiative (PFI). This is based on competitive tendering for the design, supply and operation over a number of years of each project. Quality is driven out by the need to reduce costs and minimize risk. The architectural evidence of this process is characterized by a high degree of monotonous banality, with no design innovation and no attempt to respond to changes in penal policies and ideas.

Private finance

The effect on architectural quality of the PFI approach is potentially extremely serious. The UK seems to be unique in using a device that actually drives a wedge between users and designers. Other countries employ private finance on terms that still leave the designer answerable to the Prison Service rather than to the funder.

Secret competitive tendering prohibits the dialogue between designers and the Prison Service that is the essential prerequisite of a good design. It is well nigh impossible for the authorities to resist the pressure to award the contract to the bidder who offers the greatest number of cells at the lowest price. Numbers drive out quality. It is impossible to make an impartial assessment of the subjective criteria affecting long-term quality so, in the interest of commercial fairness, they are ignored. Does an annual reduction of 1 per cent in recidivism figure in the performance specification?

The proponents of the PFI system are chiefly those with either a financial or a political stake in its success. They claim that it establishes a closer relationship between designers, builders and operators than the old bureaucracy could ever achieve. However, what is this worth if the qualitative criteria figure neither in the brief nor in the evaluation of the tenders? The lack of innovation and poor architectural quality of the PFI products is convincing evidence that the architect's contribution is completely stifled by the commercial prerogatives of the builder, the operator and, above all, the financier whose money is going to be at risk over a long period. Treasury money is a lot cheaper and better able to carry the responsibility if the unpredictable inevitably happens, but politicians will stick to their dogma regardless.

Feedback and development

Science derives its power from a recurring sequence: *hypothesis – experimental test – verification of reproducible results – confirmation of hypothesis* (a new fact), or *a new hypothesis* . . . and so on. It is equally true that the construction process in any sector in any country is as weak or as strong as its support of such a process of feedback.

In terms of prison architecture, this is provided in the USA by a continuity of senior management embodied in the Federal Bureau of Prisons; in France by centralized direction from the state; and in The Netherlands by the tradition of a strong Chief Architect to the Government. In the UK, a more scientific approach was being urgently promoted by the PSA during the 1980s and formally emerged as the PDBS in 1989, with the full support of the Prison Department and the Home Office. A number of so-called 'new generation' prisons were being designed to test different hypotheses about the relationship between design and penal reform, but the whole structure collapsed with the demise of the PSA.

None of the new generation prisons has been properly evaluated except by administrators, whose main criterion is initial cost. Woodhill

Prison in Milton Keynes, according to governors and prison staff the most successful of the new UK prisons, has been dismissed as an extravagant fantasy. A policy of rational development and monitoring has been abandoned for the easier but relatively valueless quantitative judgement.

Cynics who oppose systematic feedback claim that it is impossible to evaluate the performance of such a complex organism as a prison in a way that would make it possible to compare the consequences of one design with another, bearing in mind the overriding influence of managerial quality. The fact that a course of action is difficult does not mean that it is not worth making the effort, particularly when so much money and human happiness is at stake.

In fact there is much interesting and valuable work being done by psychologists and physiologists in Australia, The Netherlands and the USA on the response of inmates to different forms of prison design and management – the two cannot, of course, be divorced. There is much to be done to establish a systematic approach to research and development throughout the penal system.

Lessons can be learned by the Prison Service from one of Britain's major architectural post-war successes – the school building programme. The basis of this was the creation of a division of the Ministry of Education responsible for organizing the design and construction of buildings for education throughout the country. It was called the Architects and Buildings (A & B) Branch, and was headed by the Chief Architect and a senior administrator working in partnership. It developed architectural briefs, using the Schools Inspectorate as proxy clients, promoted new developments in building technology to speed up construction and reduce costs, and sponsored a series of demonstration projects hosted by local education authorities to test new ideas in practice. The results of these were promulgated to the world at large through a series of 'Building Bulletins', which established new benchmarks for architects and their clients. The results not only solved an enormous problem of growth and reconstruction, but also established for Britain an international reputation for excellence in the field of school building.

The parallel with the prison building programme is compelling. It is not difficult to imagine the Prisons Inspectorate and the Prison Ombudsman acting as independent proxy clients who can speak with authority, both for the inmates and the prison officers. It is more difficult to imagine the Prison Service investing in an effective in-house architectural skill. However, there is a very strong case for a development programme of prison design and construction that would incorporate a feedback loop and help the Prison Service to turn itself into a learning institution with a positive attitude to growth and change, rather than lurching from one crisis to another. A team of architects submitted their recommendations on design development, on behalf of the Royal Institute of British Architects, to the Woolf Inquiry in 1990. A summary of these is given at the end of this chapter, but, like the Woolf Report itself and the excellent White Paper that followed it, these ideas seem to have been abandoned by an administration that was proud to proclaim, in the face of all the evidence, that 'prison works'.

Managing demand

All countries and all administrations have a common problem in how to deal with the greatest threat to an enlightened prison building programme – the inherent instability of the penal system. This is characterized by violent and unpredictable swings in demand for prison places, which leave the system buffeted by crisis after crisis, and everybody involved with a deep sense of failure in giving their prisoners a chance to find a better life.

Whenever there is an escape or a riot in the UK, the media whip up public feeling, the Government issues decrees without having enough time to think, the police and judiciary overreact, the Home Office struggles to keep its balance, and the Prison Service, which bears the brunt, is starved of resources and gets the blame when things go wrong.

Although the United States, France and The Netherlands are all suffering from the effects of an increasingly punitive climate, they seem to manage better through a more unified system in which the police, the judiciary and the prison regime work together. The UK may surely learn some lessons from these precedents.

Conclusions

Sir Stephen Tumim, the previous Chief Inspector of Prisons, had this to say in a talk he gave to the Royal Society of Arts on 14 May 1997:

[The Woolf Report] is saying that the real trouble in prisons is the distrust between prisoners and staff, the distrust between senior staff and the Home Office. I must say that within the last couple of years of my time in the prisons, which ended in 1995, you had only to visit any prison as an inspector and the governor would be saying, 'What are they going to do to us next? What are they planning? Who's going to be blamed for what?' That was the attitude in the senior part of the service. Since then many of our best governors have resigned and gone, but the correction of grievance has not proceeded in the commonsense way which Lord Woolf proposed, and which the White Paper proposed.

In the face of such fundamental disarray, it is difficult to see how the architectural performance of the Prison Service in the UK can be improved in the short term. It needs a reforming government with a liberal philosophy and a will to keep abreast of developments and practices in other countries, and to learn from them the most appropriate lessons for the UK.

Appendix   Summary of recommendations from a report on prison design

(By the Royal Institute of British Architects, for Lord Justice Woolf, November 1990)

1. Establish a Home Office Design Group to continue the work of the team which produced the Prison Design Briefing System (PDBS). The new group should be multidisciplinary and headed by a senior architect. Its role would be to encourage and maintain high design standards, monitor results and ensure that they are fed back into future designs.

2. Strengthen the existing Home Office Prison Board and Building Board by adding experienced architects from within the Home Office and outside, to encompass the totality of environmental concerns.

3. Conduct more basic research into the effects of various prison designs on the treatment of prisoners, on the work of prison officers and on the operation and costs of running the prison.

4. Establish more open and direct channels of communication and feedback between Home Office staff and outside consultants involved in the procurement, design and running of prisons.

5. Ensure that the principles outlined in the PDBS are adopted throughout the prison estate in both new and rehabilitated prisons, and keep them under periodic review.

6. Establish a clear and detailed brief, based on PDBS principles, specifically related to a particular prison project before design work is started.

7. Appoint a Senior Manager within the Home Office to be the facilitator between the client and the design team on each prison project.

8. Further reduce, if possible, the four years taken to commission prisons.

9. If the Chief Inspector of Prisons would find it of benefit, allocate an architect to accompany his inspection teams to guide him on design implications.

10. Establish a rolling investment programme of new and rehabilitated prisons, with a plan for the phasing out of those prisons whose useful life has come to an end.

11. Do not use contractor-led 'Design Build' contracts for such complex buildings as prisons.

12. Pay more attention to the detailing of furniture and the design of landscape.

We further recommend that greater efforts should be made to increase public understanding of the role of prisons and the work of the prison service.

6 Does design matter?

Leslie Fairweather

There is often a rather vague understanding about the contribution of architects to the functional, aesthetic and financial success of buildings. Apart from certain high profile structures designed by the famous, many people have little appreciation of the role that architects play, often believing it to be no more than cosmetic. Their task, however, is more complex than that. It can involve every stage of the design and construction process, from helping clients to examine their requirements in very precise terms in the form of a full written brief through to their occupation of the completed building and, sometimes, its subsequent maintenance.

The brief is the major contributing factor to a successful result. It includes the proposed function, the cost limits and method of funding, the constraints of the site; indeed, every detail of why the building is being proposed and how and by whom it will be used. While the outcome will differ widely depending on the type of building and the skill and imagination of its architect, the briefing and design process is the same whether for a prominent city bank or an art gallery, a young offenders' institution or a maximum security prison.

It is true that architects are rarely the prime movers and mainly respond to the needs of their clients, yet their role can be of fundamental importance – especially at the early briefing stages – and can result in new ways of thinking and solving problems. Architects are trained to challenge accepted solutions and policies and, if given the opportunity, can do much more than merely design to a stereotyped brief. They can bring to bear their knowledge and experience of other building types and clients, and contribute a professional outsider's view on how to solve old problems in new ways. They are not being stretched to their full potential if used as draughtsmen and asked merely to assemble standard details within the context of conventional buildings and orthodox layouts. Yet, too often, this is what they are asked to do.

On the other hand, it could be questioned whether architects should be allowed, or need, design freedoms in what might seem to be fairly standard buildings like prisons. Are they not, in many cases, simply assemblers of standard parts? While this may occasionally be the case, there are always special features of any client's requirements, or the site, or the activities to be housed, which demand special design considerations. To give any building its own unique character it needs to be fitted into the local context and have its own individual personality. If nothing else, the assumptions of its sponsors should be challenged. Is the brief sufficiently similar to other briefs to warrant the same design solutions? Is the adoption of standard drawings merely a way of cutting corners and avoiding answering difficult questions? Is there perhaps a chance that the function or security grading may change before the prison is even completed, as often happens? How much flexibility or adaptability should therefore be assumed and allowed for in the design? Buildings endure longer than the ideas that give them substance. These are all questions an architect should ask before embarking on the design process.

Contrasting achievements

There have been only two major innovations in prison design in England during the past 160 years, both of which originated in America. These were the development of radial principles, as exemplified in Pentonville prison, and the adoption of new generation management techniques, which led to the design of small group prisons typified by Woodhill at Milton Keynes.

The first earned its place in history through a small group of powerful enthusiasts, and its actual birth to an outstanding military engineer, Joshua Jebb. The early part of the nineteenth century was remarkable for its social reform and innovation, and for its firm belief in progress and the advancement of science. Building technology was seen as a prime instrument in this fundamental doctrine, and none were greater advocates than the Royal Engineers, who were an important force in achieving reform through the planning, servicing and construction of prisons, barracks and military hospitals. Criminal reformation and army sanitation were critical concerns for Victorian social reformers.

Jebb's army training thus well fitted him for his later career in prisons. He was ingenious in his solutions, and never wavered in his belief that architecture was a crucial vessel of social reform. Although responsible for many prisons, it is Pentonville for which he is most famous and which is his enduring legacy. His brief was to provide prison accommodation in which the separate system could be enforced, and he took as his model an American radial prison, the Eastern Penitentiary in Philadelphia designed by John Haviland. However, instead of adopting it wholesale, he analysed every aspect of prison life and found new solutions. He recognized, for example, the importance of indoor air quality and warmth as having a direct influence on the health of prisoners, and devised an ingenious method of providing a flow of fresh air to each cell. He designed the cells, in particular, with great care. The cell, to him, was the key to the whole institution: 'a kind of chrysalis within which the transmutation of the criminal mind was to take place'.[1]

Although not an architect, he performed most of the functions of an architect and produced what was, for the age, one of the most splendid and advanced constructions for housing criminals. He did, in fact, employ the eminent architect Sir Charles Barry to apply an Italianate frontage of machicolations and pilasters (*Figure 3.7*); the rest was pure Jebb, developed from Haviland's basic idea. But, as Robin Evans points out:[2]

1   Evans, R. (1982). *The Fabrication of Virtue: English Prison Architecture 1750–1840*. Cambridge University Press.
2   *Ibid.*

After this, it was the fate of every prison architect to do little more than Barry had done, as the construction, detailing, and dimensioning of prison buildings were pre-ordained. All the architects could do was to fit Jebb wings onto a site and then devote attention to the appearances of facades and entrances, which became increasingly mediaeval, ornamental and meretricious.

To some extent the terms 'architect' and 'engineer' were interchangeable at that time, although Prince Albert was in no doubt about their different attributes:

If we want any work done of an unusual character, and send for an architect, he hesitates, debates, trifles: we send for an engineer and he does it.

Jebb could be said to have done it. His great achievement was to apply himself to an old problem and come up with an astonishingly new and original solution.

He had, however, a further and very powerful weapon in his crusade to improve British prisons. He held, among his many other senior positions, the post of Surveyor General of Prisons. It was through Jebb that all new prisons had to be approved, so it was hardly surprising that over the next six years following the completion of Pentonville in 1842 many new radial prisons were built, and many more existing prisons were modified. He dominated central government's penal policy and pushed his own favoured architectural solution from then until his death in 1863. Whatever his faults, and they were many, he brilliantly summed up the end of an era of chaos and confusion and pointed prison design in a totally new direction.

What happened after Pentonville?

Since Pentonville there have been many design variations on the basic theme, the most notable of which has been the substitution of closed corridors for open wings. Architects obviously played a part in these changes, but came up with no design innovations to match Jebb's achievement at Pentonville. Consultant architects employed by the Home Office (later the Prison Service) were not allowed to propose solutions that might rock the established certainties, and were servants to expediency. One such architect claims that he had to 'work within an extremely rigid brief, harshly applied, with dire threats of excommunication if any predetermined decision was questioned, or if the word "why?" was asked, or if his practice had any consultations with unauthorized bodies or sources'. He claims that his practice was subsequently ostracized for his involvement in giving evidence to the Woolf inquiry into prison riots – hardly a recipe for improved collaboration and confidence.

Some of these restrictive practices were to change with the adoption of prison designs inspired by new generation principles, when architects were given more, if still limited, freedoms. Chapter 2 describes in more detail how this came about, and how it led to the first break with tradition after Pentonville. Again, like Pentonville, the inspiration came from America. A completely new architectural vocabulary had to be devised to describe a new system of management to which design was to respond. For this to happen, the old prison briefing guides had to be totally rewritten: adaptation and addition were not enough.

The Prison Design Briefing System (PDBS) that resulted was, like Jebb's, an exhaustive and detailed examination of every aspect of prison design and use. It was produced by an architect leading a team of specialist advisers and users, and included an illustration of a possible design model. Unlike Jebb's design at Pentonville, however, this one illustrated a *general* solution. It was not site-specific, nor was it related to a particular problem or security category. The final design was to be left to the project architect to resolve for individual prisons.

Although many of the principles of the PDBS were subsequently adopted, no complete model solution as illustrated has yet been built, although there are plans to do so. However, this will be more than a decade after the publication of PDBS and after its recommendations were generally commended and endorsed. What a contrast to Jebb's Pentonville, which was widely imitated during the following decade and is still copied today in a modified form. The procurement of new prisons has now been handed over to private operators, with no apparent restrictions on what they can design and build. They do not have to stick to PDBS principles, nor to anything approximating to the model solution.

There are concerns and potential benefits about such a major swing in procurement methods from public to private sector. If the purpose of prison was unclear before, will it become more clouded when private operators have a free hand? Their priorities may be different, for while needing to provide appropriate secure accommodation and a constructive regime they also have to offer good financial returns to their shareholders; not a normal requirement for government projects.

How far will the architects attached to these operators be free to discuss and question the more fundamental aspects of regimes and staffing; to challenge government and Prison Service policies and to offer alternative solutions? Their technical competence is not in question, but if they cannot do these things will the role of the architect as an independent professional be compromised or restricted? Will it diminish any hope of breaking new ground in design and the treatment of prisoners? Will the influence of architects, as Andrew Derbyshire fears, be marginalized? Or, on the contrary, could their influence suddenly flourish, with a variety of designs and fresh thinking on offer, forged through competition, where best practice could be identified and incorporated in future prisons?

Many advantages are claimed for private sector prisons:

- that there is closer collaboration between the client, including *all* users of the prison, and architects
- that it is possible to stand back and look at the issues from first principles
- that with responsibility for running the prison for 25 years, good relations have to be fostered with the local community, with consequent benefits to the inmates and staff.

Whether all of these supposed benefits will result in real design innovation remains to be seen – there is not a lot of evidence so far of a conceptual leap. In France, where it is a legal requirement to hold architectural competitions for new prisons, nothing new has yet emerged. This could be due to a failure of architectural imagination, or a resistance to change on the part of the authorities. Much depends on how closely the private operators work in conjunction with the prison authorities in understanding changing trends in penal policy and reacting to them in a positive way.

While it is almost impossible to prove what effect the prison experience has on long-term recidivism or rehabilitation, it is possible to be more certain about short-term environmental conditions and the immediate impact of buildings and regimes on inmates and staff. To gain maximum benefit from the freedoms offered by private sector involvement, it is crucial that checks and comparisons are made between the private sector prisons and those run by the Prison Service. Each must learn from the other, but the basic requirements of an effective prison system must never be jeopardized by the desire simply to produce a good financial return.

The easiest way to cut costs and maximize profit is to reduce or downgrade staff. This in turn may limit the adoption of constructive regimes and activities, and all of these have design implications. For example, most prisons have large kitchens with generous spaces between equipment. This allows inmates to work in them with safety and affords officers clear sightlines in case of trouble. If prisoners were not allowed in, the kitchens could be very much smaller and more efficient, in line with normal commercial restaurant kitchens; but a prisoner activity would be lost. That may not be significant in all cases, but it must be recognized and weighed in the balance.

Different approaches, different results

Joshua Jebb brilliantly summed up the penal requirements of his day and, in Pentonville, produced an icon of power and authority that was copied throughout Europe. He created a prison image and style that is still instantly recognizable today. He was a single-minded and powerful man, who achieved a sufficiently exalted position to force through a large and complex building programme in an incredibly short time.

The term 'fast track' today means that designers and contractors manage to design and build in about three or four years. Jebb built, fitted out and commissioned a prison for 560 prisoners in just 18 months. This was no mean achievement, even though planning restrictions then were fewer and sites easier to obtain. With our new technology, why does it take us so long today? And why do our prisons cost so much to build?

The modern equivalent of Jebb, but without his power to enforce, is split three ways: the team that produced the Prison Design Briefing System; the Prison Service (now itself split into two units for existing and new prisons); and the plethora of architects and consortia bidding for the work. There is no one in Jebb's solo role as prison supremo, given responsibility to force design reforms through or to set and insist upon high standards of design quality.

It is true that design may now possibly develop more individually than was possible under Jebb, as there is no overriding image to sustain. In theory, more architectural talent should be released to design in new ways to cope with constantly changing penal ideas. In practice, there are fears that events will again overtake such utopian dreams, and the longer-term planning urged by architects will be abandoned in favour of short-term expediency. Money is only available when disaster looms. As one cynical prison officer put it: 'prisons don't get designed, they get built'.

Could the day ever arrive when whole packaged prisons are bought from catalogues? The Norwegian prefabricated Ready-to-Use Units

(RTUs), bought to solve overcrowding, are perhaps an indication of what might be to come.

Managing design has never been treated with the same seriousness as other aspects of prison management, and architects are not encouraged to enter into any sort of meaningful discussion about the wider questions of the purposes of imprisonment and the attitudes of society. The importance of the brief as the springboard for design has already been stressed. Design cannot be created in a vacuum, but is the result of solving clearly defined problems as expressed in the brief. The creation of the brief, through intense discussions with the client and a deep understanding of the social and penal issues, is as important a job for the architect as the actual design work that follows. Architects respond best to clearly defined problems, but they too must be involved in defining and understanding what those problems are. Their work starts long before any design sketches are produced. A brief into which they have had no input, and which is apparently unrelated to current penal policies and possible future trends, presents architects with major design problems and a deep sense of misgiving. It is not the best use of their skills – architects are trained to be problem solvers; is it not likely that they may have interesting new slants and solutions to offer if asked?

To answer the question in the title, 'Does design matter?', it has to be said that it does matter very much indeed. Design cannot solve all problems, but it is not marginal. The perennial task of prison architects is to struggle to produce acceptable solutions in a very difficult and changing climate of opinion amid conflicting advice and not a little confusion. They have to balance functional and environmental needs against the demands of security and increasingly vengeful and worried public opinion, with most politicians not sure, and seeming not to care, where they stand on any of the issues. Many reform groups are guilty, too, of paying insufficient attention to the importance of design and its effect on inmates and staff. They retain no architectural advisers, nor do they appear to appreciate the fundamental importance of the envelope within which prisoners are incarcerated and regimes enforced.[3]

Prisons are public demonstrations of what the state thinks of its offenders and how it believes they should be treated. Seán McConville believes that architecture is 'explicit, powerful and influential'. Why, then, are architects mostly excluded from full involvement in its creation when they have so much to offer?

Bibliography

The literature on Jebb and Pentonville is too vast to be listed in this very abbreviated bibliography.

Edited by Iona Spens (1994). *Architecture of Incarceration*. Academy Editions

Dale, K. W. *Sir Joshua Jebb (1793–1863) and the model prison – Pentonville 1840–1842*. Royal Engineers Journal, December 1994, pp. 272–7.

---

3   See Chapter 17.

Dale, K. W. (1992). *Within these walls*. Building Services, December, pp. 32–3.

Evans, R. (1982). *The Fabrication of Virtue: English Prison Architecture 1750–1840*. Cambridge University Press.

Fairweather, L. (1989). *Prisons: a new generation*. Architects' J., 16 March, 26–31.

Fairweather, L. (1992). *Prisons* (Woodhill Prison, Milton Keynes). Architects' J., 2 September, 28–43.

Fairweather, L. (1993). *Modernising Strangeways*. Architects' J., 2 June, 29–42.

Fairweather, L. (1997). *Prison design: a Christian dimension. Newlife*, The Prison Service Chaplaincy Review, 13, pp. 13–25.

Foucault, M. (1975). *Discipline and Punish: The Birth of the Prison*. Penguin Books.

Home Office (1988). *Prison Design Briefing System* (PDBS). Home Office Library Publications, updated 1989, 1990, 1991.

Home Office Working Party (1985). *New Directions in Prison Design*: Report of a Home Office Working Party on American New Generation Prisons. HMSO.

King, A. (ed.) (1980). *Buildings and Society: Essays on the Social Development of the Built Environment*. Routledge and Kegan Paul.

Markus, T. A. *Pattern of the law*. Architectural Rev., Vol 116, no 694, October 1954, pp. 251–6.

Markus, T. A. (1993). *Buildings and Power: Freedom and Control in the Origin of Modern Building Types*. Routledge.

UNSDRI (now UNICRI) (1975). *Prison Architecture*. Rom & London. The Architectural Press Ltd.

White Paper (1991). *Custody Care and Justice, The Way Ahead for the Prison Service in England and Wales*. HMSO.

7 Prison policy, construction and design

Sir Richard Tilt

Rising prison populations are a familiar preoccupation in England and Wales and in most, but not all, other countries. In England and Wales there has been a particularly dramatic increase in the prison population in recent years, probably rising faster than the international average. As a response to policy changes there was a steady fall in the prison population in England and Wales in the late 1980s and early 1990s, reaching a low point of about 42 000 at the end of 1992 (an incarceration rate of about 75 per 100 000 of the general population). This was followed by a sharp and sustained increase from the beginning of 1993, with an increase of about 50 per cent in the prison population over that five-year period. The population in 1999 stood at over 65 000 and was still rising. That equated to about 125 per 100 000 of the population, and was roughly equivalent to the figure in Canada but some considerable way ahead of France and Germany's incarceration rates of about 90 per 100 000. It was, nonetheless, still a very long way from the rate of incarceration in the USA, which stood at 645 per 100 000.

One of the perennial problems for prison administrators is the fallibility of population projections. The growth from 1995 onwards had not been in any way predicted by the statisticians, and an extraordinarily rapid response was needed to keep pace. The projections of long-term trends published in January 1998 suggested that there may well be a population of over 82 000 by 2005, with an upper variant that suggests a population of over 92 000. All of this prompted media speculation about the taxpayer facing a £2 billion bill for 24 more prisons. This was not unrealistic in terms of the capacity required if the trends continued, but was fairly unrealistic in terms of likely outcome. The imperatives of public expenditure would actually force politicians to change policies in some way to make sure that kind of public expenditure on prisons was not required. However, the key problem was not so much the actual increase but the speed of increase. The numbers rose by approximately 6000 (about 10 per cent) during 1997 and 1998 and continued to rise at about the same rate, at times by as much as 400 per week, which implied building a new prison about every two weeks.

As well as the required long-term planning, short-term coping strategies were needed. These relied on a range of measures, some of which were quite unconventional. However, Prison Service policy, which is to aim to match the population increases with extra capacity and with some small increase in overcrowding, was absolutely clear throughout. Levels of overcrowding in England and Wales were considerably lower in 1999 than they were in 1990, despite a much higher population, and this was a direct consequence of the increasing capacity.

Statisticians struggle to keep up with the changing behaviour of sentencers, but it is clear in this case that what led to the growth in the prison population were two factors, both occurring mainly in the Crown Courts. First, the rate of custody given to people found or pleading guilty rose from about 45 per cent to about 60 per cent over a three-year period. Secondly, the average sentence length rose from about 19 months to some 21 or 22 months over the same period. These two trends added thousands to the daily population.

The capacity of the prison estate had to be more efficiently exploited. There was necessarily some increased overcrowding, but not at the levels experienced in the 1980s. There was, however, a need for increased prisoner movements to utilize capacity on a daily basis, and in the summer of 1997 there was the bizarre situation where people were being moved large distances every evening simply to exploit the last few vacancies. In July of that year the Service was on the edge of reaching absolute capacity for a number of weeks, and was obliged to resort to extremely extensive prisoner movement. This was, of course, counterproductive in relation to many other objectives – for example, it obviously disrupted family links and caused great hardship both to families and to prisoners. It was not an ideal solution, but the alternative would have been to use police cell accommodation at huge cost, which simply sucked money out of the main programmes.

The overall figures revealed significant fluctuations in the size of specific groups, with particularly sharp rises for women and juveniles. For some reason the rate of increase for female prisoners had been twice the rate for male prisoners, so that the female population had been increasing at about 20 per cent a year. In 1995 the female population was about 1500; by 1998 it had reached about 3000. Over a longer period of time, between 1992 and 1998, the female population rose by 70 per cent, and the projection showed it set to continue to rise at a faster rate than the male population. By 1998 it represented over 4 per cent of the total prison population, 1 per cent up from an earlier fairly steady figure of about 3 per cent. This rapid increase required readjustment to some of the existing accommodation, and the roles of a number of male establishments were changed. Some existing female establishments were enlarged, and plans were set in train to build new facilities. Planning permission for female prisons at Peterborough and Ashford was sought, and further changes were clearly necessary to keep pace with the growth of the female prison population.

Changing to female accommodation is not straightforward, and there is a particularly difficult problem in ensuring that female prisoners quickly have access to appropriate facilities – particularly visitors' facilities – as well as mother and baby accommodation. The Prison Service did not always recognize the implications in good time. It has always been difficult to change the staffing mix quickly enough and, although mixed staffing is beneficial in female establishments, there does need to be a majority of female staff.

Considerable effort has been invested in defining the kind of regime standards that ought to be provided for both women and young offenders. That, of course, has significant design implications.

The politics of imprisonment

There were three phases during the 1990s that underpinned the prison population trends outlined above, and these directly affected the Prison Service's investment in prison building and design.

First, in the late 1980s, the Home Secretary was saying that he believed prison was an expensive way of making people worse. This attitude was reflected in the criminal justice legislation in the early 1990s, particularly the Criminal Justice Act 1991, and was echoed in the Woolf Report and the White Paper that followed the Strangeways riot.[1] Lord Woolf provided a very perceptive analysis of the problems facing the Prison Service, and his recommendations were warmly welcomed by the Prison Service. This preoccupation with conditions and treatment did allow for substantial capital investment in the prison estate. Some new accommodation was provided, which, together with the refurbishment of much of the older Victorian accommodation and a gradual reduction in overcrowding, helped to match accommodation to declining prison numbers. Through a major programme of capital work (completed in 1996), it was possible to achieve an end to the degrading practice of slopping out by providing for 24-hour access to integral sanitation. It is probably sensible to suggest that the implementation of much of the Woolf agenda may also be the reason why the Prison Service managed to cope with the population surge without prisoner disorder.

A second political strand that replaced the earlier liberal approach arrived in about 1993, and was characterized by the mantra 'prison works'. It was a very significant switch in political stance, so much so that the success of the Government penal policy came to be measured almost by the size of the prison population. 'Prison works' was the rhetoric of the then Home Secretary, Michael Howard, which talked about measuring success in terms of public safety by keeping serious and violent offenders secure and providing respite for communities through temporary absence of high volume criminals. This was a corollary to new forms of policing which involved targeting known offenders, and came to be known as incapacitation. It was also accompanied by substantial investment in prison security following the well-publicized escapes from Whitemoor in 1994 and Parkhurst in 1995. It was clear that those events were wholly unacceptable and an indictment of the Prison Service; a signal that people had become too lax and that there was a need to tighten both control and security. The sustained and successful emphasis on security since then very significantly reduced the escape rate until it became one of the lowest rates in the Western world. This period saw substantial investment in security and new establishments, but the Prison Service was also subjected to stringent efficiency targets.

The third political strand was the 'tough on crime, tough on the causes of crime' approach. These were two very clear New Labour election commitments that related to the Prison Service. One was to provide regimes that tackled offending behaviour, and the other was to provide for voluntary testing for drugs and the increase of drug treatment in prisons. This led to a very positive and constructive agenda for which funding was made available through the Comprehensive Spending Review, and the aim was to expand regimes such that all prisoners received 35 hours of constructive activity a week. This was through a mixture of work, education and treatment programmes, known as the Offending Behaviour Programmes, that tackled the treatment of particularly violent and sexual offenders and encouraged a considerable expansion of substance abuse programmes.

---

1 Woolf, A. and Tumim, S. (1991) *Prison Disturbances April 1990*, Cm. 1456. HMSO. *Custody, Care and Justice: the way ahead for the Prison Service in England and Wales* (1991) Cm. 1647. HMSO.

The private sector role

The involvement of the private sector was a radical change for the Prison Service. This contribution can be assessed under three headings: competition, efficiency and innovation.

Competition

The Conservative Government (pre-1997) introduced the private sector as a matter of policy, very much to provide competition and stimulus for the mainstream public sector service. There were two phases to this, the first being contracting out, and four such establishments were built as a result. The second-phase prisons were known as design, construct, management and finance (DCMF) under the Private Finance Initiative (PFI). Not only was the management contracted out, but also the whole design, building and financing. Three such establishments were seen operating, and four more are due for completion by 2000. Initial scepticism was replaced by confidence. There was a clear recognition from many outside commentators that the first four prisons to be run under contract – Blakenhurst in Worcestershire; Doncaster in West Yorkshire; Buckley Hall in Rochdale, Lancashire; and the Wolds in Everthorpe, North Humberside – were performing extremely well. A very firm regulatory framework was established, with daily onsite monitoring of contract performance, and this made sure that the private sector contractors kept very strictly to the contract.

Efficiency

Comparative studies were made over about three years, which proved that the initially contracted-out prisons showed substantial savings in comparison with the public sector prisons. As a result of the competitive stimulus and tight efficiency improvements in the public sector, the gap between private and public sector costs started closing at about 2.5 per cent per year. The data suggested that the private sector management contracted-out establishments were some 10–15 per cent cheaper on a cost per place basis than their public sector equivalents. However, the principal reasons for the reduced costs in the private sector were lower staff costs, lower staffing levels, lower pay for staff, and poorer pension and sick pay provision than in the public sector.

Innovation

Bringing in new operators, sometimes with international partners, may have injected some new ideas into prison management. While these were not as many as had been expected, a valuable exchange of good practice between the public and private sectors was forged. There was no doubt that the private finance initiative encouraged innovation by defining the required ends, outcomes and number of prison places required, and by delivering a service to a particular level rather than over-specifying the means of doing so – although requirements of deliverability and quality had to be satisfied. The PFI approach provided innovation in a variety of ways. In terms of design, Parc prison in Bridgend, South Wales made greater use of IT to reduce staffing levels. In terms of construction, this prison and the Altcourse prison in Fazakerley, Liverpool were completed ahead of schedule at a time when accommodation was desperately needed. They were built using the very latest techniques, comparing well with the old public sector construction methods, which were always bedevilled by high cost and long time-scales. The contracts have a life of 25 years, with suitable breaks during that time if necessary to re-evaluate the management of the prison.

Emergency accommodation

Innovation was also a key feature in the emergency accommodation project, both in conception and construction. In addition to completely new prisons, new houseblocks were built very quickly indeed, sometimes within six months. Other measures included: the refurbishment of old unused wings; some quick-build prefabricated accommodation bought from companies that had been providing accommodation for oil rig workers; some very small place-creating schemes; and lastly, perhaps most innovatively of all, a floating prison in the form of a ship moored in Portland harbour and providing 400 very good quality prison places. There was some small increase in overcrowding, but overall the long-term aim is to eliminate it altogether. Prisoners should not be required to share accommodation against their will. The opportunity for exploitation of individuals where they are forced to share is very high indeed and extremely undesirable. Overcrowding must be eliminated in all establishments.

Conclusions

The Private Finance Initiative has been very successful and offers a way of replacing old, inefficient prisons, particularly some very small ones, using the private finance route. It is doubtful that the prison population will continue to grow as rapidly as in the past – expenditure implications will push politicians of all persuasions to look for community-based measures as alternatives to imprisonment. New prisons need more high-quality activity spaces to allow opportunities for constructive experiences and events that can change behaviour and attitudes.

Electronic tagging, for home detention curfew, will afford a much more flexible way of using prison, with periods shared between prison and community care.

The problem with prison buildings is that they endure while ideas change. About one-third of the prison estate dates from the nineteenth century or earlier, and these prisons were built for quite different philosophies, in quite different social climates and with very limited space to expand. For control purposes they actually remain a very good design, but they simply do not have the space and facilities required in a modern training prison.

8 Building for growth

Elaine Bailey

The scale of the problem of space has been outlined by Richard Tilt, and was due to the rise in prisoner population, segmentation of the population, and financial and political constraints. The practical consequences demanded an Emergency Accommodation Programme to keep pace with the increasing numbers. The Prison Service was running out of places for prisoners, and the alternative solution of using police cells at a cost of £120 000 per prisoner per year – more than four times the cost of a prison place – was unacceptable in the long term.

The Prison Service therefore embarked on an ambitious building programme consisting of:

- the construction of two or three new prisons each year via the Private Finance Initiative (PFI) route
- bringing mothballed accommodation back into use
- the provision of new accommodation blocks within existing prisons
- reclaiming cells
- the provision of temporary accommodation, which resulted in the purchase of a prison ship, HMP The Weare, from America, and mooring it in Portland Harbour.

The need for so many different types of accommodation was due to a number of factors. First, the previous Government had promoted the provision of public services using private finance – the Private Finance Initiative – due at least in part to the Government's desire to reduce the immediate public sector borrowing requirements (PSBR). PFI projects involving the provision of services (i.e. prisoner places) rather than buildings had the effect of converting what would have been capital expenditure into current expenditure. As a result, whereas in the case of traditional public sector building the payments for the prison buildings had to be made as significant capital payments during the two- to three-year construction period, the payments in respect of PFI prisons could be spread evenly over a much longer period as part of the running costs.

Secondly, additional accommodation was needed quickly and at phased intervals to match the rise in population. PFI prisons take two to three years from inception to come on-stream, but additional places were required by the end of 1996 – only six months after the launch of the Emergency Accommodation Programme.

Thirdly, there was a growing awareness within the Prison Service that it needed to tailor its accommodation to the differing needs of different prisoner groups. For example, women generally do not try to escape, nor do they attack structures; there is therefore no need to provide as robust a building fabric for women's accommodation as for adult males who pose a security risk. On the other hand, experience has shown that people on remand are more likely to try to escape, to harm themselves and to attack the fabric of the building, and therefore accommodation for this inmate group has to be more robust. The introduction of an earned incentive programme, which gives inmates the reward of better conditions and regime in return for good behaviour, also enables the provision of accommodation of varying degrees of robustness and austerity of internal finishes.

The fourth factor was finance. The Home Secretary of the time had to obtain additional funds from the Treasury, who had to be convinced that the proposed building plans represented good value for money. In all, the Treasury provided over £250 million to fund this building programme.

New prisons

Contracts for new prisons are awarded under the PFI initiative, with contractors responsible for the design, construction, management and finance (DCMF). These prisons are dealt with by the Prison Service Contracts and Competition Group. All other prisons are the responsibility of the Prison Service Construction Unit.

To date, 3100 places have been provided by five operators under the PFI initiative – 800 at Parc in Bridgend, 600 at Altcourse in Fazakerley and, most recently, 500 at Lowdham Grange. Contracts have been awarded for two further prisons, Forest Bank, Swinton (800) and Ashfield, near Bristol (400), which are due to come on-stream in the year 2000. Two further prisons are currently being planned.[1] The basis of the contract between the Prison Service and the operator is detailed in Chapter 14.

New accommodation within existing prisons

In order to meet the short delivery time-scales of six months upwards, the Construction Unit considered standardization of design and modularization of construction. There simply was not the time to develop a wide range of differing designs. What was needed was a small number of designs that could be repeated many times over at different establishments throughout England and Wales.

In terms of modularization of manufacture, the more that can be manufactured off site – in a factory or in laboratory-like conditions – the better. The quality that can be achieved in a factory is higher and more consistent than that which can be achieved on site, which means that there is less snagging to be done. The time-scale in which buildings can be manufactured is also much shorter in a factory than on site, because factory manufacture is not affected by weather or the number of daylight hours. A factory can simply keep going for the requisite number of hours to produce the structure within the time required.

---

1 Details of all the prisons mentioned are included in Appendix 8.1 at the end of this chapter.

Figure 8.1
Houseblock cell unit built as part of the
Emergency Accommodation programme.

Another advantage of standardization and modularization is cost. Costs can be driven down because of the repetition, and it is easier to predict what the out-turn costs are going to be, which is essential given that funding from the Treasury was a fixed amount.

Houseblocks

The most common type of accommodation used in the Emergency Accommodation Programme was the houseblock, which provides accommodation to Category B standard[2] (*Figure 8.1*). A houseblock typically consists of two wings, each providing 60 cells arranged over two floors with a central area providing showers, association, offices and other facilities. The cells are arranged on each side of a central gallery, which is open from ground to roof. There are clear views along each wing from the central area. The shape of the houseblock can be configured to fit the site; the block can be straight, cranked, provided with spurs of different lengths, or have just one spur. It can be two or three storeys in height. What does not change is the use of a standard cell and central area.

The houseblocks can be built in either steel or concrete. They are prefabricated in a factory and brought to site in sections of four cells, which are then fixed together. As an example of speed of delivery and installation, Garth prison at Preston was brought into use in May 1997, just over eight months after work started on site and at a cost of just over £6 million.

However, as more and more houseblocks were built, the cost of individual schemes began to rise. This is because the easier sites were picked off first – easier in terms of planning approval, ground conditions, lead-up services and the number of ancillaries required. Taking ancillary accommodation as an example, in the first phase of houseblocks, workshops were the most common and generally the only

2 Security categories are listed in Appendix 8.2.

additional facility required. However, in later phases the number of ancillaries has increased significantly. For example, at Styal prison, Cheshire, which cost £10 million, a new workshop, kitchen, library and car park have been provided, the visiting facilities extended, the gate and reception modified, and the existing library converted into a chapel and the old stores into a works department. However, even here construction took no more than eight months from start to occupation.

The scale of the houseblock programme was such that 3700 places in 29 houseblocks were provided. Over 700 places were provided within one year of project start-up (the equivalent of one large prison); the remainder within the following three years.

Ready to use units (RTUs)

The second type of accommodation that the Construction Unit provided is the Ready to Use units. The population crisis was such that providing houseblocks could not entirely solve the problem of providing the right type of accommodation in the right location and at the right time-scale. Places were required by February/March 1997, and this could not be achieved with houseblocks. The problem required an innovative solution, and led to the use of RTU accommodation – which had not, and probably never would have been, considered in the past.

It was pure chance that a catalogue arrived advertising second-hand construction workers' accommodation for sale. The units provided a prefabricated solution, like the houseblock, but for category C rather than category B accommodation, and they could be installed even more quickly than the houseblocks. This type of accommodation was clearly suitable, although it has a shorter life than the houseblocks. The useful life of RTUs is reckoned to be from 15 to 17 years; possibly longer. Each RTU unit provides 40 places, and to date there are 20 units at 15 different locations.

Ten second-hand units were bought from Norway because places were needed quickly. The remainder were purchased from both Norwegian and British companies following a competitive tender. Buying new units enabled certain improvements to the design to be made. These units have been a resounding success, and governors have been using them as part of their differential regime. Inmates on the enhanced level of the earned incentives and privileges programmes have been accommodated in the RTUs, and there have been very few problems with vandalism. That is hardly surprising given that, in most cases, the RTUs are the best accommodation at the establishment.

The Weare

The Weare is another example of an innovative solution to the problem of providing the right type of accommodation in the right location at the right time (*Figure 8.2*).

The Weare was used as a floating barracks during the Falklands war, and was subsequently purchased by the New York Department of Corrections for use as a rehabilitation centre for those involved in drug crime. The Weare is a flat-bottomed barge, and its superstructure consists of steel containers stacked on top of one another to provide five levels of category C accommodation. It arrived in Portland Harbour on

Figure 8.2
The Weare, moored at Weymouth, Dorset, formerly used as a floating barracks. This provided an imaginative solution to an acute accommodation problem, and it is now popular both as a prison and as a tourist attraction.

13 March 1997, but there was no planning permission. The application had been rejected at the beginning of February, mainly on the grounds that it would be a blight to tourism. Fortunately the Department of the Environment reviewed the matter very quickly, and planning permission was granted at the end of March.

When comparing the Weare with traditional establishments, the sea represents the foundations. The Weare's foundations move – they are capable of rising and falling up to six metres in certain weather conditions, and the vessel can also move two metres forward and two metres aft, two metres outwards and one metre in compression. Throughout all these potential movements, the Weare must remain fully operational. To allow this, all methods of access have been carefully designed and all service connections are by means of flexible umbilical cords. The vessel also has ballast and trim systems to keep her at the correct plane. The ship is secured to the shore by ropes, and is also restrained by anchors. To date she has withstood winds of 96 miles per hour.

The vessel is unique in that she has a 24-hour qualified marine crew on board to ensure that the ship's systems and moorings are kept within the tolerances and at optimum performance. The crew has access to an on-board weather station, the meteorological office and ship-to-shore radio. It was discovered in New York that the vessel had been inadequately mothballed, and consequently all the mechanical and electrical systems had to be overhauled and recommissioned once it reached its berth in Portland, and the fire precautions substantially upgraded to bring them in line with UK standards.

It took just four months to refurbish and bring the Weare back into use, and it was finally handed over to the Governor in the middle of July 1997. It seems that the planners' worries that the Weare would badly affect tourism were unfounded.

Whilst the Weare was a fast response to an immediate problem, the layout of the ship in operational terms has proved very efficient because of the short distances between the accommodation and any one of the ancillaries.

To sum up, the Prison Service delivered four new prisons (including the Weare), 29 houseblocks, 20 RTUs and four refurbished wings, all within budget and on time. Just as importantly, the accommodation – whether houseblocks, RTUs or the Weare – is of a very good quality. The programme has been a spectacular success, and this is reflected in the fact that, with the prison population continuing to rise, it has been extended, and more houseblocks and RTUs are being commissioned.

Planning problems

Problems in obtaining planning approval, which the Prison Service nearly always encounters, considerably affect the speed at which new accommodation can be delivered. Whilst the Prison Service has, in theory, Crown immunity from the procedures, in practice this exemption is not used. The typical response from a local planning authority is to resist any proposal for a new prison. This is often emotive, based on the concept that a prison stigmatizes an area. The planning issues are not looked at objectively, nor are the economic advantages and the job creation that a new prison brings to a community considered.

Both Altcourse in Fazakerley and Agecroft in Manchester were initially refused planning permission by the local authority, and both went to a public inquiry which decided in favour of the Prison Service. The Prison Service has also had planning applications refused for temporary prisons in Yorkshire and the North West. The Weare was initially refused, and a public inquiry was required for a houseblock at Brinsford, Featherstone, Wolverhampton. There was also a public inquiry over a new prison at Peterborough.

However, the Department of the Environment, Transport and the Regions recognized the problems, and issued local planning authorities with a new planning guidance circular drawing attention to the need for new prison accommodation.

Maintenance

The Prison Service has a large and very diverse estate of over 130 establishments built at various times to various designs. There are four main building types: Victorian, country houses and ex-service camps, the 1960s hotel style of prison layout, and the 1980s PSA programme.

The maintenance of such a large and diverse estate is a major task, a problem that is compounded by the relatively high age profile. Only 46 prisons have been built since 1960, and around 50 are over 100 years old. However, the age or date of first occupation of the prison is not necessarily an infallible guide to its condition. In general the worst conditions are found at prisons built in the 1960s and 1970s, due largely to poor design and construction methods. For example, many of the prisons have flat roofs, which leak and deteriorate quite rapidly.

In comparison, many Victorian prisons have in recent years benefited from major refurbishment schemes that have enhanced their fabric, services, and living and working environment.

It has been estimated that over the last seven years £600 million has been spent on maintaining the prison estate. Whilst this may be perceived to be substantial expenditure, when compared with other public sector departments – and indeed with the private sector – it actually represents a large under-investment. The Construction Unit assessed the backlog in 1999, and over £300 million worth of maintenance work was identified. A continuing programme of condition surveys is underway, and a database has been established with schemes listed by category – for example, roofs, electrics and heating systems. A procedure is also in place for prioritizing maintenance needs, which is essential given that on the one hand there is a backlog in excess of £300 million and on the other a baseline for capital expenditure of £100 million per annum. Prioritization is essentially a matter of risk assessment – what is the likelihood of a failure occurring, and what would be the consequences of such a failure?

The database has one other important function, which is to aid future planning. Now that the extent of the backlog is known, with evidence to support the amount that needs to be spent annually to maintain the estate, the Unit is better placed to make bids for funds from the overall Prison Service budget and also from the Treasury.

The legacy of the past

Lancaster Castle is one of our oldest prisons. Some of the earliest buildings on the site, such as the so-called 'Witches Tower', named after the Lancaster witches incarcerated there in 1612, are traceable back to 1229. Lancaster Castle was remodelled in 1793 as a male, female and debtors' prison. This building is typical of many early prisons, where old castle gatehouses or dungeons were pressed into use to detain criminals because of the robustness and official ownership of the structures.

The first 'official' prison building programme was ordered by the Assizes of Clarendon in 1166. In 1423 Newgate was rebuilt, and Bridewell opened in 1556, having previously been used as a palace for Henry VIII. In 1773 the first self-styled prisons' inspector, John Howard, High Sheriff of Bedfordshire, started his work, and in 1816 Millbank Penitentiary was opened on a site now occupied by the Tate Gallery. The prison estate also has a fort from the Napoleonic period masquerading as a prison at the Verne; and Dartmoor, which was built by prisoners of war from both the American War of Independence and the Napoleonic wars. Pentonville (1842) was the most influential example of prison architecture in the nineteenth century, known when it was built as 'The Model Prison'. It embodied two principles: a radial plan for ease of supervision, and a separate cell system that aimed to reform prisoners by isolating them from one another.

Wings of this period built to house prisoners were three or four storeys high, with cells on either side of a central gallery. The design of the wings aided supervision in that both the straightness and the openness of the wings allowed a prison officer to stand at the end or in the middle of the wing and have a clear uninterrupted view along its whole length. This same principle has been revived and reflected in the design of new accommodation since the 1980s.

Designs for this type of radial prison, which can also be seen at a number of inner city locations (including Wandsworth, Manchester and Leeds), can be traced back to English and European models and, in particular, proposals for lunatic asylums in London and Cornwall. The radial plan was refined and developed in the USA. The best example is the state penitentiary near Philadelphia, Cherry Hill, which was completed in 1836, housing about 450 inmates in solitary confinement. Heating, ventilation and plumbing all proved problematic. Criticism of Cherry Hill generally centred on four issues:

- cost
- the adverse effects on the physical and mental health of the inmates
- the comparative cruelty of the separate system
- the low degree of inmate reform.

Trenton Prison, New Jersey, whilst similar in design to Cherry Hill, had a different regime philosophy. Inmates worked together in silence in large workshops rather than being in solitary confinement as at Cherry Hill. England opted for the Cherry Hill system, and Pentonville opened in 1842, housing inmates in strict isolation prior to their transportation to penal colonies in Australia or elsewhere.

In 1877 the Prison Commission was set up, and existing local prisons (hitherto administered by the justices) were nationalized. The first prisons erected under the Prison Commission were Dorchester, which has a cruciform layout, and Bristol, which has a telegraph-pole layout. The latter design was first used at Wormwood Scrubs, which was built between 1874 and 1881. Wormwood Scrubs has four parallel cell blocks, originally linked by a central spine corridor but now linked by a new rear spine block. The wings were oriented north–south to ensure that every cell received some sunlight during the course of the day.

Radial prisons of the mid-nineteenth century displayed a simplicity of outline that is in marked contrast to their present appearance, surrounded as they are by a multitude of other buildings. Because regimes were based on separate confinement, all that was required at that time were cells and a few limited support services, which included offices, a chapel, a kitchen, a laundry, infirmaries for men and women, and staff quarters. The proliferation of other structures, including ablution towers, workshops, hospitals, visits and receptions, occurred subsequently as changes were made to the nature of the prison regime.

At the end of the nineteenth century many older prisons were extended, and the radial wings of the newer prisons had additional floors added to accommodate the consolidation of the prison system. Approximately half the local prisons were closed after nationalization. Regime facilities were also added at this time in response to the report of the Gladstone Committee, which recommended an expansion of the number of inmates permitted to work together in community rather than alone in their cells. This necessitated the building of workshops and the removal of treadwheels. The Committee also recommended classification of inmates in local prisons, and special treatment for drunkards, juveniles and habitual criminals.

Separate wings for drunkards, or inebriates as the Victorians called them, were built at prisons like Aylesbury, and in 1906 the Borstal system was set up for juveniles. For habitual criminals, preventive detention prisons, less institutional than conventional prisons, were built. An example is Camp Hill on the Isle of Wight, which opened in 1912 and was described as a sort of garden village.

Women were generally housed in male establishments in separate smaller wings with completely separate systems of movement, particularly to chapel. In addition, work was provided, usually a laundry attached to the female wing.

The second stage of expansion of the national prison estate began when the Prison Service acquired a number of country homes, such as the Grade II-listed Hewell Grange in 1936. The expansion continued after the war, and also included surplus army and airforce camps. None of these buildings had been constructed with prison use in mind, but they were available at a time of need – the country houses because owning families were unable to pay death duties, and the army and RAF camps because of the end of the Second World War. After the Ministry of Defence, the Prison Service is the largest government department owner of listed buildings. It has 170 Grade I and II listed buildings, which include many country houses and also, rather less obviously, statues, ice houses, pig sties, a fort, a theatre, a wash house and a sewage aqueduct; there used to be a crypt, and there are still some ruins!

The next stage of prison building came in the 1960s, when the hotel style of prison was constructed. This phase of building is exemplified by Risley and Hindley, which have narrow central corridors with small cells on either side. These have proved difficult to supervise and manage in a safe economic way. Inmates feel less safe in this environment because of the lack of defensible space and poor sightlines in comparison to the open galleried wings. In construction terms, the fabric of the building is far less robust than Victorian prisons, being quasi-domestic in nature with flat roofs and cavity walls. Consequently, this form of prison building has proved to be very expensive in running costs and maintenance terms.

Following a number of serious escapes, the dispersal system was set up in the 1960s to house the most dangerous inmates. Security at prisons going into the dispersal estate was substantially increased. Following the Whitemoor and Parkhurst escapes in 1994 and 1995, the Woodcock and Learmont reports have resulted in further enhancements to security at dispersal prisons.

The next phase of new prison building was the PSA programme in the 1980s and 1990s. Twenty-one prisons were built of varying designs, although one design, known as the Bullingdon repeat, was built at six locations. The designs for Woodhill, Lancaster Farms and Doncaster were influenced by visits to the USA. All three have triangular living blocks, with two storeys of cells along two sides overlooking an open association area. This area is flooded with natural daylight from floor to ceiling, windows forming the third side of the triangle. The design is easy to supervise and is popular with both staff and inmates.

The spatial design of today's houseblocks and DCMF prisons has come full circle from Victorian times. Accommodation blocks have open galleries, and the layouts of Agecroft and Lowdham Grange follow the radial and cruciform configuration of early Victorian prisons. However, although the layouts are very similar, the rationale behind them is very different. Whilst the main aim of prisons in both Victorian times and today is rehabilitation through work, education and self-awareness, the methods of achieving this differ. The Victorians generally tackled this through isolating prisoners, who lived, ate and worked in their cells, whereas nowadays the idea is to provide ease of supervision together with a safe and secure environment for prison officers and inmates alike. Both the Victorians and today's Prison Service came to the conclusion that galleried wings are the most effective layout for achieving their respective aims.

The future

The need for new prisons will continue – either to accommodate a continuing rise in the prison population, or to replace existing prisons with high running costs. Designs will continue to evolve. For example, there is a pilot scheme for a new safer cell design with fewer ligature points. Small numbers of these cells have been installed in both existing establishments and new houseblocks, and are currently being evaluated by the Suicide Awareness Unit. Subject to this evaluation, more such cells are likely to be built (*Figure 3.1*).

The move towards standardization and modularization will expand the public/private sector partnership beyond the scope of DCMF prisons. The ability of the Prison Service to deliver such a large number of places in such a short period of time under the Emergency Accommodation Programme was due, in part at least, to an informal public/private sector partnership. The first modular houseblocks were developed by the public sector for Buckley Hall, Rochdale, Lancashire – a publicly funded and privately run prison. This signalled to the private sector that the Prison Service would accept modular buildings, and thus created a market. The private sector operators utilized the same design of houseblock for the DCMF prisons, which resulted in more suppliers entering the market. The Prison Service benefited from this expansion, and contracts were placed for houseblocks with multiple suppliers.

However, while elements of prison design will continue to evolve and new prisons may be funded and managed differently to the current DCMF prisons, it is likely that new prisons will be built in accordance with the fundamental principles of design layout that were first introduced by the Victorians and have stood the test of time.

Appendix 8.1 Details of prisons mentioned in the text

Name and location	Opened	CNA[1]	Category
HM Prison & YOI[2], Altcourse, Fazakerley, Liverpool	1997	600	Male local
HM YOI Ashfield, Pucklechurch, Bristol	1999	400	Closed YOI
HM Prison Blundeston, Lowestoft, Suffolk	1962	408	B male
HM Prison Buckley Hall, Rochdale, Lancashire	1994	350	C adult male
HM Prison Bullingdon, Bicester, Oxfordshire	1992	635	Male local

HM Prison Camp Hill, Newport, Isle of Wight	1912	469	C male
HM Prison Dartmoor, Princetown, Yelverton, Devon	1809	619	B male
HM Prison Doncaster, Marshgate, Doncaster, W. Yorkshire	1994	756	Male local
HM Prison Forest Bank, Salford, Greater Manchester (formerly called Agecroft)	2000	800	B local
HM Prison Garth, Leyland, Preston	1988	512	B male
HM Prison Hewell Grange, Redditch, Worcestershire	1949	136	D male
HM Prison Hindley, Wigan, Lancashire	1961	267	Male local
HM YOI Lancaster Farms, Lancaster, Lancashire	1993	548	Closed YOI
HM Prison Leeds, Armley, Leeds, W. Yorkshire	1847	591(*)	Male local and remand centre
HM Prison Lowdham Grange, Lowdham, Nottinghamshire	1997	500	B male
HM Prison Manchester	1868	967(*)	Male local
HM Prison Parc, Bridgend, Mid-Glamorgan	1997	800	B male
HM Prison Parkhurst, Newport, Isle of Wight	1838	286	B male and protected witness unit
HM Prison Risley, Warrington, Cheshire	1965	692	C male and female local
HMP and YOI Styal, Wilmslow, Cheshire	1895	189	Closed female
HM Prison The Verne, Portland, Dorset	1949	552	C male
HM Prison Wandsworth, Wandsworth, London SW18	1851	965	Male local
HM Prison The Wolds, Everthorpe, N. Humberside	1992	360	Male local
HM Prison Whitemoor, March, Cambridgeshire	1991	534	Dispersal
HM Prison Woodhill, Milton Keynes, Bucks	1992	566	Male local
HM Prison Wormwood Scrubs, Du Cane Road, London W12	1890	472(*)	Male local and lifer wing

[1]CNA Certified Normal Accommodation
[2]YOI Young Offender Institution
* Numbers actually held in some of the older prisons exceed the CNA.
For example, in Leeds the average roll in 1997 was 846, in Manchester
it averaged 1113, and in Wormwood Scrubs it was 667.

Full details of all prisons in England and Wales are contained in *The
Prisons Handbook*, Leech, M. (1997/8) Pluto Press.

Appendix 8.2 Security categories in English prisons

Category A   Inmates are housed in one of the six maximum-security dispersal prisons. There are three groups: standard risk, high risk and exceptional risk

Category B   For those inmates for whom escape must be made difficult

Category C   For those who are unlikely to escape

Category D   For those who can be trusted in open conditions

9 Responding to a fourfold increase in population: the experience of the Federal Bureau of Prisons

Scott Higgins[1]

Population growth

It is hard to believe that in 1981 the United States' federal prison system had slightly less than 24 000 prisoners and it was actually planned to close the three oldest penitentiaries. From that point on the prison population began to rise, and overcrowding rates increased accordingly. Most state correctional systems in the country also faced similar overwhelming population growth. The largest states of California and Texas have had expansion programmes even larger than that of the federal system.

By 1983, the Federal Bureau of Prisons had resumed its capacity expansion programme until, by 1999, the federal prison system had an institutional population of over 100 000, with an additional 10 000 or so offenders in various contract facilities.

During that time 38 major new institutions were completed, representing a planned capacity of over 40 000 bed spaces at a cost of over $2 billion. Another 20 new institutions are in some stage of development, representing an additional 20 000 inmate beds and another $2 billion. This trend is likely to continue.

Within the federal system, population growth was driven initially by:

- an increase in mandatory minimum sentences, particularly for drug law violations
- the abolition of parole for the federal system
- the development of Federal Sentencing Guidelines, which increased average sentences and decreased the percentage of offenders who received probation as their sentence.

More recently the mood of the country has become more punitive, and the trend has been compounded by additional legislation increasing the type and number of offences placed under federal jurisdiction and the

---

1 Scott Higgins is the Chief of Design and Construction for the Federal Bureau of Prisons. The opinions expressed in these remarks are those of the author and do not represent the official policy or position of the Federal Bureau of Prisons or the US Department of Justice.

amount and length of mandatory sentences, particularly those related to drug and firearm offences.

Increasing capacity

The federal system addressed its capacity needs with a four-pronged approach:

- increased use of contract facilities
- expansion of the capacity at existing institutions
- acquisition of facilities and their conversion to prison use
- construction of new prisons.

Contract facilities are now used for virtually all the 'halfway house' inmates. More secure contract facilities have been used largely for lower security inmates, and particularly for illegal immigrants serving relatively short sentences.

The Bureau has now almost exhausted the possibilities of adding additional housing spaces within the confines of its existing institutions.

Various other types of institutions have been acquired for conversion to prisons. These have included small colleges, military barracks, psychiatric hospitals and, in one instance, an abandoned monastery. While these have presented some interesting challenges, they have mostly been suitable only for minimum or low security use.

While significant capacity has thus been added by the first three alternatives, most of the capacity expansion has been through development of new institutions, and these are divided into two broad categories. The first category is those intended primarily for sentenced offenders, which represent the majority of the population. These institutions are typically located in rural areas with adequate sites available for campus layouts, and one of their defining characteristics is the reliance on a very secure perimeter to allow for more freedom and flexibility for operations within the secure compound. Another feature is the subdivision of inmate housing into functional units operated under direct supervision by staff, which remains part of the core philosophy of the Bureau of Prisons.

The second type of new institution is the detention centre, which is intended primarily for pre-trial or pre-sentenced inmates still with direct involvement with the federal courts. In America this type of facility is often called a jail; in the UK it is referred to as a remand centre or local prison. For the Bureau, these detention centres are typically located in cities where the federal detention population is large enough to warrant such a facility. They are generally of mid- or high-rise construction, and where possible they are located in close proximity to the federal courts they serve.

Related responses to population growth and overcrowding

The levels of overcrowding facing the Bureau and the need to justify and defend the level of funding required for new institutions led to re-examination of many of its policies and its operational philosophy, and generated a number of significant changes.

During the 1980s, the rated capacity of Bureau facilities was based on single-person cells or single bed spaces in dormitory cubicles. Double bunking was considered a necessary but temporary solution to crowding. In recent years the Bureau has determined that some double bunking is manageable. Current policy calls for the rated capacity to be determined by providing 100 per cent double bunking of cubicles in minimum and low security dormitories, 50 per cent in medium security correctional institutions, and 25 per cent in high security penitentiaries. These levels, of course, are often exceeded due to overcrowded conditions, to the extent that many secure institutions are currently operating at levels in excess of 100 per cent double bunking.

Another major change in the 1990s was the development of institutions with increasingly larger planned (or rated) capacities. Throughout the 1980s, Bureau facilities were planned with about 500 cells for general population with single bunking. This increased to the point where a typical secure institution is now built with 768 cells for the general population. The double bunking guidelines have therefore increased rated capacities to 1152 for medium security and 960 for high security facilities.

The cost per bed for these institutions has been reduced by means of this large increase in housing capacity with only a slight increase in support and programme spaces, most of which could serve the larger population with only small incremental increases in staff or building areas.

Almost all the secure institutions are developed with an adjacent satellite minimum security camp. This allows the housing of those inmates who can function in that environment by providing the least expensive type of housing possible, with any required administrative and support functions shared with the main institution. This group of inmates also provides a workforce for maintenance and support of the overall facility.

At several locations, correctional complexes have been developed with more than one institution located on the same site. Here, too, they share many administrative and support functions. Complexes also allow savings through consolidation and distribution of site development costs between the separate institutions. The close location of facilities with different security levels also generates operational cost savings related to movement of inmates and reassignment and relocation of staff.

The role of prison architecture

No matter what accommodation the buildings provide, they can still house a good or bad prison operation. Any well-run prison operation is dependent upon and supported by a tripod of three elements: well qualified and highly trained staff; a classification system to identify and separate inmate predators and those with special requirements for protection; and established procedures, policies and an underlying philosophy of how to operate and manage the inmate population.

The buildings are not part of this essential support – even the best-designed prison is doomed to fail if such an operational foundation is absent. The facility and its designers cannot ensure a safe, secure or humane operation. However, careful planning, well thought out design and quality construction can support such a programme in many ways and help those correctional professionals who must carry out these operations as a day-to-day responsibility.

This support can include the provision of spaces that allow for flexibility of use and future growth, separation and classification of inmates, and facilitation of security or other procedures. Well-designed facilities can contribute to a sense of pride in those who work there and help to attract and retain good staff.

Buildings also send messages to both staff and inmates about how they are expected to act and, particularly for a prison, how they can expect to be treated. Terrible things still happen in prisons, and the absolute highest priority must be the provision of a safe and secure environment for both inmates and staff.

Perhaps more important than any architect's ideal layout is the need for any design to have the support and acceptance of both those managing a facility and those in the front line of daily contact with inmates. People who plan and build these institutions must constantly strive for a cooperative effort with those correctional professionals who have the day-to-day responsibility, and must take into account the problems and responsibilities they face. This is usually a very difficult task. As with any complex human endeavour, there are widely divergent opinions among those who are charged with managing such a facility, and these differences must be sorted out and decisions made if the design of the project is to proceed efficiently and in an orderly manner to avoid confusion or costly delays. Even within the Bureau, which is fortunate to have a high degree of management continuity and philosophical consistency, there are numerous operational issues that continue to surface and must be resolved and often reconfirmed as a project develops. These building design problems become even more challenging when they must be combined with establishing a management and operational framework.

Prisons will continue to be constructed. How well they are built will depend largely on how this cooperative effort by planners, designers and correctional practitioners is performed. Together these professionals can ensure that the architecture of prisons can 'make a difference' and provide a positive influence on their management and operation.

10 Prisons in the USA: cost, quality and community in correctional design

James Kessler

The environment of incarceration can be designed to reduce tension by creating an atmosphere of human respect. It is in such an ambience that the opportunity for self-rehabilitation can flourish. This approach does not necessitate spending inordinate amounts of money in the construction and operation of facilities; rather, manageable inmates can result in more efficient operation.

In tailoring designs for clients – the owners and administrators – it is helpful to consider the balance of three competing influences: cost, quality, and community.

Cost

The United States' incarcerated population in 1997 was about 1.6 million adults. In the state and federal correctional population alone, spending was close to $30 billion a year on agency budgets, with an increase of about 1 per cent every year. Generally, these expenses were supported by voters, and many politicians gained advantage by relating this spending to enhanced personal safety of the public.

The operational cost was about $54 per day per inmate, or $20 000 per year. This cost grew steadily over the decade, while construction cost per bed remained relatively level at $30 000 for minimum security beds ranging to $80 000 for maximum security beds. This indicates that while construction costs were kept steady in spite of inflation, operational costs increased by about 12 per cent during the same time. In 1997, 11 per cent of budgets were allocated to construction and 89 per cent to operations, with approximately 75 per cent of the operations budget being spent on staffing. The implications are that if operating costs – primarily staffing – can be reduced through innovative design, this is a feature well worth paying for.

Quality

Quality consists of two aspects. The first relates to conditions in correctional facilities, including security, safety, and meeting the constitutional threshold against cruel and unusual punishment. The American Correctional Standards for Accreditation have been accepted by the courts as satisfying this constitutional principle. The standards provide operational procedures as well as establishing physical plant criteria.

The second aspect of quality is the relationship between capital and operating costs. This form of quality maximizes long-term savings although it increases initial expenditure. An example of potential savings is in the decentralization of inmate activities. The relocation of a large central outdoor exercise area to smaller spaces at the housing pods initially adds to capital costs, but savings can be found in operating costs if the housing officer is able to observe the exercise area while performing other duties.

Cost savings can also be found by performing certain medical procedures on site rather than escorting an inmate to off-site facilities. Spending money to address officer satisfaction, such as providing adequate locker and break rooms and designing a building that inspires pride, may pay dividends with reduced officer turnover. It may also attract more capable staff.

Space for conducting inmate programmes will, if successful, more than pay for itself if the programmes lead to lower recidivism rates. Technology, if effective, can replace staff as well as reduce long-term maintenance costs.

Direct supervision

Direct supervision of inmates is now accepted by the US national correctional institutes and by the American Institute of Architects as a major quality enhancement. Direct supervision is considered by many to be the state-of-the-art for inmate management and housing unit design. The concept is founded on the mutual respect of the officer and inmate, and the imposition of immediate sanctions on the inmate if conflict occurs.

Direct supervision has evolved from indirect supervision, where an officer in a secure control room observed a series of relatively small pods of inmates. This design was useful in providing multiple levels of classification. However, the remote location of the officer and the impediments to direct contact limited the officer's effectiveness in understanding the behavioural dynamics of the pod.

Direct supervision was instituted in order to make dayroom officers more effective. Officers in control rooms are merely observing inmates and activities. When they are in the space, they have the opportunity to influence the behaviour and become proactive with regard to inmate behaviour. The physical design of direct supervision pods affords architectural opportunities unavailable in the design of indirect supervision pods. The strict geometry necessary for sightlines from a control room into multiple housing pods often results in a configuration that produces wasted space. Direct supervision pods, not linked to a control room, may give priority to more cost-effective construction and greater operational efficiency.

Direct supervision of dayrooms is enhanced by the following key points:

- *Visibility.* Visibility is important. The design should promote visibility from wherever the officer is in the dayroom. The correctional officer acts like a police officer on the street or a teacher in a classroom and knows what is going on throughout the area.

- *Information.* Correctional officers, through the use of computers, can supply inmates with information about activities such as visiting, court dates, and operational details. This not only establishes a relationship of authority between the officer and the inmate, but also allows a cooperative relationship to be reinforced.
- *Outdoor recreation.* Outdoor recreation at the pod can allow natural light to enter the dayroom. It also provides continuous access to outdoor activities at the discretion of the pod officer. This means that the outdoor recreation area can either be open all day or shut down, depending on the degree of cooperation received from the inmates.
- *Acoustic control.* Acoustical ceilings and wall panels reduce noise and help the dayroom officer establish control, letting his or her voice be heard.
- *Comfortable furniture.* Comfortable furniture is viewed as an amenity that can be withdrawn from uncooperative inmates.
- *Immediate sanction.* Immediate sanction reinforces the authority of the correctional officer. Housing units devoid of dayroom amenities and controlled indirectly must be available without delay for non-cooperative inmates.

Technical advances

Quality can also be enhanced by technology, and operational cost savings can be derived by using proven technological advances. Two examples being employed are touch-screen control systems and pneumatic locking devices. The inherent ease of touch-screen controls allows control room staff to follow more closely the changing workload patterns during daily shift changes. Pneumatic locking devices have proved to be more reliable and require less maintenance than their electromechanical counterparts.

Community

Prisons are an integral part of every community. They are next door to homes and highways. Sometimes they were constructed in a remote area and communities have grown around them; often they were built in an urban area to be close to courts and to minimize the use of police time by placing the facilities at the locus of criminal activity. The buildings can express the enlightened attitude now evolving from a better understanding of the implications of incarceration. The vast majority of inmates will be re-entering society, and their experience in prison may have an effect on their ability to reintegrate. The prison's task is to prepare the inmates for this. The design of the buildings should express to the community the professionalism of the administrators and correctional officers, and reinforce the advantage of a positive approach to incarceration.

Facility examples

The following projects demonstrate various ways in which communities have addressed the issues of costs, quality, and involvement.

Wake County Public Safety Center, Raleigh, North Carolina

The Wake County Public Safety Center, designed by Hellmuth, Obata & Kassabaum (HOK) in association with O'Brien Atkins Architects, comprises three major components, consisting of the jail and detention facility; the Sheriff's Office, hearing rooms for the Magistrates' Courts, and other public offices; and a 250-space parking facility. The building is designed to be functional and to respond to its setting by blending in with the city's emerging skyline. It breaks away from the sombre tradition of public buildings by being a lively piece of civic architecture (*Plate 4*).

The building responds to the three bordering streets in different and appropriate ways. The front door of the building on Salisbury Street gestures to the existing County Courthouse and County office buildings in an effort to create a unified complex of County buildings. This side of the building is set back to emphasize its importance, as well as to allow space for a landscaped buffer and establish a streetscape that may be continued across Salisbury Street. The mass of the jail tower is further stepped back to allow the lower floors, which comprise the building base, visually to eclipse the housing tower from the entry plaza. The tower location also enhances the separation of the tower from neighbouring high-rise buildings.

The jail tower is the most dominant visual element of the building. The placement of its elevators provides the key to the building's internal organization. The jail elevators accommodate all inmate traffic, and their location on the first floor is in direct view of central control and anchors the circulation for the intake and discharge areas. On the ground floor, the elevators are incorporated within the food service area to facilitate distribution. Inmate visiting on the second floor and support services on the third floor are arranged around the elevators.

The Salisbury Street lobby serves as the organizational focus for the Public Safety Center. This skylit space provides orientation and information, and symbolically expresses the openness and efficiency of the Center.

Baltimore Central Booking and Intake Facility, Baltimore, Maryland

Approximately 60 000 people are expected to move through Baltimore's Central Booking and Intake Facility each year – the equivalent of 45 per cent of those arrested in the State of Maryland. This high-tech facility consolidates and streamlines all booking and intake operations for the City of Baltimore, formerly conducted at nine separate police districts throughout the City. The facility was designed by HOK in conjunction with SOJ Architects (*Figures 10.1, 10.2*).

Several innovative features maintain the efficiency of this high-volume facility and expedite inmate processing, thus improving safety throughout Baltimore's criminal justice system and the City itself. First, the facility consolidates the location of court commissioners, pre-trial services, public defenders and state attorneys; this centralized approach facilitates early prosecutorial review and saves taxpayers the expense of costly jail beds for defendants whose cases would later be dismissed. For those cases that proceed through the system, an interactive video system allows judges in two distant district court buildings to conduct video bail reviews of prisoners (who remain at the booking facility); this feature greatly reduces inmate movement and transportation requirements system-wide, making

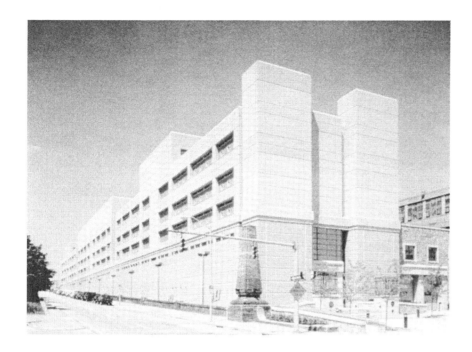

Figure 10.1
Baltimore Central Booking and Intake Facility – a very urban solution, reflecting the architecture of the neighbourhood.

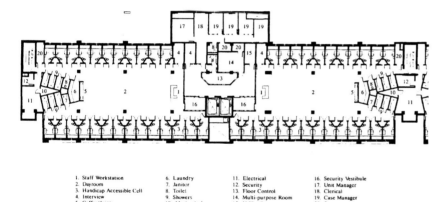

1. Staff Workstation	6. Laundry	11. Electrical	16. Security Vestibule
2. Dayroom	7. Janitor	12. Security	17. Unit Manager
3. Handicap Accessible Cell	8. Toilet	13. Floor Control	18. Clerical
4. Interview	9. Showers	14. Multi-purpose Room	19. Case Manager
5. Coffee/Juice	10. Mechanical	15. Utility Room	20. Storage

Figure 10.2
Typical housing pods at Baltimore, with cells enclosing a central association area. Compare with the triangular plan shown in Figure 10.6.

Figure 10.3
Precast concrete units being lowered into position during construction of Fairfax Adult prison.

more police available to patrol the streets. The podular units of the Booking and Intake Facility provide a total of 811 beds for reception and general housing in single-cell, double-cell and dormitory arrangements. Direct supervision is the management method employed. Recreation, interview, examination and multipurpose spaces are located at each housing pod, further reducing the need for inmate movement.

The five-storey building's brick and precast concrete façade is meant to reflect the architecture of the surrounding neighbourhood. The massing, texture and colour of the building's two-level base relate to the stone security wall of the existing, adjacent Jail Administration Building, creating a visual and functional extension of that wall. The housing units above have a finer texture than the base, reflecting the smaller-scaled rooms and the residential nature of this part of the building.

Fairfax County Adult Detention Center, Fairfax, Virginia

The expansion and renovation of Fairfax County Adult Detention Center (ADC) is part of a complex of several criminal justice buildings located at the Fairfax County Public Safety Center. The expansion will add housing and support areas to the Center's existing detention capabilities, accommodating the county's increasing inmate population. The new structure will be linked to the existing ADC building by a vehicular sallyport at the ground level and bridges at the first and second levels. Another secure bridge will connect the new buildings to the site's existing courthouse, also designed by HOK.

The expansion will contain 796 beds, including 16 medical cells, 96 forensic cells, 12 special housing cells, 96 diagnostic and treatment cells, and 576 direct supervision cells serving the general population. The whole complex will be serviced by support areas in the expansion facility, including a new kitchen and laundry facilities, a central receiving area, accommodation for bulk trash removal, a large warehouse serving both food service supply and storage requirements, the commissary and associated inmate finance offices, and a centralized locker and shower area for employees working in this support area.

The entire structure, including cell modules, will be made from precast concrete. Cells are to be fabricated, finished and furnished off site; these components will then be stacked, eight high, onto a cast-in-place concrete support base. This precast approach not only speeds construction but is also a cost-effective technique for buildings of this type (*Figure 10.3*). The masonry and precast façade responds appropriately to its site context. Renovation of the existing facility will accommodate the intake-processing function for the complex, which includes the police processing area, magistrates, booking/holding areas; property; and accommodation for video magistrate and arraignment appearances. Expanded facility administration, visiting, public waiting and information areas are also provided in the renovation. These components are designed to support a potential inmate population of 2000.

Virginia Women's Multi-Custody Correctional Facility, Richmond, Virginia

HOK, in a joint venture with the Moseley McClintock Group, designed a new 1354-bed facility dedicated to the special needs of women incarcerated in the Commonwealth of Virginia (*Figure 10.4*). Double dry cells (i.e. without integral sanitation) will house the general population, offering

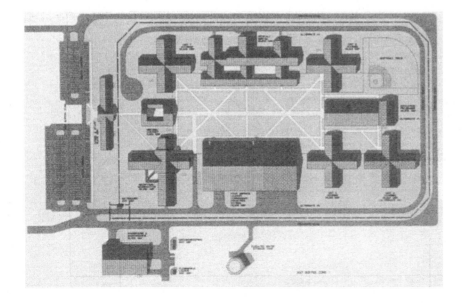

Figure 10.4
Site layout of Virginia's Women's prison. It is similar to the PDBS layout shown in Figure **2.1j**, with small-scale cruciform cell blocks arranged around a central courtyard.

important advantages to the inmates and reducing project costs. As opposed to a dormitory arrangement (which has typically been used in this correctional setting), double cells are shared by only two inmates and provide greater privacy. Inmates are also better able to protect themselves and their property. Because dry cell inmates have access to central lavatories, plumbing and ductwork costs will be significantly reduced.

Nearly 60 per cent of the facility's beds will be assigned to the general population; the remaining beds will be designated as reception/classification, medical/mental and segregation areas. Direct supervision will be employed in the general housing areas.

The facility's organization around a secure, central courtyard, with the housing units anchoring each corner, is another cost-effective design solution. The ring of buildings will surround the courtyard and create an inner security perimeter. The courtyard will serve as the primary inmate exterior space, and provide access to the numerous programmes, industries and other available decentralized activities.

The facility's accepted construction bid of $28 000 per bed, which includes extensive medical/mental, vocational and industrial programme elements, reflects an extremely economical, innovative and cost-effective design.

Youth Services Command Supermax Component, Polk Youth Institution, Butner, North Carolina

Located on the campus of the Polk Youth Institution, the 100-bed Supermax component, designed by HOK in joint venture with Little and Associates Architects, will accommodate the most aggressive youthful offenders in the North Carolina Department of Corrections (*Figure 10.5*). These inmates, aged between 19 and 23 years, have been

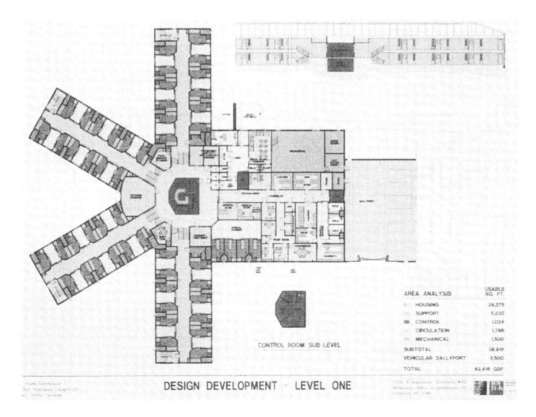

Figure 10.5
A much tougher solution is chosen for the Youth Institution at Butner. Very little communication is allowed between inmates; cells are arranged more traditionally off a fairly narrow corridor.

DESIGN DEVELOPMENT - LEVEL ONE

administratively assigned to this component because their serious assaults against other inmates or staff threaten the safety and manageability of other facilities within the youth command. The mission of the component is to exercise maximum control over prohibited inmate actions until acceptable behaviour is demonstrated over a period of time.

The facility is designed to withstand inmate abuse. Regular maintenance to the cell plumbing duct is possible by access from outside the facility to avoid the need to move the inmates. Exercise areas are located between each pair of cells, and allow direct entry from each cell. This arrangement reduces dangerous and staff-intensive movements of the inmates. The cells are designed with special security doors that allow for the delivery of food and programmes to the inmate in the cell. The food pass is notched into the side of the door so that inmates may be cuffed and tethered when they are escorted to centralized services. The lockable vision panel and food pass also serve as a means to interview and counsel inmates from the exercise area. Interaction of this sort provides the inmate with the opportunity to demonstrate cooperative behaviour.

Each cell has a window with a view to the outside as well as a strategically located corridor window. The window limits intimidation between inmates, while allowing full cell visibility by the officer. The cells also are equipped with individual showers. As inmates demonstrate cooperative behaviour, they will have access to a larger outdoor exercise area as well as supervised contact programmes.

Mecklenburg County Work Release and Restitution Center, Charlotte, North Carolina

Emphasizing responsibility, inmates at the Mecklenburg County Work Release and Restitution Center work throughout the day, using money earned to pay for the expenses of living in the Center (*Plate 5*).

Completed in December 1996, the Center houses inmates who qualify to be relocated from the county's other detention facilities. In the five floors of housing, resident bedroom suites are grouped around a two-level dayroom to provide a normalized environment. Scheduled visiting takes place in the dayroom or on the adjacent outdoor terrace.

The building's exterior is massed to give it a more residential and less institutional appearance, in keeping with the nature of the facility and the surrounding townhouse-style office buildings. Locating support and administrative programmes in an older county office building saved construction time and expense. Future planning includes the expansion of the facility.

HOK, in joint venture with Little & Associates Architects, designed this urban facility adjacent to the existing Charlotte government complex. A planned expansion will allow for an additional 392 beds.

Mecklenburg County Jail, Central Charlotte, North Carolina

Jail Central, designed by HOK in a joint venture with Little Architects, integrates the programme requirements of a single-cell, direct supervision facility within the constraints of a prominent downtown government complex. Phase 1, consisting of 1004 secure beds, was completed in December 1996, with a 900-bed expansion planned to follow its completion. The housing pods are organized horizontally around a circulation spine and vertically by the stacking of cells and dayrooms.

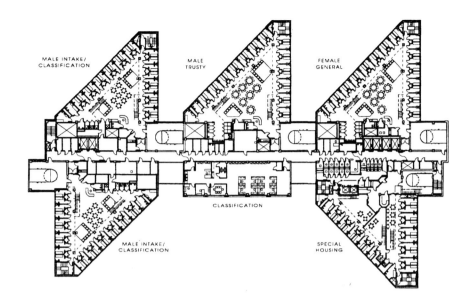

MALE INTAKE/
CLASSIFICATION

MALE
TRUSTY

FEMALE
GENERAL

CLASSIFICATION

MALE INTAKE/
CLASSIFICATION

SPECIAL
HOUSING

Figure 10.6
A series of triangular house pods is arranged off a central corridor at Mecklenburg County Jail. Triangular plans of this sort were popular when new generation first took hold, but now many different geometrical shapes are used.

Arrest processing, public reception, administrative and medical treatment areas occupy the lower three floors (*Figure 10.6*).

Direct supervision and the extensive use of dry cell pods fosters a normalized environment and saves money in construction and equipment costs. In these areas, inmates are allowed free access to the dayroom and toilet facilities, enabling them to retain some privacy and personal territory. The pod officer will establish the dayroom schedule and remotely control door locks. Costs are saved in the elimination of security hardware, security doors, plumbing fixtures and special chases.

An open-plan processing area with colour-coded airport-style seating zones encourages a more relaxed atmosphere for officers and arrestees. The assumption is that arrestees are cooperative when they are respectfully treated, although facilities for restraint are readily accessible throughout. The planning allows flexibility of movement, custody and staffing to adapt to variable intake loads and to alleviate bottlenecks. Staff lounges, a physical conditioning room and a cafeteria with an outdoor dining terrace and landscaped garden give staff the opportunity to relax in non-secure areas that are directly accessible to the security circulation core. Each elevation of the building responds to its urban context. To the north, a linear park features planting in the natural pattern of the adjacent old courthouse. The formal public entry is provided from a south-facing entry plaza in the tradition of the neighbouring civic spaces.

11 Prisons in the USA: supermax – the bad and the mad

Norval Morris

Architecture and technology have recently joined with prison policy in the United States to build a series of supermax prisons that raise the level of punishment close to that of psychological torture. I am unfitted to describe the electronic and engineering innovations that permit this new development, but I can briefly describe its growth in the United States.

Most prisons, including maximum security prisons, already have their own prisons – their punishment cells and disciplinary segregation – and now those prisons have spawned yet further prisons to which the prisoner may be sent without any further court order. These are the maxi-maxis, the supermax prisons. There are now, depending on the definition preferred, more than 30 such institutions in the United States.

A survey published by the National Institute of Corrections[1] defines the object of their study as:

a highly restrictive, high-custody housing unit *within a secure facility, or an entire secure facility, that isolates inmates from the general prison population and from each other due to grievous crimes, repetitive assaultive or violent institutional behaviour, the threat of escape or actual escape from high-custody facility(ies), or inciting or threatening to incite disturbances in a correctional institution.*

Read quickly, that sounds just like another segregation or punishment unit, but in practice much more is involved. Note that it is not only prison offences that can attract this placement, but also the threat of escape, or threatening to incite a disturbance. Note also that the isolation is 'from the general prison population and from each other'.

Supermax prisons make extensive use of technology to facilitate control of the institution and all those in it. There are all the usual state-of-the-art electronic controls for drugs and contraband upon entering the facility; hand, voice and other identification techniques far surpassing the precision of fingerprint controls for entry into the secure section of the facility by staff, visitor or prisoner; video cameras everywhere; multiple electronic controls of inner passage entrances, which are generally underground; walkways of steel grates over the corridors where the prisoner is moved from the cell to the exercise yard so that a guard armed with a gun or a gas gun can control the scene – generally a brave new world of technical controls that pass my understanding but not my perception of their invasiveness.

---

1 Rivland, C. (1999). *Supermax Prisons: Overview and General Considerations.* US Department of Justice.

I have visited the federal supermax at Florence, Colorado, on two occasions, and its predecessor at Marion in Illinois several times. Marion was designed to take many prisoners then held in Alcatraz when that institution in the Bay of San Francisco was abandoned, and now Florence has taken over from Marion. The various states then followed suit in a splurge of extensive and expensive building, with California, as usual, in the lead. Not one of these state supermax prisons is necessary, and all are a grave error in the sad tale of man's brutality to man.

Instead of relating the history of this spread of a new type of highly restrictive prison, let me focus on one institution and try to give a view of the processes of its operation – the Tamms prison in the far South of Illinois.[2] This outline of Tamms may be compared with those of some other states – there are, for example, Human Rights Watch surveys of Indiana and Virginia Supermax prisons. Tamms is an expensive Illinois investment; it cost over $73 million to build, and it runs at a cost of $35 800 per prisoner per year, roughly twice the annual cost per capita of a maximum security prison in the same state.

There are two categories of prisoners in Tamms. First, there are those who come to Tamms while serving a disciplinary sentence for a prison offence in another prison, a term of disciplinary detention imposed on them in the prison from which they came – thus it is for them a prison's separate prison for prison-adjudicated prison offences. Secondly, there are those who, at the time of their transfer, were not being punished for any prison offence. There are thus *disciplinary detainees* and *administrative detainees*, and the prison population of 200 is divided approximately equally between these two groups.

To be legalistic about who goes to Tamms, the pertinent regulation, Section 505.40(b) of the Illinois Administrative Code, reads:

Among other matters, a committed person who the Department has determined has engaged in the following activities or who may be planning to engage in these activities may be referred for placement in the Tamms Correctional Center:

- Escaping or attempting to escape;
- Assaulting staff, inmates or other persons which caused death or serious injury;
- Engaging in dangerous disturbances;
- Having influence in activities of a gang or other unauthorized organization;
- Engaging in non-consensual sexual conduct; or
- Possessing weapons.

Consider the amplitude of the phrase 'who may be planning to engage in any of these activities', and consider how many prisoners at one time or another 'possess weapons' or 'engage in dangerous disturbances'.

However, there are a further six concerns that those responsible for sending a prisoner to Tamms, pursuant to Section 505.40(d) of the Code, must bear in mind:

Placement in the Tamms Correctional Center shall be based upon the following considerations, including but not limited to:

---

2   For a general overview, see: Rivland, C. (1999). *Supermax Prisons: Overview and General Considerations*. US Department of Justice.

- The safety and security of the facility, the public, or any person;
- The committed person's disciplinary and behavioural history;
- Reports and recommendations concerning the committed person;
- The feasibility of transfer to another facility;
- Medical concerns; and
- Mental health concerns.

The theoretical arguments offered for the creation of supermax prisons are straightforward. It is argued that it is worthwhile to hold this group of prisoners, described by the proponents of these institutions as 'the worst of the worst', in absolute solitary confinement and to reduce their living conditions severely to prevent them injuring a staff member or a prisoner and to stop them fomenting disturbances in the prisons from which they are sent. In brief, get the very worst apples out and the barrels will be safer and easier to control. It is also believed that if the conditions in the supermax prisons are known to be substantially more punitive even than those in the segregation units of the maximum security prisons, that in itself will deter misbehaviour and violence in those prisons. There is no hard evidence to support either of these arguments, and no studies are underway to test them, but there is no lack of belief among politicians in their truth – and it is certainly true that increased punishment plays well with the voters.

The life of a prisoner in Tamms

Your cell measures ten feet by twelve feet (three metres by just over three and a half). It is made from poured concrete with a steel door – no bars, just a lot of small holes, smaller than the tip of a little finger, punched through it. The cell has a stainless steel sanitary unit, which it would not be easy to destroy. There is a small window, high and narrow, which lets in a little outside light. There is a mirror made of polished metal, again tending to be indestructible. Your bunk is also of poured concrete, an integral part of the cell, with a slim plastic foam mattress to put on it. There is a well-protected fluorescent light and a light switch. At night, the light cannot be turned off entirely; it gives out a continuous dim light, bright enough for the guards to peer in. There is a small trapdoor, low down in the cell's steel door, through which food can be pushed.

When you are allowed into the exercise yard for an hour, you will find that you are alone in a concrete square, somewhat larger than your cell, with a small grating high in the corner of the roof through which you can see the sky. Recently there seems to have been some show of weakness on the part of the Department of Corrections; the exercise yard still has no exercise equipment whatsoever in it, but some prisoners are now being allowed to have tough rubber handballs to throw against the yard walls.

Your clothing consists of three jumpsuits (tan), three T-shirts (white), three pairs of undershorts (white), three pairs of socks (white), one pair of soft-soled shoes and one knitted cap (blue); you also have two towels (white) and one washcloth (white). Provided you remain of good behaviour (which really means no bad behaviour, since the opportunities for other than promptly conforming behaviour are limited), you may also have a wristwatch, a wedding band, a pen, a religious medallion (provided it represents no threat of being converted to a weapon), a dictionary (provided it has only a soft cover), a plastic cup, a coffee cup, and a reasonable supply of paperback books. No picture frames are allowed, but you may have up to 15 photographs.

So much for your cell and accoutrements. What about contacts with the world outside Tamms? You are given three pre-stamped envelopes a month, and you can pay for more. Depending on your punishment status and behaviour (of which more later), visiting privileges range from once a month to four times a month – but of course Tamms is a very long haul for most prisoners' families (generally 350 miles), so visits remain infrequent for all but a very few prisoners. Phone calls are not allowed except in certain emergency situations.

To continue this account of contacts with the world outside the cell, there is a distinction between the two categories of prisoners in Tamms – disciplinary detainees and administrative detainees. The disciplinary detainees, during the term of their disciplinary sentence, receive fewer privileges at Tamms than the administrative detainees, though the differences are not of transcendent range. They are as follows.

- Disciplinary detainees: first 90 days, one shower per week, one hour in the exercise yard per week, one visit per month, and one commissary (order of goods from the prison shop) per month.
- Administrative detainees: first 90 days, one shower per week, two hours in the exercise yard per week, one visit per month, no commissary. After 90, if of good behaviour, two showers per week, five hours in the exercise yard per week, two visits per month, and one commissary ($15 maximum) per month; in addition, inmates with their own televisions may watch educational or religious programmes.

After six months of good behaviour, these privileges blossom for both groups into four showers per week, seven hours of exercise per week, four visits per month and two commissary days per month; inmates may also be allowed a television set in their cell, the available programmes of course being centrally controlled.

It bears repetition that these functions – showers, yard and commissary – are not pursued in the company of other prisoners. When going to take a shower the prisoner walks a line, clad in a towel, to the small shower room, under observation by an armed guard looking down from above through a metal grate. The guard can also release a swift-acting disabling gas to encourage any recalcitrance on the way to or from or during the shower. Going to the exercise yard normally involves three guards accompanying the heavily shackled prisoner, and one armed guard observer walking above the entourage looking through the steel grating to inhibit any hint of aggression by the prisoner. The performance is repeated on the return journey an hour thereafter. These few prisoner–staff contacts tend not to be harmonious – curtly, they foster a 'we/they' relationship of considerable hostility.

All in all, this amounts to solitary confinement far more severe than the solitary confinement imposed in the segregation units of the maximum security prisons, more punitive than 'the hole'. Prisons thus now have not only their punishment cells and withdrawal of congregate and private privileges, but also further prisons – thus prisons' prisons' prisons.

The minimum term for all prisoners in Tamms is one year – as predicted and so far enforced.

Visits, when they occur, are the prisoner's longest flight to a less hostile world. The prisoner is taken, shackled, to a small booth, and seated facing a thick wall of glass. The visitor or visitors are seated on the opposite side of that glass. There is no opening in it through which anything can be passed, and conversation is via telephones on each side of the glass.

Family visits are hard on the visitors. They have to travel long and expensive distances, and must receive specific permissions in advance for each visit. As they enter the outer grounds of Tamms and approach the buildings, they are likely to be vigorously checked for alcohol, drugs or nicotine products. They will be gruffly ordered out of the car that has brought them to Tamms. The order will be barked by the leader of a team of near riot-clad men – 'barked' is not inappropriate, since this team is accompanied by a dog that assists in the inspection of the visitors and their car by diligently searching, sniffing and rooting about for contraband. It is, visitors tell me, an unsettling experience.

Within the building, your visitors will be further checked electronically. Once in the visitors' room, communication is not easy. Usually, there is not much to talk about; the prisoner is, after all, denuded of recent experiences other than those occurring within the curtilage of the mind and skin, and is probably not skilled in light badinage. In the result, visits tend to wane in frequency for all but a very few Tamms prisoners. Visiting privileges, ranging from one to four a month, are for most prisoners a rhetorical flourish rather than a reality.

Visits by your lawyer, if you are fortunate enough still to have such a luxury and if your lawyer actually visits you rather than confines him or herself to an exchange of letters, will take place in slightly different circumstances. There will be the same glass divider and the same telephone communication, but in addition a prison guard will sit in another little booth which abuts the side of the visiting booths. There will be slots between the guard and you, and between the guard and your lawyer, through which documents can be passed back and forth under the guard's close observation for any contraband going either way.

Should you not have a lawyer for your appeal, or for any other legal action, civil or criminal, in which you may be involved, you may wish to seek out the relevant law for yourself. This is possible, but difficult. In a long series of cases, the federal courts have established the range of law books that a prison library must contain to facilitate prisoners' access to the courts. The constitutionally minimally adequate law library has been defined, and Tamms has one. Also, Tamms employs a prisoner to work in the law library to copy whatever extracts from law books you or any prisoner may require. All that sounds very reasonable until one reflects what little knowledge all but the most exceptional Tamms prisoners have of the law. The law clerk knows very little more. Nevertheless, it seems clear that Tamms has abided by the Constitution.

You are not, of course, isolated from the Tamms staff. The clergyman visits regularly, as does the social worker and the psychologist, the nurse, and various categories of guards who are checking on you or passing your food to you. All these contacts take place through the multi-holed steel door. If you need medical attention you will be shackled and escorted, as if going to the exercise yard, by a team of guards, and shackled to the floor while, for instance, you are talking to the visiting psychiatrist. The medical and dental services are adequately available – there is no desire to have to transport you to an outside hospital.

Should you, as some prisoners have been known to do, throw urine, faeces, your food or anything else at a guard through the little openings in the steel door to your cell, the remedy is easy – a plastic shield is superimposed on the far side of your cell door. This will have a secondary effect. While the steel door remains uncovered it is possible by shouting particularly loudly to have some sort of communication with the prisoner in a neighbouring cell. This is seen by many who work in Tamms as a design defect of the building. If the plastic cover goes up, that distant noise of another is effectively inhibited.

Should you or any other prisoner prove recalcitrant at any time, swift action will be taken. For example, suppose you decide to disobey an order to facilitate coming out of your cell – that is, to come forward in the proper manner so that your hands and feet can be shackled without risk to the guards. You will be told again what to do. On your third refusal to obey promptly, you will be 'extracted' from the cell. There are no ifs or buts, no hesitation or second thoughts about an extraction. On the third recalcitrance it will take place.

To extract you from your cell, five men dressed, armed and protected rather like Darth Vader enter your cell and, with a large plastic shield, pin you to the wall. This facilitates two of them safely chaining your feet to each other, and your arms to each other at the wrist behind your back. You are then removed from your cell. The extraction is complete. Extractions are not pleasant to observe; nevertheless all extractions are videotaped so that any allegations of excessive force can be rebutted.

That may not be the end of the matter. Perchance you had precipitated the extraction by throwing food at the guard, or maybe in the melee of the extraction you had lashed out at or struck a guard assisting in the extraction. If so, it is likely that you will be charged with battery or aggravated battery for that offence. The preliminary hearings prior to trial will be heard by a visiting judge in a small courtroom deep in the bowels of Tamms, adjacent to the State's execution chamber. If you insist on a jury trial, the trial itself will be held before a jury in a courtroom in a nearby town. You will not find it easy to controvert the video recording of the incident before a jury when most of them have relatives or friends working in Tamms, or are appreciative of the business Tamms has brought to this otherwise impoverished region. Acquittal is unlikely, but the prolongation of your time both in Tamms and in other prisons is far from unlikely. There seems no end to the belief in deterrent controls.

If you manage to avoid such miseries as extractions impose, how do you stand? Month after month you are thrown back on your own inner resources, a commodity usually not generously present in Tamms prisoners. Is there work to do? Not in Tamms. Education? Entertainment? No and no, other than the 'library's' supply of paper-covered books, which tend to the western and sickly romantic. You do have a bible and a dictionary and writing paper, and they help. But, as Churchill said of his brief time in a Boer prison, 'the minutes crawl by like constipated centipedes'.

The consolations and inspirations of religious belief are delivered through the steel door. There are no congregate ceremonies. The insights of professional counselling, such as they are, are also available, but they too are offered through the thickness of the steel door.

Misbehaviour is swiftly sanctioned. An 'extraction' is a not inconsiderable threat, and to back it up there is the likely prolongation of your residence in Tamms. In any event you will be in Tamms for a year, and you are on disciplinary segregation until the term of that punishment has expired; thereafter there is a chance, a realistic chance, of returning to the relative comfort and conviviality of a maximum security prison – unless you are found to have demonstrated undesirable behaviour while in Tamms.

All in all these are harsh conditions for anyone, but they are formidably harsh for the mentally ill and those teetering on the brink of serious mental illness – of which there are not a few in Tamms. For example, on the day I first visited Tamms there were either nine or eleven prisoners taking prescription psychotropic drugs – the visiting psychiatrist was not sure! He did recall that there had been two prisoners transferred to the mental hospital-prison run by the Department of Correction, and many more have since been transferred.

What purposes does this expensive regime at Tamms serve? The warden answers that first, it removes the worst troublemakers from the other prisons and thus makes them safer for staff and prisoners alike; and secondly, by its notorious harshness – a notoriety spread and even exaggerated throughout the entire prison system – it serves as a deterrent to those who might otherwise cause trouble in the other prisons. Hence you fall for your country in Tamms; you suffer so that many more will not suffer.

A defect in this analysis of the functions of Tamms and similar supermax prisons is that these two purposes are offered as a mantra, as a fixed belief beyond cavil, supported by selected hearsay prison stories. The mantra has never been tested, and it is doubtful that it is true. It could be tested empirically, and it should be. However, even if it were true, does it justify the degree of adversity visited on the Tamms prisoners?

Even in your prison cell in Tamms you will not find that an easy question to answer with any precision. How much suffering by one justifies the avoidance of other suffering by others? While you are meditating your answer, let me tell you by what decisional processes of the prison administration you found your way to Tamms.

The courts are, of course, necessary to get you into prison, but judges do not sentence you to serve your term in Tamms. You are sent there by an administrative decision, not a judicial decision. Under the US Constitution, due process is the condition precedent to punishment. If Tamms is a punishment added to your properly imposed prison term, then it attracts this constitutionally sanctified due process. What does due process mean in the context of Tamms?

The Code requires the warden of Tamms to appoint two staff as a 'transfer review committee' to advise him on your suitability for detention in Tamms, and the wisdom of its continuance. They are directed to interview you within ten days of your arrival at Tamms. Thereafter, every 90 days they must review your record, although there is no requirement that they interview you on these subsequent occasions. Their recommendations go to the warden, who may recommend to headquarters at Springfield your further detention at or your transfer from Tamms. For those in administrative detention, as distinct from disciplinary detention, every year you will also be afforded an interview at which you appear in person before the transfer review committee. Of course, the hearing may be held at your cell's door.

To risk a little amateur philosophy: how does one choose between sensory near-isolation for a year for 'A' and a greater risk of violence to 'B'? Surely in utilitarian terms the choice thus stated is impossible; the two are incommensurable. The answer seems to me clear: only in the most obvious and extreme cases should sensory deprivation be imposed. There are such cases, but they are rare indeed, and they are certainly not adequately defined by the regulations and procedures that put prisoners in Tamms.

The mentally ill

In conscience, I cannot omit further discussion of the mentally ill in Tamms. Throughout the United States, the mental health deinstitutionalization movement of the last quarter of the twentieth century, and the closure of many mental hospitals, had the expansion of community-based treatment and shelter for those evicted from the institutions as its corollary and necessary promise. The promise was not kept. Shelters and community-based care remain in exiguous supply, and even what little is available often excludes the indigent mentally ill and has been captured by those with some funds to meet the costs of care. This has resulted in hundreds of thousands of mentally ill indigent and other than wealthy patients finding themselves consigned to prison-like hostels, to the streets, to jails and to prisons. Prison and jail populations swell as the mental hospitals constrict.

For the time being, this cruel process shows little sign of reversing, though a few private institutions do meet the needs of some patients, and families harbour others. However, the political reality is that an increasing and now large number of the prison and jail slots of this country are occupied by the mentally ill, the weight of their treatment or neglect falling on the prison and jail mental health services. It is a matter lacking precision, but the best current estimate is that over 30 per cent of the population of US prisons and jails suffer from diagnosable and treatable mental illness; and the supermax prisons hold more than their fair share.

I find it hard to imagine what it must be like in Tamms cells at night, isolated from everyone and everything that stimulates life, your half-sleep filled with terrors and then waking yet again with the mind racing from imaginary conversation to imaginary conversation, none of them significant. There is hope only for a very distant future, and thoughts of suicide and its means are pervasive. If you add to that, for the mentally ill, periods of hallucination of visual and audible stimuli, many of them powerfully threatening, which yet at one distant level you know not to be there but are nevertheless very real to you, the pain becomes unimaginable.

The uncertain purposes claimed for the imposition of this psychological torture, which are most likely wrong, are grossly inadequate. This is psychological torture; no other description seems adequate. Of course, psychotropic drugs can reduce the pain and engender a dull, shuffling and somnolent blankness, but the Tamms regime intensifies even this.

All of this leads to the question of whether the mentally ill should be held in Tamms. It seems an almost merely rhetorical question, requiring an immediate negative reply, but in reality it is more pointed than it seems.

Divide the world of the seriously mentally ill into two parts – clearly a superficial division, but bear with it. One group is of those who are withdrawn into their own fantasy life, deeply depressed, catatonic, passive and unassertive; they will not normally find their way to Tamms. They are indeed the residue of the seriously mentally ill to be found in our mental hospitals, or homeless on the streets, or in jails, or scraping by in marginal circumstances; however, they do not manifest the behaviour that would bring them to Tamms. It is the others – the aggressive, the bizarre, the acting out mentally ill – that can become Tamms inmates.

The problems of causation of human behaviour are not easy. In the previous paragraph I introduced the weasel words 'seriously mentally ill', as if those words described a clearly diagnosable class. They do not. The line between aggression precipitated by a sense of injustice and aggression precipitated by mental illness is not clear, and nor is the line between malingering and mentally disturbed hostility. In practice, those who run maximum security prisons tend to see the proper site for the passive seriously ill as being in mental hospitals or special medical treatment prisons that now exist in the federal prison system and in some state systems. By contrast, they see the others, the hostile and aggressive, unless their symptoms are particularly bizarre, as properly to be held in prison or in punishment blocks in prison or in institutions like Tamms.

There is a more insidious aspect of the processes that put the mentally ill in jails, prisons and supermax prisons. More than the community at large, the criminal justice system and those who serve it rely on deterrence as a system to control human behaviour. A substantial proportion of those who suffer from mental illness, are marginally retarded or are trembling on the brink of those conditions tend to respond unfavourably and with increasing resistance to punitive controls. The supposed equilibrium of misbehaviour and deterrent punishment is thus ratcheted up step by step, so that the inadequate and troubled personality may be jailed for a minor offence and, by virtue of repeated processes of deterrent punishment and increased resistance, moved through the graduated severity of different prisons and ultimately to a place such as Tamms.

The Department of Corrections has rules to exclude the mentally ill from Tamms. When a warden recommends a prisoner for transfer to Tamms, 'except in cases of emergency, the medical and master record files' of that prisoner 'shall be reviewed by a mental health professional prior to the committed person's placement at Tamms Correctional Center'. The mental health professional conducting the review, who need not be a psychiatrist or a psychologist, is merely required to check the prisoner's criminal and prison records to be sure that they do not contain data indicative of severe mental illness.

The fatal defects in this provision are that it relies on records that are notoriously imprecise and incomplete concerning the prisoner's proper encounters with mental hospitals, and that it does not require a face-to-face interview by any trained mental health professional prior to the prisoner's transfer to Tamms.

Orders like the above are not self-enforcing; they depend for their efficacy in the first place on the quality of record keeping in prison, and secondly, prior to the prisoner's arrival at Tamms, on the perception of people entirely untrained in the recognition of mental illness.

When the prisoner arrives in Tamms, there is still no mandatory psychiatric examination by anyone trained in that discipline. In the result, certainly at the time of writing, there are several floridly psychotic prisoners in Tamms and a number more teetering on the brink of clearly diagnosable psychosis. No prisoner should be placed in Tamms without having been interviewed at reasonable length by a psychiatrist, and once in Tamms the prisoner should undergo at least a quarterly interview by a psychiatrist whose daily practice is not concerned with that prison.

As to where and how to control the criminal and dangerous mentally ill, the best we can do is to recognize the reality of the pressures of mental illness on human behaviour and to provide systems of control, support and treatment in specialized institutions, a few of which currently exist in the United States and in Europe.

The official, legislatively approved, publicly proclaimed mission of the Department of Corrections is to:

protect the public from criminal offenders through a system of incarceration and supervision which securely segregates offenders from society, assures offenders of their constitutional rights and maintains programs to enhance the success of the offender's re-entry into society.

Is that what is happening at Tamms? It is hard for anyone who knows the place so to believe, and that scepticism includes some of those leading the Illinois Department of Corrections, including its senior medical staff. Only professional politicians, resolutely turning their eyes from reality, can so believe and prosper by proclaiming the myth of effective prison control rather than the reality of psychological torture. No evidence is offered to justify this overkill or technologically sophisticated utter isolation of prisoners by supermax prisons – it is a political knee-jerk reaction. At a time of booming prosperity, it provides further work for the building industry and the placement of new and expensive prisons in rural areas that are falling behind economically. It is, of course, not economically unwelcome, although the public and political discourse on punishment is largely confined to reiterations of the 'tough on crime' mantra and to the alleged 'realities of inefficiencies and corruption in the treatment of the mentally ill in community settings'.

Conclusion

In such a situation, what role does architecture, design and technology play? At our conference I described Tamms, and one of the distinguished architects in the audience later said in the public discussion that if asked to build such an institution he would refuse. The problem is that others would step in.

It is clear that modern technology worsens the conditions of prisoners in supermax prisons and greatly helps the slide to torture in this steep decline of decent punitive values. Prisoners are more isolated, observed and controlled, afforded less human contact and suffer more sensory deprivation than in earlier dungeons. To the staff, the prisoners become more dehumanized, the temptation is strong to treat them as less than another human being. It is the same process we bring to bear in wartime – the enemy, soldier and civilian alike, are demonized, and whatever happens to them is of little concern.

The contained solitary situation precludes other than dreams of escape, and powerfully inhibits social contact with any other human. The walls of isolation are monstrous, but no higher than the walls of ignorance and cruelty that built them. It is to be lamented that our technological and design skills are turned to such ends.

So, what does the architect, designer or technologist troubled by these new dungeons do about them? The usual distinction between one's role as a citizen and as a professional is unavoidable. As a citizen, the architect, designer and technologist is as obliged as the butcher, baker and candlestick maker to oppose politically imposed cruelty when he or she sees it – and those who help to build supermax prisons see it. As a professional involved personally or through professional associations in the building of a supermax prison, the obligation is, I submit, higher. The professional should insist on being advised of the necessity of every element of isolation that is being sought, and should advise on every possibility of allowing the prisoner in solitary confinement to communicate with staff, family and friends without negating the justified purposes of the isolation.

Likewise, when solitary confinement is necessary, it can be accompanied by a variety of in-cell activities that allow prisoners to be productive and to develop their own capacities without risk to the staff or other prisoners or the community. The architect, the designer and the technologist can help a great deal if they are constantly on the right side of this argument; they will find that by and large the prison administrators share their views and that the opposition is political, remote and ill-informed.

12 Prisons in Europe: France

Jean François Jodry and Michel Zulberty

Categories

There are three categories of prison in France: remand centres, detention centres and central prisons.

Remand prisons

These are establishments located in the vicinity of the courts that take in those awaiting trial. If prisoners are convicted and receive a sentence of less than one year, they remain in a remand prison until they are discharged.

In practice, the lack of overall prison capacity has meant that convicted prisoners, the remainder of whose sentence lasts for more than one year, are also kept in remand prisons. Furthermore, the need to have prisoners to work in general services (catering, laundry, cleaning and so forth) has often led the prison administration to keep prisoners in remand prisons even if sentenced to more than one year. These prisons must therefore be capable of coping with very different types of personality and lengths of sentences. In establishments of this sort, the range of possible activities is limited by the average length of stay (four and a half months) and by the restrictions on contacts between prisoners while judicial inquiries are being conducted.

A reception and connected observation area permits the personality and profile of new prisoners to be assessed during the early days of detention so that they can then be assigned to appropriate accommodation units. Communication with the outside world – examining magistrates, lawyer and family – is a priority, as is the link between inmate accommodation and the visitors' entrance to the prison. Communal services are more restricted.

Detention centres

These take in prisoners whose sentences range from one to five years (sometimes longer, but not more than ten years). This is a sufficiently long period of time to justify the encouragement and organization of social life. The prime aim of these establishments is the rehabilitation of prisoners and their successful return to the community. Communal services are important, as are the workshops and the educational and social facilities. In contrast, accommodation for legal representatives is more restricted, since it is considered that contact with the outside world serves less purpose.

Central prisons

These take in prisoners serving long sentences lasting more than five years. Their design is not noticeably different from that of detention centres, except that better, more commercial workshops are provided.

The production procedure can be organized on a more specialized technical basis. Security is usually more developed, as central prisons deal with the most dangerous prisoners and those most likely to be tempted to escape. By contrast, the way of life is more open inside the prison and more freedom is allowed.

State of the prison system in 1987

From the 1970s onwards, overcrowding in prisons had reached an intolerable level and provoked numerous mutinies. At the same time, the increasing severity of penal doctrine aggravated this situation to the point where public authorities were forced to adopt a ten-year construction plan as a possible solution.

However, the coming to power of the socialists, convinced as they were that imprisonment was not the only solution, put a brake on the planning of new establishments. Then, faced with reality, the Ministry of Justice set up a number of experimental institutions (Brest, Epinal, Mauzac and so forth). Unfortunately, these establishments were very expensive to build and run, and took too long to bring into service. However, this humane attempt led to a re-examination of the role of imprisonment and the problem of rehabilitation of prisoners.

In 1987 the prison population in France stood at 49 000, with only 32 500 places provided. The situation was all the more explosive because 60 per cent of available prison space (18 000 places) dated from before the turn of the century and was therefore very ill-equipped to meet current needs so far as work, training, rehabilitation, space and the fitting-out of cells was concerned. The new Prisons Minister, aware of how long it would take public authorities to build and commission the running of 14 500 places, presented an outline proposal for handing over the prison programme to the private sector.

There was an outcry. The Minister was attacked by political parties and the press, but one goal was achieved: agreement to a special budget of 4000 million francs to create 15 000 places. A double challenge emerged from this:

- to create each prisoner-space for a cost of 270 000 francs as opposed to the 400 000 francs per prisoner for the prisons built in 1987
- to carry out the programme in only three years.

The plan of action

To meet these demanding conditions, the Ministry of Justice set up a strategic organization, with a new set of procedures.

Organization

The masterstroke here was to entrust the overall management of the project to a specific administrative centre directly answerable to the Minister – the Delegation for Prison Development. This small organization was composed of top level executives, 15 engineers, six assistants and an accountant. Alongside the managing director and his assistant, there were four project teams each made up of two or three engineers and an assistant.

Procedure

For a programme of this scale, a movement away from the standard regulations was essential and inevitable. Both an organization and an ad hoc procedure were set up on the basis of a specific legislative brief outlining an overall consultation proposal. This was in two parts: design/construction, and a whole range of functions involved in the running of the establishments covering a ten-year period from the date of their opening.

The State thus guaranteed the financing of the construction and gave its backing to the management and security functions. The other items – accommodation, catering, laundry, work, transport of prisoners, maintenance, upkeep and operating – were handed over to private operators.

Programme

Twenty-five establishments were planned, mainly remand prisons and detention centres. They were distributed over four geographical zones, north, south, east and west, with the remand prisons situated in urban districts. Twelve architect–construction firm consortia were consulted, and for each zone candidates were required to draw up two complete preliminary schemes, with sketches for the remaining projects. The outcome of the consultation was the selection of four winners with distinct proposals each making specific reference to one of the zones.

Two contracts were agreed with each of them:

- a conception (design)–construction contract
- an operational contract (except for four establishments whose administration remains in the public sector, one per zone).

The operational diagram clearly identified two areas positioned around the central security point. The first was the detention area, comprising accommodation, socio-educational and medical facilities, and the second was the non-detention area, with general services, administration and work facilities.

Results

The construction permits were all obtained before the end of 1988, and all the establishments – providing 13 000 places – were fully operational before the end of 1991.

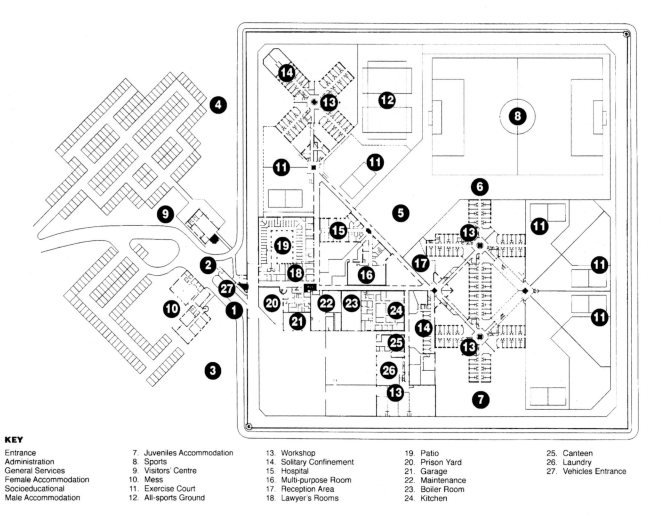

KEY

1. Entrance	7. Juveniles Accommodation	13. Workshop	19. Patio	25. Canteen
2. Administration	8. Sports	14. Solitary Confinement	20. Prison Yard	26. Laundry
3. General Services	9. Visitors' Centre	15. Hospital	21. Garage	27. Vehicles Entrance
4. Female Accommodation	10. Mess	16. Multi-purpose Room	22. Maintenance	
5. Socioeducational	11. Exercise Court	17. Reception Area	23. Boiler Room	
6. Male Accommodation	12. All-sports Ground	18. Lawyer's Rooms	24. Kitchen	

Four teams, four perspectives

The west zone design was a fragmented solution, which had the advantage of adapting to hilly sites and providing separate well-identified buildings. One condition had to be observed: the socio-educational, medical and reception facilities had to be situated between the entry screen lock and the accommodation units.

The north zone design emphasized the differentiation of the functional areas – accommodation, socio-educational, general services and visitors' rooms. Each of these had its own character and specific exterior space (*Figure 12.1*).

The south zone design offered two overall building plans, each of which exploited the same elements and principles. One, specific to remand prisons, organized the accommodation units in a star shape (*Figure 12.2*); the other, designed for detention centres, articulated these same elements in a horseshoe pattern.

The east zone design exploited the visibility of connections. The communal services, as well as the activities, were placed at the centre of the design and linked to the different accommodation units by a semicircular pathway. 'The street' was an original concept around which activities could be organized. As an assembly point, this street is under the control of the central security point (*Figure 12.3, Plates 7–9*).

Figure 12.1
North zone: cruciform solution in various configurations for use as a remand prison.

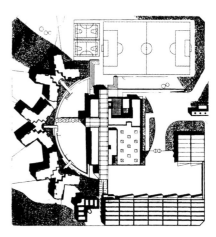

Figure 12.2
South zone: star-shaped remand prison.

Figure 12.3
East zone: cell units linked by semicircular 'street'.

Economic appraisal
The total cost of the operation came to 4300 million francs in 1991, in other words about 330 000 francs per place; the total administrative cost per prisoner averaged 170 francs per day, at 1997 values.

Assessment and the new programme

The programme of providing 13 000 places left its mark on the development of French prison architecture in the form of units of accommodation which were as secure as possible and allowed different ways of living and types of supervision, with the movement of prisoners controlled by passive security systems.

The extent of the 13 000-place programme meant keeping designs as standardized as possible. Even so, the four models showed considerable local variations. Other forward-looking establishments have been created both before and since then (for example, Val de Reuil and Cayenne).

A new programme for 4000 places was put out to competition, for three establishments in mid-1998 and a further four in 1999. Its aim was not to provide an urgent response to need, but rather to re-establish a balance in the current occupancy levels of the different establishments by splitting the ones that were overcrowded into two.

The 4000-place programme was designed to have a widespread effect and to serve as a point of reference for future prisons. The Minister gave priority to the quality of life in detention, and to the professionalism with which the prison staff conduct their duties.

The following three objectives were decided:

1. To extend the range of areas and times offered to prisoners for socializing.
2. To give more value to socio-educational activities by making them more accessible and improving the facilities.

3. To improve staff working conditions by installing, for example, an active security system. This gives priority to the contract between staff and prisoners, making the latter more aware of their responsibilities and developing better teamwork.

On the basis of these general objectives, the 4000-place programme was aimed at six prison establishments. These were to be situated in urban areas, and to some extent diverse in character, comprising different types of establishment, whether remand prisons or detention centres – prisons for men, women, young people and those needing medico-psychological treatment.

Functional organization

The overall functional organization remained similar to that of the 13 000-place programme, although it differed from it on a number of essential points.

Outside the compound
In order to create links with the town, bring about a convivial atmosphere for staff outside working hours and reduce the degree of security needed in the main building, a complex of buildings was situated outside the boundary, bringing together the socio-educational, recreational and staff trade union functions.

Within the precinct and outside the accommodation area
The shared facilities and activities for prisoners were supplemented by the creation of a gymnasium (which can be transformed into a multi-purpose hall), a football pitch of French Football Federation standards, and a family living unit, placed close to the visitors' rooms. This unit is reserved for convicted prisoners who are not allowed to go out on 'weekend permission', so that they can receive their family and have a relatively normal life for one or two days.

The accommodation area
The principal development of the 4000-place programme was at this level, since life in detention follows two regimes depending on whether the individual has been remanded in custody or convicted, or needs to be placed in solitary confinement or under supervision:

1. *Mode 1 (termed 'open door')* applies to that group of prisoners who can meet in the same accommodation sector and have permanent unaccompanied access to some communal activities, and is the preferred mode for convicted prisoners in detention centres and prisons.
2. *Mode 2 (termed 'closed door')* applies to all other prisoners who require a high level of supervision. They are accompanied at all times and do not have access to communal activities on their own; it is the preferred mode for those in custody in remand prisons.

Within the accommodation area, each cell is equipped with:

- a sanitary unit (shower, WC, basin)
- a kitchenette (refrigerator, hotplate)
- a study and dining corner

- a bed (two in double cells)
- a television stand.

The cells are grouped into living units of 30 prisoners, made up of 20 individual and five double cells. The living unit comprises the following communal spaces:

- an activities room (refectory, lounge, games etc.)
- an office (with dustbin area)
- a storage unit
- a sanitary space
- a launderette for mode 1 (open door) prisons.

Where possible, the living units belonging to the same category of prisoners are grouped in pairs around a single supervisor's office. This is not simply for ease of supervision, but also to act as a focal point from which the staff member goes out into the living unit to meet prisoners.

The living units are generally grouped to accommodate 180 prisoners per unit for mode 1 (open) and 210 prisoners for mode 2 (closed). To ensure greater flexibility, an area designed to function according to mode 1 has to be able to function in mode 2. Each unit is controlled by a fixed information and control point, and from there all movements within the area and entrances and exits from the area are supervised.

Some of the general facilities open to prisoners are grouped centrally, for example:

- the service office
- socio-educational rooms
- a newspaper stall/information point
- the library
- a fitness room
- an exterior space for mode 1
- a bank/shop for mode 1
- a cafeteria for mode 1
- telephone booths for mode 1
- a launderette for mode 2.

Prisoners can go from the living unit to the exercise yard and the above facilities, depending upon whether they are in mode 1 or mode 2 accommodation.

Each unit also contains rooms and workspace for staff, including an office, appeal room, interview rooms and a waiting room.

Although the units are based on general principles, they are nonetheless specifically equipped to meet particular needs. These will vary according to whether the prisoners are women, young people in reception or solitary confinement, or prisoners who are allowed to go back to their families under certain conditions and, for a period of time, have them to visit in a family living unit.

The total prison establishment is thus made up of three or four distinct sections. Apart from the accommodation areas, the two modes of living function in a very similar way. However, in mode 1, prisoners can decide when to move about and only one door at a time is opened and then closed behind them. In mode 2, prisoners are under supervision from the moment of leaving their cell, in a group, until they reach their destination.

Competition procedures

The procedure for selecting the winner for the 4000-place programme differed from that for the 13 000-place programme in that it related to architectural conception and construction costs and did not include management. The latter will be the subject of another competition in conjunction with the 'programme 13 000' contracts. In order to give priority to architectural creativity and to minimize any prior interdependence of interests, participating architects and construction firms were separately selected by the Ministry of Justice and came together only afterwards. In the last year, ten teams involving architects, construction and engineering companies have been selected. Their proposals have been examined, and a new concept of prison is now being finalized (*Figures 12.4, 12.5*).

Figure 12.4
Competition design concept. L-shaped cell blocks are located diagonally within a square enclosing wall.

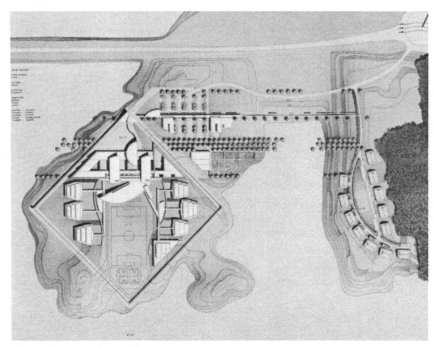

Figure 12.5
A further variation, with an undulating 'street' connecting the cell blocks.

Conclusion

At the end of the 1980s, the French penal estate was showing signs of age and was seriously deficient in capacity. In response, the French government has taken successful measures.

The first initiative (commencing in 1987) was directed at the lack of capacity, and was called the '13 000 programme'. Legal and regulatory measures were accompanied by specific organizational steps, including the involvement of private sector partners.

The second initiative (commencing in 1995) was intended to deal with some local overcrowding problems. This was called the '4000 programme'. This programme has recently begun to be implemented, and is based on the same process as the 13 000 programme although it incorporates some important improvements for prisoners and staff.

The third initiative, for which the first studies are beginning, is intended to update the old penitentiary estate. For financial reasons, this will take many years to complete.

Beyond rethinking the operation and organization of the traditional establishments, the Ministry of Justice is considering the establishment of a new type of prison which will hold non-violent prisoners in conditions that permit them to preserve social connections and employment. The Ministry is also exploring alternatives to traditional imprisonment, such as electronic tagging.

Taken together it is our hope that these programmes and initiatives will provide a reasonable, timely and cost-efficient solution to France's prison problems.

13 Prisons in Europe: The Netherlands

Peter van Hulten

Until about 1970, the prison capacity in The Netherlands was expanded only marginally. There were a number of institutions that dated from about the turn of the century, and with limited expansion by adaptations and extensions, and an occasional new building, the situation could more or less be managed. However, this limited growth led, at the end of the 1960s, to a serious lack of cell space. This was rectified by two new complexes: the PIOA (Penitentiare Inrichting Overamstel) in Amsterdam, and a similar but smaller prison in Maastricht. Together they contained 900 cells, and they came into use from the middle of the 1970s.

These complexes were high-rise solutions, called 'stacked pavilions'. They evolved from the idea that small groups, or communities, of inmates could be better managed and treated than the large groups of the old wing or domed prisons. However, it soon became clear that these new prisons were cumbersome and expensive to manage. They needed too many staff, and it was a complex and time-consuming procedure to move groups of inmates around the high-rise building.

Some ten years later, in 1985, a new expansion programme was conceived by the Sacri-plan (Society and Crime plan). A limited number of prisons provided about 2200 places. These institutions were large and extensive in layout because the cells all looked out onto courtyards, with the outer wall of the building doubling as the first perimeter wall of the complex. This type of design has cells on only one side of the corridor, and the corridors are therefore very long and wide and have to carry a lot of traffic. Inevitably the design also led to high building costs (about f300 000 per cell; £80 000 or US$130,000), which in turn prompted immediate social and political opposition.

In the late 1980s, influenced by social developments, the internationalizing of crime and the rise of organized crime, more severe opinions on crime and punishment led to social dissension. This coincided with the early release of or refusal to accept offenders because of lack of prison space. A two-pronged operation was therefore initiated to address the problem; judicial capacity was increased by erecting 20 new court buildings in six years, and penal capacity was increased using much lower building and management costs. This last development was named Cap '96, and was intended to increase the capacity by 1996. It was succeeded by a similar programme, Cap '98 (*Figures 13.1–13.3; Plate 10*).

Figure 13.1
Interior of cell wing at Zutphen. Central access is widened slightly to provide association space.

Figure 13.2
Brick exterior of prison at Zutphen.

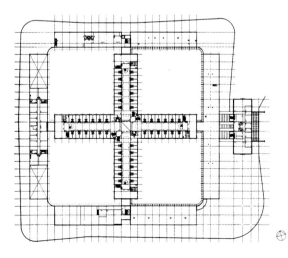

Figure 13.3
Courtyard layout at Sittard.

Detention in The Netherlands

In The Netherlands, the standard punishment is by fine or detention. There are also specialized programmes for the treatment of drug addicts, psychiatric patients and positively-motivated inmates. Approximately 75 in 100 000 people are currently in detention.

The enforcement of prison sentences is the responsibility of the National Agency of Correctional Institutions of the Minister of Justice (Directie Justitiële Inrichtingen). The DJI is responsible for all aspects of enforcement, within the framework of security, effectiveness and human dignity.

Great importance is attached to outcomes and economic costs, introducing, for example, new initiatives in the care of convicted drug addicts. Stress is placed on work as a means of creating discipline and self-respect, and improving the chances of prisoners' re-integration into society – which is, after all, the long-term objective.

An important part of the job of the DJI is planning penal capacity and, in conjunction with the Government Building Agency of the Ministry of Housing (RGD – Rijksgebouwendienst), realizing that planning. It is notable that the DJI tries to supply almost all the different forms of penal 'products' in one judicial division, so that prisoners can have their whole penal 'career' in one region. This helps to maintain continuous links with prisoners within the penal system, keeps them in contact with their social background, and makes it easy to keep in touch with them after release. These requirements determine what is built where and when, on the basis of the total requirements of a particular region.

A number of specialized institutions are not provided regionally – notably facilities for the detention of foreigners and for the care of psychiatric prisoners. For Cap '96 and Cap '98, DJI has, with the RGD, formed a specialist team responsible for the planning, finance and realization of the programmes.

Government buildings in The Netherlands

In The Netherlands, state buildings are not built by the ministries themselves; the RGD is responsible for the housing of the various branches of government. The Government Building Agency RGD is part of the Ministry of Housing (VROM – Volkshuisvesting, Ruimtelijke Ordening en Milieu), and it controls and maintains all government buildings, including prisons. It deals with matters concerning those buildings, including designs and project management, and has its own in-house architectural and engineering office.

An advantage of the RGD is that the work is done by an organization whose core business is housing and construction. By being involved in building itself, it creates and keeps hands-on knowledge of all aspects of the accommodation of the range of government departments and agencies. The Netherlands employs a Chief Government Architect, who maintains architectural standards in government buildings and is also responsible for appointing architects for all the projects and for supervising and reviewing the design processes. In addition, the Chief Architect is responsible for the provision of art in projects for government buildings on the basis of a percentage of the building costs. This approach to architecture and art also applies to the building of prisons. Each project, however, has its own priorities and issues. Because Cap '96 and '98 had short time-spans, friction arose from time to time between the DJI and the RGD.

Current programmes and objectives

Cap '96 was started in 1994. The objective was to provide 4500 extra cell spaces by 1996; an increase from 9500 to 14 000. An important issue was the reduction of the cost per cell. In 1996 Cap '98 followed, aiming at another 2500 cells. By the end of 1999 the total objective was 16 500 cell spaces to achieve our doubling in a decade. Because most of the increase in crime appears to be in the more serious drugs-related offences, the emphasis of Cap '98 was to increase capacity for long-stay psychiatric prisoners and drug addicts. There will be a continuing need to increase capacity for the foreseeable future.

The new Dutch prisons are based on groups of 24 inmates, or multiples of that number, with prisons ranging from 144 to 384 cells. Those numbers are sometimes exceeded by double occupancy of cells.

Almost all the older complexes, including the 100-year-old domed panopticon prisons, are being or already have been upgraded. All possible capacity has been brought into service to create cell spaces, and this has the advantage over new construction of relatively low costs and greater building speed. This type of expansion also assists the Government Chief Architect in the preservation of significant monumental buildings.

Analysis of existing buildings

The expansion of penal capacity is mainly through the extension of existing complexes, and the running of these institutions then becomes cheaper per capita through the sharing of support services. More 'penal products', more differentiation, can be housed in one institution.

The RGD, together with the DJI, methodically analyses the existing capacity of a building. This allows assessment of the possibilities and limitations of extensions and adaptations, especially in the fields of use and management, in order to get the best fit between the complex and the type of inmates.

New developments are mainly in three areas:

- shorter periods of detention for certain categories of crime (mostly light), in order to improve the effect of the punishment
- restricted regimes with fewer facilities, especially work, for short-term prisoners (under three months)
- SOV (Strafreshtelijke Opvang Verslaafden) regimes for drug addicts who repeatedly cause problems on the streets.

These types of prisoners all have their own special needs, and the new prisons are largely built within or adjoining existing institutions.

Can design change behaviour?

When building prisons, a great deal of consideration is given to the structural environment. This arises as much from the government's desire to play a leading part in the wider cultural debate as from the design of prisons themselves. This suggests something about the way inmates are seen: they are citizens temporarily removed from society, but almost certain to return there, with all their civil rights.

Whether prisoners make clothes pegs or a complex piece of carpentry makes a difference to the way they regard themselves, and thus influences their chances of re-integration into society. The building must therefore be able to accommodate this kind of work. The same applies to other activities such as sports, counselling and visiting. Buildings must make them possible, in a practical sense, and this requires good (at least inventive) design within the limitations imposed by the logistics of the prison system. In a more qualitative sense, the formal and spatial qualities of the prison complex are an important part of how prisoners experience custody (the complex being more or less all they have to look at). The signals that emanate from the quality of their environment will have an effect on the inmates who, after no more than a few years, will once again regain their places in the community. The answer to the question 'Can design change behaviour?' is that design can certainly *help* to change behaviour, and denying this means leaving a potentially powerful instrument unused.

14 Public/private partnerships[1]

Leslie Fairweather

A mixed economy in custodial services

The net value of the UK Prison Service's Private Finance Initiative (PFI) prison programme at the end of 1999 was £642 million for three contracts. A further four contracts in the following procurement programme doubled this. Significant as these figures are, they are only part of a much larger package of United Kingdom custodial contracting. At the beginning of the decade starting in 2000 (*but using 1997–8 prices*), the value of the current let contracts in England and Wales, including a secure training centre and two immigration detention centres and the prison escort system worth some £89 million per annum, will exceed £160 million. The addition of four more PFI prison contracts takes this beyond £230 million. The level of expenditure for let contracts is approximately half of what is spent on the Crown Prosecution Service, and the estimated forecast future level is over half of what is spent in England and Wales on the probation service.

When the Prison Service let the first three PFI contracts, for Bridgend, Fazakerley and Lowdham Grange in Nottinghamshire, in 1995/6 and 1996/7, it had already built up substantial experience of contractual management, beginning with the 1992 contract for the management of Wolds prison. The further 1900 places since then have become part of a prison estate where some 4 per cent of the prison population are held in contractually managed prisons (*Table 14.1*).

The existence of an established market for custodial operators, together with an in-house ability to work equally well with potential new DCMF (design, construct, manage, finance) contractors, was a key factor in explaining the Prison Service's ability to let PFI contracts and the speed at which the service was delivered.

What was remarkable was the reduction in delivery times for prison places. The previous PSA-managed programme of 21 prisons in the 1980s and early 1990s had seen average construction times cut from seven to four years. Under PFI, times were further cut to an average of two years. Lowdham Grange was constructed in one year (two years from receipt of the design brief); a pacemaker for the future.

This is clear evidence of what an operator-led PFI team can achieve. However, although the building contractor, architects and other specialists may be very good, without a strong and effective lead being taken

---

1 This chapter is based on briefing documents provided by Tim Wilson, David Kent and Elaine Bailey.

Table 14.1 DCMF prisons (England and Wales)

	Location	When ITT/ITN	How many companies tendered bids	When contract signed	Contractor (preferred supplier)	When construction finished (planned)	When first prisoner received (planned)	CNA (Certified Normal Accommodation)	Type of prisoner	Net Present Value (NPV) of contract (£ million)	Contract term (years)
Parc	Bridgend, South Wales	Jan 94	6	4 Jan 96	Securicor + Costain/Atkins/Skanska	2 Sep 97	17 Nov 97	800 (500 + 300)	Cat B local and YOs	266	25
Altcourse	Fazakerley, Merseyside	Jan 94	6	20 Dec 95	Group 4 + Tarmac	12 Nov 97	1 Dec 97	600 (500 + 100)	Cat B local and YOs	247	25
Lowdham Grange	Nottinghamshire	Nov 95	6	7 Nov 96	Premier Prison Services + Kvaerner	23 Jan 98	16 Feb 98	500	Cat B (sentenced)	137	25
Forest Bank	Salford, Greater Manchester	June 97	4	02 July 98	UKDS + Tilbury Douglas	(Dec 99)	(Jan 00)	800	Cat B local	197	25
Ashfield	Pucklechurch, Bristol	June 97	4	29 June 98	Premier Prison Services + Kvaerner	(Oct 99)	(Nov 99)	400	Young Offender Institution	121	25
Marchington	Marchington, Staffordshire	Nov 97	5		(Premier Prison Services + Kvaerner)	(Dec 00)	(Jan 01)	800 including 200	Cat B Training including therapeutic community	240	25
Onley	Rugby	Nov 97	5	22 July 99	Group 4 + Tarmac	(Sep 00)	(Oct 00)	600	Cat B training	154	25

All contracts are for 25 years.
CNA, certified normal accommodation.
NPV, net present value.

by the operator who will manage the contracts there will be no synergy between operation and design, which is the hallmark of a successful PFI scheme. In addition, substantial savings are possible compared with more traditional procurement routes.

The search for new public/private partnership models

The DCMF contract will not necessarily be the model for future public/private partnership prisons. The government had reservations about the principle of contracting out prison management, but their initial approach had necessarily been determined by the situation they had inherited – a sharply rising prison population and expenditure plans that relied on new prisons being designed, constructed, managed and financed by the private sector. The government had to decide whether the responsibility for the incarceration of prisoners should as a matter of principle be discharged through direct management in the public sector, or whether it could properly and effectively be discharged by private contracts under a regulatory framework.

The Home Secretary accepted the conclusions of the two reports relating to the review of private sector management of prisons, which he had announced on 19 June 1997. The first report examined the case for transferring the management of existing private sector prisons back to the public sector. It concluded that the cost gap between the sectors could not be closed quickly, and that any attempt to impose less generous pay and conditions of service on the public sector would result in a substantial industrial relations confrontation. The second report examined whether it might be possible for the private sector to design, construct and finance (DCF) a new prison under PFI, whilst leaving the management of the prison in public hands. The report concluded that to adopt DCF would increase the cost of new prison places by at least 10–12 per cent, reduce the transfer of risk to the private sector to an unacceptably low level, and weaken incentives for innovation on the part of a winning consortium.

The Home Secretary confirmed that the transfer of existing contracted-out prisons back from the private sector to the public sector would have to be done within existing resources and as budgets allowed. He therefore decided that the public sector should be allowed the opportunity to demonstrate best value for money in competition with the private sector. The first occasion for this was an in-house bid under competition for the management of Doncaster and Buckley Hall prisons, whose current contracts expire in 2000.

Key elements of the DCMF contract

There are a number of key elements to the DCMF contract:

1. There is a single fee for the total service. Government does not provide or finance any form of business interruption insurance to finance the underlying debt should the service fail significantly or altogether.
2. Payments will only be made for available places. The contract requires the prison to be built, and that certain physical requirements,

for example a minimum ambient temperature, should be achieved in various parts of the building. Each cell must be properly equipped, and basic services such as the distribution of mail, the response to calls for medical assistance and the provision of food must meet clearly stated minimum criteria. Levels of security and safety in the prison and the control of prisoners must meet approved operating procedures which, reflecting the sensitivity of this area of the public service, includes compliance with the Prison Service's own security manual. Only when the specified elements are in place will a payment be made.

3. The payment stream is subject to deductions for poor performance. In the most recent DCMF contract there are 45 performance measures, and their value will vary depending on the significance of the measure and the contractor's ability to control events. For example, a failure to comply with approved cleaning schedules is half the value of the failure to effect a repair within 48 hours. Both result in substantially lower deductions than the release of a prisoner in error.

4. Failure in respect of such measures can result in a maximum deduction from the revenue stream of 5 per cent each year. This reflects the judgement made in the first procurement competition about the degree of uncertainty in respect of this element of risk distribution that would be bankable. There is, however, an additional provision that allows for a deduction from revenue that is not subject to a maximum figure should a prisoner escape. In the Lowdham Grange contract, an escape from the prison itself would result in a deduction of £50 000. Material failure resulting in the termination of the contract also includes action 'either by itself or in addition to any other failure or failures (whether or not remedied), which casts, in the Authority's reasonable opinion, serious doubts on the competence or suitability of the contractor to provide the service'.

5. On or after the fourteenth anniversary of the prison coming into operation, the Prison Service can choose to initiate a price review to assess whether the contract continues to represent value for money compared with other providers in either the public or private sectors. The trigger is not cost irrespective of quality or range of service; all are of equal consequence.

6. The arrangements for compensation on termination of contract are complex and vary according to circumstances. There are two key elements that fully illustrate the nature of the PFI contract:

   • If the asset cannot be built, or the special project budget or its construction subcontractor runs out of money before it is completed, the Government will not pay compensation for a partly completed asset. It will not take over responsibility for ensuring that whatever has been built can be turned into a prison capable of taking inmates. The risk of delivery remains firmly with the private sector. Indeed, late delivery will result in the contractor paying liquidated damages that reflect the probability that this would result in the Prison Service having to use police cells at £300 per night to cover part of the shortfall in places.

   • The Prison Service looks for a significant equity (or equity/subordinated debt) investment by contractors. At a minimum this has been at about 8 per cent of the capitalized cost of the project. Should the contract be terminated because of material default, there would be no compensation from Government to cover the loss of equity. Compensation could be reduced to less than the value of outstanding debt if, as a result of terminating the contract, prisoners had to be temporarily relocated. The lease for DCMF contracts gives the Prison Service exclusive possession in these circumstances.

Risk allocation

The Prison Service's approach has been to achieve sufficient risk transfer for the Home Office, Treasury and National Audit Office (NAO) to be confident that the DCMF contracts are indeed off-balance sheet transactions, and also to acquire the service at an affordable price. This has meant seeking to identify optimum rather than maximum risk transfer.

- There are no volume-related payments except for overcrowding, which features increasingly in specifications for local prisons. This currently amounts to an option to increase the number of inmates to up to 130 per cent of design capacity without a significant reduction in regime activities (including education and work routines). The scope for revenue provided from elsewhere (e.g. private manufacturers using prison labour) is essentially confined to the extent to which this reduces the costs of providing a demanding and purposeful regime for prisoners. For example, in one contract two-thirds of the population have to be provided with 35 hours of work or vocational training in the industries – an ambitious target for any prison. If it cannot be delivered, the payment stream will be reduced for poor performance.
- There is a substantial transfer of risk to the private sector in terms of pricing, as the service payment does not vary with the underlying cost base. In general, it is inflated by pre-agreed factors that reflect movements in the retail price index. There is, however, provision for a price review if the operator's costs increase by more than 5 per cent for reasons outside his or her control. As for the operating cost risk, the Government undertakes to meet the cost of implementing changes in prison legislation.
- There is no residual value risk to the contractor. The asset reverts to the Prison Service at the end of the 25-year contractual period, and it must do so in a suitable condition with all work identified by a final dilapidation survey completed at the contractor's expense. The contractor is not expected to offer the Prison Service a discounted price to cover the residual value for an asset that remained with him or her after a contract term as long as 25 years.

Serial/template procurement

PFI procurement clearly works better when neither the agency nor the contractors are restricted to a single competition, as improvements are usually achievable the second time around.

- However well the public sector comparator is prepared, the previous competition inevitably begins to provide more realistic benchmarks for unit costs.

- The learning curve on both sides is much steeper; it is not without significance that Lowdham Grange had a much shorter procurement time-scale, despite having to substitute one merchant bank for another.
- It is possible to prime contractors about the objectives for the next competition, for example by placing considerable emphasis on the need to reduce unit costs during the debrief following the first competition.
- In the Lowdham Grange competition, a two-stage process was employed to reduce a field of six down to two. This enabled the Prison Service to gauge through negotiations to what extent improvements in risk allocation were likely to be bankable. It is easier to be more decisive the second time around.

Results of the Bridgend and Fazakerley competition

The National Audit Office Report on the first DCMF procurement competition, for Bridgend and Fazakerley, drew the following conclusions about the benefits of PFI:

- The procurement, design, construction and pre-occupation periods, 40 months at Bridgend and 41 at Fazakerley, are significantly shorter than many prisons built by the Property Services Agency on behalf of the Prison Service. They opened 45 per cent more quickly than the average of a sample of PSA prisons previously examined by the National Audit Office.
- The PFI solutions enabled some innovative building design and operational methods to be proposed and implemented.
- The PFI solutions produced aggregate savings of 10 per cent compared with similar types of public-financed prisons where the operations were contracted out to the private sector; this reflected economies of scale (Fazakerley has 200 less places). The design at Bridgend was more innovative.
- The Lowdham Grange contract was let six months after the invitation to tender was issued, which was approximately 65 per cent faster than the time-scale required for Bridgend and Fazakerley.

While the main objectives had been to secure value for money and risk transfer, the NAO also commended the close working relationship with the chosen contractors to ensure that issues were resolved quickly without the need to go to arbitration. Opportunities for developing the projects in a mutually beneficial manner were reflected in:

- the arrangements whereby the contracts provided for the Prison Service and the contractors to share in any benefits arising from the new security technology
- close on-site cooperation between the Prison Service, their contract monitoring engineers and the contractors to achieve a 'win–win' situation for *all* parties
- the contractual facility for the contractor to propose changes to the design, operation or other aspects of the contracts, which could be accepted or rejected by the Prison Service
- agreed procedures for resolving any disputes.

This partnering approach helped to identify and test new designs, technology and operational procedures that could be implemented across the prison estate.

The NAO acknowledged that the £1.6 million spent on advisers and consultants reflected the work required for new and complex methods of procurement. The cost, however, was more than double the estimate of £0.6 million because the Prison Service had no previous experience of a major PFI contract, underestimated the amount and complexity of work that was necessary, and did not expect to have to re-tender during the procurement. Procedures were established to monitor and cap expenditure on legal advice (the biggest single item).

Conclusion: learning points

Three important lessons were learned in the first experiments with PFI:

1. PFI needs to be driven by a strategic approach that will encourage both competition and confidence in the market place if the service itself, contract prices and terms are to represent the best deal for the taxpayer. Eventually, this may make possible significantly different models for public–private partnerships.
2. The process needs to encourage innovation in operation and design if the benefits well beyond the PFI contracts themselves are to be fully realized. The Prison Service has a unique opportunity to learn from the private sector in the testing of different approaches.
3. Whether it is developing the nature of the service to be purchased, learning lessons, improving terms or achieving good value for money, the task is immeasurably easier with serial procurement. Where there is not a single contractual authority, it may be possible to adapt a template approach. Colleagues and their advisers need to discuss issues frankly and share information in such areas.

15 Providing the complete prison package

Michael Gander

The previous chapter explains the process by which the Prison Service procures new prisons under the Private Finance Initiative (PFI), with contractors responsible for design, construction, management and finance (DCMF). This chapter describes how private sector contractors actually provide and run the new prisons within the DCMF framework.

Purchasing and contracts

The process of purchasing can take between 12 and 18 months, from the Prison Service making its requirements known to the signing of the contract. There are five individual steps:

1. First indication (OJEC Notice)
2. Shortlisting
3. Invitation to tender (ITT)
4. Preferred supplier
5. Contract.

The process begins with the publication of a notice in the Official Journal of the European Community (OJEC). This notice is required by European legislation, and gives details of all government contracts over a certain figure (currently £60 000) for professional services.

In some cases, officials may give advance notice to potential contractors of whom they are aware or with whom they have done business before. This personal approach is not anti-competitive; government departments have a responsibility to their ministers to ensure that the best deal is done. It therefore makes sense to ensure that those who are known from their track record to be capable are at least alerted to the opportunity. The next stage is normally for the competing contractor either to submit a full pre-qualification statement, often in answer to a questionnaire, or, if it is a competition in which the contractor has already pre-qualified, an expression of interest to confirm that the contractor is still interested in pursuing the new opportunity.

It is often wrongly thought that in competition for large government contracts there is an agreement that all the contractors in the market are given, in turn, sufficient contracts to keep them viable and to maintain their interest in future business. This is not the case. As each contractor knows, contracts are awarded on the best total value for money represented by their proposals. The cheapest bid may not necessarily always win. There is a finely balanced judgement on the part of the Prison Service over not only the cost but also the quality of the proposal and the ability of the contractor to deliver. Although this apparent dilution of the economic argument could result in a market dominated by the major players, with the barriers to entry proving overly difficult to new contenders, experience proves that the main players already in the international prison management market are not the only ones to win PFI contracts. For example, in the tendering for prisons at Fazakerley (outside Liverpool) and Bridgend (South Wales), the first was won by Group 4, which had been successful in the tender for the first managed prison at the Wolds, while the second went to Securicor. Up to that point Securicor had no prison management experience, although they had gained, over the years, a certain amount of experience of immigration detainees. This result was despite the market including two major international players: Corrections Corporation of America (CCA, known in England as UKDS – United Kingdom Detention Services – now a joint venture between Sodexho of France and CCA), and Wackenhut Corrections Corporation (WCC).

The hard lesson for the losers was that lifetime economic cost is a major, if not deciding, factor in the decision of where to award contracts. This early failure galvanized private prison providers to look at their design and costing structures to ensure that their solutions reflected this economic emphasis, while retaining the quality of vision required to operate the prison for the benefit of both staff and prisoners.

Tenders and contracts

There are two major components of the tendering process: the DCMF contract itself and the operational requirements. These also include the issues of contract compliance, contract monitoring and performance measurement, which are the main concerns of all contractors. By this stage the major issues within draft contracts will have been agreed on previous prisons, and the evidence is that they will therefore form the basis of the model agreement for new contracts, with any amendments necessary to reflect the particular aspects of each prison tendered.

The Prison Service has developed a clear set of operational requirements, and the contractor must either commit to these or provide detailed management information to demonstrate that the question has been understood and the requirement to deliver accepted. This procedure is somewhat different in the United States where, typically, state legislatures rely on the accreditation requirements of the American Correctional Association (ACA).

The ACA is a voluntary body in the United States, which over the years has developed comprehensive quality standards and requirements for all aspects of prison management. States involved in the procurement of privately managed prisons will usually insist on the contractor subscribing to the ACA accreditation requirements. Although the English Prison Service approach is becoming more comprehensive, the contractor is obliged to spell out how these services will be delivered and the standards employed to audit output. Detailed standards and requirements, which must be met by all contractors, are not issued in the interests of achieving better value for money through innovation. It will be interesting to observe the development of the Prison Service's own standards audit process in the future and to see whether the American model will gradually become adopted, even if the detailed requirements of the process are different.

The measurement of performance has changed less than the method of requiring operational responses. There have been considerable returns to the Prison Service from the imposition of 'fines' on various contractors for breaches of contractual terms of performance measurement. In many cases these breaches are minor, and a view is growing amongst contractors that the operation of performance measurement is perhaps more concerned with revenue reduction to the contractor than with performance improvement.

Under a straightforward management-only contract, calculating the cost is simple: how many staff are needed to manage the prison; what are they to be paid; what other costs are there (such as maintenance and food), and what is a proper reward for the skill and management required in running the enterprise? With the advent of the PFI prison, however, financing arrangements have become more complicated. In addition to the continuing requirement to pay staff over the 25 years of the contract, design and construction also need funding. This involves careful consideration of the different ways that finance can be achieved on the open market and of how this finance can be used to allow the contractor to provide for this considerable proportion of the total project cost most economically. Various methods have been tried, but the wish of the Prison Service to transfer risk to the private contractor acts as a considerable restraint. The most obvious solution – that the contractor arranges for a large pot of money to be available from which money is drawn as and when required for various projects – is unlikely to be a successful route. Prison construction and management contracts usually run for 25 years, and to have a large amount of money focussed on a single project for this length of time does not always make sense for corporate finance arrangements. Instead, typically, contractors will arrange loans for a specific project from one or more banks. This gives both the contractor and the Prison Service comfort, since the money is committed for a specific purpose and does not depend upon maintaining the viability of the company in its other operations to ensure its continued ability to support long-term debt. The cost of money to a private contractor, however, is always going to be more expensive than the cost of money to the government. The challenge to the contractor is to manage the financial arrangements so that this cost penalty is reduced as far as possible, and so that it is more than offset by the savings provided by the operational approach. In the end, therefore, the contractor's ability to be successful depends on the quality of the proposal in the round, since that quality should translate into a more efficiently designed institution and a more efficiently staffed management approach.

Risk transfer

The transfer of risk is a serious and demanding issue that goes to the heart of the private provision of a public service. It is a very powerful tool available to the Prison Service. It can ensure that the contractors provide best value for money and are so organized that the Prison Service does not have to bail out a failing contractor. It can act as a further test on the contractor's proposals by early exposure of risk, which may be so great as to leave the contractor in mortal danger and thus incur further costs and difficulty for the Prison Service in having to deal with the aftermath of failure. Sensible risk management strategies will reduce the actual risk to the contractor, but still permit the Prison Service to pass on to the contractor the risks of doing the job. It is thus able to ensure that the service required is delivered at the cost agreed with no 'hidden extras'. A significant element of the transferred risk comes early on in the contract. Typically, prisons are to be constructed on land already in the government's possession and, as part of the process of requiring a tender, the preferred approach is to achieve outline planning permission for the construction of a prison of the required size on the site. This does not bind the contractor to proceeding with the Prison Service's outline design, since the purpose of the outline application is to gain acceptance that a prison will be built on that particular site. Transfer of risk comes with the awarding of the contract and the requirement for the successful contractor to achieve detailed planning permission. This will include not only the overall design, but also involves the environmental impact of the prison and any benefits to the community that may be achieved.

Commercial confidentiality and competitiveness

There is no 'cartel' that operates amongst prison contractors, nor even an industry body that speaks on their behalf. This has undeniably been of significant benefit to the whole prison procurement process. It has resulted in true competition between the various contractors, and has driven down the cost of providing the service while improving its quality. All contractors, therefore, are obsessive about ensuring that their insights into prison design and prison management and staff are as jealously guarded as their financial arrangements.

Although there have been a number of people recruited from the public sector Prison Service into the private sector, there is still a very competitive attitude between those private sector employees and their public sector counterparts. Such rivalry, like competition between contractors themselves, is of benefit, and has driven up the quality of provision of prison services throughout the whole estate – not just in private prisons. For the future benefit of the Prison Service as a whole, it remains essential that there is no cosy relationship between the Prison Service and the private sector, but rather one in which a competitive approach is allowed to flourish.

The costs to the contractor

The Prison Service does not pay for the costs of competition. It will not pick up the tab for the unsuccessful competitor, nor will it contribute to the successful competitor's costs, both of which can be high. The legal and financial advisory costs for the typical PFI proposal, even when successful, are huge.

To a certain extent, some costs are inevitable and sensible to avoid the company walking blindly into a situation that could imperil its other activities. A more quality-standard prescriptive approach would nevertheless significantly benefit contractors by reducing financial and legal costs in particular, which would then translate into reduced total costs for the successful prison. This approach, however, would require fully standardized contractual terms and minimum quality requirements. The cheapest way of financing prisons could be for the government to reimburse, out of current income or even borrowing, the full construction costs at the completion of the construction phase. The difficulty is that this approach cannot be pursued under present government accounting rules. The rationale of the PFI process is to take the costs of prison provision off the government's current balance sheet and hold them on the contractor's balance sheets until such time as their value is extinguished, in financial but not in physical terms. At the end of the 25 year contract, the assets are transferred to the government from the books of the contractor at effectively nil cost.

There might be a danger that such arrangements could lead to less efficient methods of prison provision. This is possible, though not likely while there is such a strong competitive element between the contractors. Such potential arrangements should not be confused with the old 'cost plus' contracts entered into between the government and defence suppliers. Those contracts usually included considerable development work, which the government paid for as part of the total procurement process. The same situation would not hold true within the prison sector since, although there is some very complicated and sophisticated technology within prisons, they are by and large rather simple to construct. Their competitive edge is more in their design and operation than in the overuse of highly sophisticated and expensive leading-edge technology.

The fact remains, however, that both the supply of money and the costs of that supply are an extra cost to private prison provision. If a way could be found of reducing these costs, this would quickly translate into a more cost effective procurement solution. The experience of the past few years has nevertheless shown that, even bearing these costs, the private prison providers have managed to bring down the cost of supplying a prison of comparable size by a factor of between 40 and 50 per cent. Set against these savings, perhaps, the extra costs outlined above are relatively small.

Briefings and pre-qualification

In the first years of both outsourced prison management (management-only contracts) and full PFI outsourcing (including design, construction and financing), the Prison Service was keen to ensure that the contractors invited to tender knew what they were doing in terms of general prison management and also appreciated the particular idiosyncrasies of the English prison system. This was not meant to inhibit contractors from importing, often from America, new ideas and practices for the delivery of prison services.

Nevertheless, the successful companies had mostly either recruited permanent staff with considerable experience of prison management, including relevant experience as the governor of a prison, or utilized, as consultants, those who had recently left the Prison Service. The latter were often at a high level, and could still be assumed to have an intimate working knowledge of the English prison system. In addition, a considerable effort was made by the Contracts and Competition Group (CCG), and especially those who were the operational advisers, to check out the depth of understanding and the thinking behind the proposals being put forward. On occasions these 'clarification sessions' inevitably began to look like debates as to whether a particular solution was acceptable or not. This discussion was invaluable. It elucidated those issues on which the CCG might be persuaded to accept the risk of a new way of doing things, and those areas where, although the contractor was confident that the proposals would be acceptable in operational practice, it felt that the risk of failure might be too high and the contractor should be encouraged to review that particular part of the proposal.

As the market has developed, however, the need for the CCG to undertake such debates has disappeared. Clarification sessions are now almost exclusively for the contractor to expand upon what is proposed, rather than to discuss and modify it. In turn, the Prison Service is more inclined to accept a contractor's innovative proposals as confidence is gained, through actual prison practice, in that contractor's ability to deliver.

Teamwork

One of the issues that has arisen for all contractors following the PFI programme is the need to ensure that the group or consortium of companies, or even the operator, has properly identified all the elements required within the PFI process. These include the legal and financial aspects, as well as the more obvious design, construction and operational ones, and they must all be brought together in a winning combination.

Team experience in design and construction of prisons can be an advantage, together with a mix of skills from those with previous experience of prison work and those without. Some contractors have even gone so far as to bring the designers and architects into the consortium of companies and into the provision of equity in the final product. Others have taken a simpler route by regarding the prison's construction and later operation as the responsibility of a separate, wholly-owned subsidiary, which subcontracts the design and construction, and the later operation, to the main companies within the group of companies that make up the bidding team. This has the distinct advantage of ensuring that each part of the group concentrates on the activities at which it is best, whilst remaining welded together by the operator who will be going on to manage the activity, after the tender has been won. The only other ongoing involvement with any other part of the group is that of the financing banks. Even this relationship has a twist, since the Prison Service ensures that there is a 'direct agreement' between itself and the banks so that, should the operator fail in such a way as to be unable to continue to manage the prison, the banks and the Prison Service can seek an alternative operator to carry on its management.

Although the activity has been described above as being that of a group or consortium of companies, the key element in the PFI provision of prisons is that of the operator. All successful contractors learn very early in the process that the key to success is to ensure that the operator is involved from the very beginning and steers the project to its conclusion. It is the operator who will be responsible for the 25 years of the prison's contractual life. If the operator does not ensure that the core design of the facility and the quality of its construction closely match the operating vision and requirements, then although the prison might look new and the design might appear innovative, the end result may be cumbersome and awkward to maintain, manage and live in.

Most contractors either recruit someone for the specific purpose of running the new prison at an early stage, or identify someone within their own ranks who will be doing that task. After the original detailed work has been done, that person must be given the opportunity to contribute to the 'design development phase' and the final details to turn the project from a building site into a living entity. The original design team's solution may need tweaking in the interests of operational reality once those who will have full and final responsibility for the prison's management are brought into the picture.

It might be thought that the best solution would be to have such people on site and involved from the earliest days. Where the company has such people within its own ranks, this is possible but still expensive. Where it does not, the cost and risk to employment if the contractor should not win has to be weighed against the benefits. In practice, contractors have built up a considerable wealth of knowledge on what is constructionally possible and what is operationally required. They have developed a particular style of construction as a result of their operational visions.

PDBS and the bidding system

From the earliest days of tendering opportunities for the new PFI prisons, the 'gold standard' of the Prison Design Briefing System (PDBS) was emphasized in the documentation dealing with prison design and construction. The Prison Service encouraged bidders to use PDBS as a guide, although they fell short of requiring it as a condition of design. This still continues. But how did contractors view this attempt to describe rather than prescribe the standards and the approaches used in PDBS?

Companies' views differed considerably, at least in the initial rounds of PFI bidding, about how much they had to include of PDBS and how much they could safely leave out. While some companies decided to take the encouragement within the tender documents as an instruction rather than a guide, others, while careful to ensure that the core requirements for security of different parts of the construction were followed, took the view that innovation was all, and produced designs that owed little to either new generation or PDBS concepts. Two extremes were seen in the successful competitors for the new prisons at Bridgend and Fazakerley. Bridgend in South Wales, now known as Parc Prison, was won by the consortium of Securicor, WS Atkins, Scansca; while Fazakerley near Liverpool, now known as Altcourse, was successfully tendered for by Group 4, whose design very largely followed the individual PDBS-type rectangular blocks of the Housing Units. In the event, the competition was decided on other parameters rather than the relative merits or disadvantages of the two offerings, at least as viewed by the Prison Service, since both had achieved the minimum threshold mark for quality and deliverability. The decision was based on two other important criteria: cost and value for money. This is the point where a cheaper but effective design will assist a contractor by reducing the overall price; however, it must be emphasized that the cost of construction and the ensuing cost of maintenance is but one part, and by no means the most expensive part, of the 25-year operating cost. It is not possible to give firm proportions, but on average it would be expected that only about 20 per cent of the final total price for the 25-year contract would be capital cost, including debt service to the project. Cheaper buildings, therefore, are by no means the determining factor for success in the PFI competition. It is important to emphasize that the government is buying a service under the PFI requirements, and not just purchasing assets on a delayed basis. In order for the service to be delivered there must of course be a building, and the building therefore becomes part of the total service cost. However, the significant factor in a total project costing is the contribution made to economy and efficiency by the operating proposals. Obviously, a building that is extremely cheap when compared with the competition might edge into success a total project whose operational costs are more expensive than the competition. Given the difference quoted above, the construction would nevertheless have to be extremely cheap and the extra costs not that much more for this trick to work. In the final analysis, therefore, to attempt a strategy of cheap building in the hope that this will win the contract is unlikely to be successful.

On the other hand, a project efficient and economic in its use of manpower, and therefore resulting in a lower operating cost, could afford to spend more on its buildings. The secret of lower operating costs for any particular contractor may be just that fact: that by spending more on the building – the 'spend to save' strategy – it might make it possible to reduce operating costs. However, there is no absolute guarantee that an expensive building will be offset by correspondingly low operating costs. Attempts to create winning strategies by the manipulation of such factors will not necessarily lead to long-term success. Rather, both operating costs and construction costs should always be kept in balance because, once past the quality and deliverability thresholds, value for money becomes dominant.

Research into prison design effectiveness

As explained in Chapter 3, there is no body of well-attested research into the link between prison management effectiveness and prison design. What is known, however, even if only by the prison practitioners themselves, is what works and what does not. The privatized management of prisons has slightly distorted the search for the 'right' solution, since inevitably those solutions tend to be rather more expensive both in construction time and in staffing requirements. As in much else, the pragmatic answer is a compromise between the ideal and the lowest common denominator. The answer for modern prison specifiers – and this means almost exclusively private companies – is to ensure that the most effective overall solution is adopted (*Figures 15.1–15.3*).

In-house research

Of more use, if only to the companies involved and their clients, is the continuing improvement in design brought about within the major companies in the United States and in the UK. This has occurred as the designs from one generation are subject to the scrutiny of actual operational practice, and the good and less good features are either incorporated or rejected in the new design. Some of these issues have to do with the design of the ancillary buildings (workshops, education facilities, healthcare etc.) rather than the main accommodation units. In the UK, the major companies that have been successful in providing more than one or two establishments have also been able to use their operational experience to improve their design and reduce costs. Obviously, as the market is still a competitive one, such improvements are not made public until incorporated in the latest design.

Figure 15.1
Site layout for HM Prison at Moreton Lane, Marchington, Staffordshire, which is being built by Premier Prison Services. Small-scale radial prisons are becoming popular again.

Figure 15.2
Entrance to HM Prison at Kilmarnock, Scotland.

The effect of technology on prison design and management

Most technology in prisons is concerned with information management. Built structures may be difficult or slow to change, but the management of those spaces inside can change very rapidly, and this change has to do with information. Both public sector and private sector prisons are using increasing amounts of information management as they seek to grapple with the demands of prison management economically and efficiently. It is wrong, though, to imagine that the easy answer to prison development and organization is increasing technological sophistication, either of information or security management. Nevertheless, the modern

Figure 15.3
Cell hall at Kilmarnock. This is a standard design for almost all prisons built by Premier Prison Services.

private prison does have more technology than standard public sector prisons, even those that are relatively new. The reason for this is the need to ensure that staff are not wasted doing repetitive and clerical tasks when they could be using their expensively trained time in the direct management of prisoners. However, technology must always be anchored in the operational requirements of the operator. A sensible operator will ensure that increasing levels of technological sophistication are matched by their ease of use and their contribution to the overall management of the prison in a positive way, and, crucially, that they do not stand in the way of day-to-day contact between staff and prisoners. Technology that assists this process rather than gets in its way is the technology that will succeed in prisons. Complex security systems and information management whose sole objectives are meant to reduce the need for prison staff will pose problems for prison managers, since the human contact and relationships between prison staff and inmates are the bedrock upon which any prison management must be founded. So although there may be considerable temptation to seek ever more cost reduction by investment in technology, the point at which that investment actually harms the central relationship between prisoners and staff must be carefully watched.

One major use of technology is for perimeter security. Sophisticated detection devices built into fences and walls coupled with CCTV cameras, both controlled and fixed, will enforce the physical strength of the perimeter and improve internal observation and control. Prison officers can therefore discharge their duties with greater confidence and without the fear of being unobserved and therefore open to harm in areas of the prison where they might feel vulnerable. There are obviously similar benefits for prisoners.

The management of prisons

As noted earlier in this chapter, with every prison procurement project a comprehensive and challenging series of operational specifications must be met. These operational specifications represent the current best practice within the Prison Service – their view of the ideal prison regime. The incorporation of those practices required must be done by statute as well as the best practice of general prison management, where statutory obligations are silent. What may be thought of as a trivial example, but is in reality an important one, is the service of meals. Statutory obligations merely demand that prisoners be fed. Best practice, however, requires that their meals should be hot (as required), nutritious, well presented, available at acceptable intervals (not, for example, having the last meal of the day at 4 pm and then nothing until breakfast at 7.30 am the next day). Additionally, the contractor will seek to improve the general service delivery to prisoners, since that is what prison management is all about. Although management of security and internal discipline within the prison may be thought of as being the prime requirements, even these depend upon an acceptable level of service delivery for prisoners. If that level is not there, prisoners rapidly become disaffected and take that disaffection out on the staff or, in extreme cases, cause major disturbances and riots. Best prison management therefore, as with all effective government, seeks to manage and govern with the consent of the governed. In the case of meals, it may be possible to improve the service by providing an individual choice, ideally chosen no earlier than the day before, and guaranteeing delivery to the person who ordered it – even though delivery may be at the canteen. Such a system has been pioneered in the privately run prisons and, despite original scepticism by many in the public sector, has now been adopted by them as a standard at which to aim. Other examples abound, from the management of bullying and intimidation within the prison and the improved management of prisoners who are exhibiting suicidal behaviours, to the management of the reception and admission processes and the base relationship between staff and prisoners. In most privatized prisons, staff routinely address prisoners by their name and wear a name badge themselves. This may not always be the case elsewhere.

The inspection of prisons

All prisons in England and Wales are inspected on a regular basis by HM Inspectorate of Prisons under the control of the Chief Inspector. These inspections are carried out on a regular basis. Some are full inspections usually lasting at least a week; others are short inspections lasting about two days. In addition, there are unannounced inspections where the Inspectorate team just turns up at the prison gate. These regimes apply to private sector prisons as well as the public sector, and the Inspectorate team treats its task as the inspection of prisons, and not the inspection of a particular prison operator – be it public or private. These reports are published, and currently the Chief Inspector is attempting to improve the speed of publication so that they become reports on practices that are current in the prison under inspection, and not reports on a situation that may have existed some 12 months earlier.

These reports are taken seriously by private prison operators, who will obviously be keen to ensure that any shortcomings or improvements noted and recommended by the Inspectorate team are attended to. It is a matter of pride to the private sector companies that inspections of their prisons have, almost without exception, generally proved their management to be at least the equal of the public sector prisons, and in many cases better. Numerous examples of best practice identified by the Inspectors from private operator practices have been recommended to the rest of the Prison Service.

The original intention, therefore, for the involvement of the private sector in prison management to improve standards in the rest of the Prison Service by its two-pronged strategy of better economic management and an improvement in the management of prisons seems to have been a well placed trust.

It is also highly significant that private sector prisons have managed to turn in such good performances while at the same time achieving extremely challenging performance standards – which are not, as explained elsewhere, a feature of any public sector prison.

A glance at the performance specifications for HM Young Offender Institution Pucklechurch, for example, now taken as the industry benchmark, shows the detail and the extent of the targets set. Additionally, of course, targets carry with them penalties for failure. Private contractors can be, and have been, fined for failing (by no matter how small a margin) to achieve any one or a combination of these targets. This situation does not apply in the public sector. Not only are there no comparable targets, but also if a governor agrees to an operational target with the area manager and then fails to reach that target, no penalty ensues – the governor is not demoted; neither is the prison 'fined' for its failure. Therefore, there are – at least in the view of the private contractor – two totally separate measurement systems for the operational effectiveness of prisons; a challenging system for the private sector, and a soft or absent one for the public sector.

Much is sometimes made in the press and Parliament of the 'failures' of private sector prisons. The fact that they are failures is known only because the contractors concerned declare them, honestly. Were the same candour to exist in the public sector, it is absolutely certain that the true difference between the private sector and its operational effectiveness and that of the public sector would be seen.

Financing the DCMF

The mechanisms by which DCMF prisons are financed are very straightforward. Essentially, the provision of the prison under DCMF arrangements means that the government is buying a service. It is not purchasing assets on a delayed purchase plan; nor is it purchasing assets plus a service. It is purchasing a service from the operator which, of necessity, must operate within fixed premises. It is the operator's responsibility to make sure that the buildings and other support necessary for providing this service are properly designed and obtained.

This, of course, means that there is a requirement for the building to be paid for, since there is a cost to the contractor for erecting it. Therefore, in the charge to government that features in its bid (the bid price), there are elements for the debt repayment arising from the need to procure the buildings for the delivery of its service, and a charge for that service delivery.

The actual money found for the payment of constructors is arranged through the normal money markets in London, and the financial close for any deal is always after the contract signatures. When all contracts have been agreed and signed, the deal is then ready to be put to the market and the price agreed for the money over the lifetime of the contract or other period as decided.

The profit motive

In the early days of privatization, the cry from objectors was insistent: that once let in, contractors would show what they were truly made of; the profit motive would take over to the exclusion of all else, and prisoners and society would get a bad deal. The reverse has been the case. Instead there has been a recognized and increasing benefit. Prisoners spend more time out of their cells and on useful, rewarding and training activities; staff have a real job to do instead of just guarding the inmates; and prisoners are contained more securely. With the advent of the new prison at Moreton Lane in Marchington (*Figure 15.1*), with its 200-bed Therapeutic Community for prisoners as an integral part of its activities, even the most intractable of offenders will benefit from the 'profit motive'. The question should not be whether shareholders in those companies managing prisons are permitted to make a profit, but whether the criminal justice system, indeed the country as a whole, is getting best value out of the arrangement.

In other countries of the European Union, the picture is not so clear. For some time France has had a number of its prisons supported by private contractors for the provision of catering, education and so forth. The French, however, have fought shy of allowing private contractors to be responsible for security and the close management of prisoners. Other countries in the EU are tracking the outcome of the UK approach without indulging in any similar experimentation themselves. However, for the moment it appears likely that prison procurement under PFI, or its new equivalent Public Private Partnership (PPP), is here to stay in the UK.

16 What needs to be done?

Sir David Ramsbotham

In Gosport, Portsmouth, you can still see the remains of one of the most interesting military architectural mistakes that I suppose were always likely at the height of the Raj. There are a number of bungalow buildings, with verandas, which should have been built in Hyderabad in India, and – yes – in Hyderabad you can still see the barracks that should have been built in Gosport. I am not going to pretend that anything like that has happened in the prison system, even with a Major General, Sir Joshua Jebb, being the designer of the large radial prisons such as Pentonville and Wandsworth, that are still in use today.[1]

I would like to outline some of the penal ideas that I hope will emerge in the United Kingdom in the next few years, and consider their architectural needs, rather than suggest particular architectural innovations. My commissioned service began in what were called Hitler blocks, barracks built by Hitler in the 1930s, to house his expanding army. I wonder if he, or any of his architects, ever dreamed about the different uses that these buildings would be ultimately put to by the British Army, and indeed are still put, any more than Joshua Jebb dreamed of what use would be made of his concepts. But each is an example of how essentially simple and practical designs have lent themselves to modern adaptations, to satisfy changing needs over the years, each imposing penalties because of their limitations but offering advantages because of their strength. How magnificently they have exceeded their sell-by dates, and what lessons they still have to teach us today.

I accept that financial realities will always be the final arbiter of any proposed development, but I do not intend to let them deter me from my theme. Penal ideas are bound to involve some expenditure, and any householder will know that there is always a need to spend money on improving and maintaining both fabric and fittings. I see no reason why all proposals should not be evaluated against operational efficiency as well as financial cost, in considering whether or not they should be adopted. But let me first attempt to set those penal ideas into context by a brief resumé of our current position.

For many years, adult male prisoners in England and Wales have been categorized according to risk – risk of escape, and risk to the public if they escape. They start at the highest, A, and end at the lowest, D, which categories define the whole system by type. Naturally the highest degree of security is to be found in high security prisons, some of which contain

---

1 Major General Sir Joshua Jebb, RE was the first Surveyor General of Prisons. In 1850 he also became the first Chairman of the Directorate of Convict Prisons. (see Chapter 6.)

Special Secure Units in which the prisoners whose risk of escape is deemed highest of all are housed. Line prison management, below the Director General, consists of two regional Directors, North and South, and 13 Area Managers of particular parts of each region, with a separate Director for the High Security estate. Recently a Director of Regimes has been added who is responsible for determining what regimes should be implemented for all types of prisoner. Assistant Directors are responsible for particular parts of the system such as adult males and life sentence prisoners, women and young offenders. This management structure is required to cope with the current rise in numbers held in prison, which, being greater than what is called Certified Normal Accommodation, is causing overcrowding throughout the system. Until 1 May 1997 this position was the responsibility of a government that put security, security and security at the top of its priorities.

Since that date responsibility has been assumed by a government that increasingly puts prison regimes, or the work done with prisoners, at the head of the list. The days of the catch phrase 'prison works' seem, mercifully, to be over, and replaced by the understanding that prison must be made to work as well as possible. I always thought that 'prison works' was about as negative a concept as you could imagine, because it implied only that people in prison could not commit crimes on the public. That is of course true, but the inevitable conclusion has been the inexorable rise in numbers, with over 66 000 (or 120 per 100 000 of the population of this country) in prison, at an annual cost of just under £2 billion. The USA, where the same policy applies, has seen its prison and jail population rise to 645 per 100 000, or in excess of 1.8 million, which translated into the UK would mean nearer 400 000 in prison at a cost of over £10 billion. What is more, 'prison works' ignores the simple truth that, of the 66 000-plus currently in prison, all except 30 are going to come out. The question that surely must be asked is, 'in what frame of mind are they going to be when they come out?'. If the soft option is taken and nothing done to challenge their offending behaviour while they are in prison, we have only ourselves to blame if they come out embittered, re-offend, and return to prison. If we take the hard option, hard, that is, for both staff and prisoners, and attempt to use the time that a prisoner is inside on sentence to address and tackle his or her offending behaviour, then there is a chance that some, at least, will come out and not re-offend. It is absurd to pretend that all will see the light, but what gives the lie to the equally simplistic phrase 'prison does not work' is that some of them may, and that must justify the effort.

I believe therefore that now is a most appropriate time for a re-examination of the current organization and all those factors that contribute to tackling re-offending, to determine what adjustments could and should be made to them. Let me therefore try to give you my overview of some of what I think this should include, beginning with management. As I have mentioned, the organization of the Prison Service is currently being adjusted to provide better directed and consistently delivered regimes appropriate for different categories and types of prisoner in different parts of the country. There is recognition, at last, that the needs of women and young offenders are different to those appropriate for adult males. I hope that this will move on to examining the different needs of training as opposed to local, or reception, and resettlement prisons. Separate plans need to be made for juveniles, i.e. those under the age of 18, while they still remain in the hands of the Prison Service; also for mentally disordered offenders, even after (as I hope) responsibility for

Prison Service healthcare is made more closely the responsibility of the National Health Service.

However, closer to home than any of this, consideration needs to be given to responding to the evidence that three factors – a home, a stable family relationship and a job – are those most likely to contribute to preventing re-offending. This says to me that it is most important to keep prisoners as close to their homes or home areas as possible, so that family contacts can be maintained, and also that resettlement, including job training, is related to conditions and opportunities in his or her local area. This is why I am such a strong protagonist of Lord Woolf's suggestion of community clusters of prisons, near a prisoner's location, consisting of sufficient types of accommodation to cater for the types of prisoner likely to come from a particular area. This development was one of the 12 priorities in the 1991 White Paper *Custody, Care and Justice*, designed and authorized by Parliament to be the blueprint for the Prison Service into the next century, only one of which, the provision of integral sanitation in cells, has been implemented so far.

Currently, too many prisoners are confined far away from their home area, which adds enormously to the cost of imprisonment in such practical ways as transporting them there and transporting their families to visit them. It is also expensive in terms of money wasted on inappropriate training that is designed around the area in which the prison is situated rather than training related to job opportunities in a prisoner's home area. Of course, to rectify the situation will require re-designating existing prisons to satisfy the population requirements of particular areas, but, heaven knows, that has been done often enough in the past for it not to be a meaningful deterrent.

These geographical areas are bound to be determined by political direction, and I am delighted that this seems to be moving towards establishing coterminous boundaries for the criminal justice system as a whole in the country. (That is to say, administrative units for police, courts and prisons should match.) I say this because it reinforces my contention that prisons should be regarded not in isolation but as a part of this system, with a very particular role within it. I liken that to the role of hospitals in the National Health Service; they have no control over who comes in, but have to try to make them better. The process involves an assessment of the prisoner's or patient's needs, followed by planned treatment over the period that the individual is in prison or hospital, which is continued in the form of aftercare in the community. This requires passage of information about the individual concerned, from the community and those agencies working in it to the prison, and from the multidisciplinary team who have conducted the treatment in prison to those who will continue with it on release. That is a diversion from my theme, but it is important to match and coordinate the various components of criminal justice administration in order to satisfy some penal advances. The Prison Service must then estimate what categories of prisoner are likely to come from each area, so that provision for them can be made. Recently I completed a study of women in prison, during which we established from where in England and Wales most women prisoners came. The distribution was 28 per cent from London, 11 per cent each from Bristol, Birmingham, Manchester and Leeds, 8 per cent from Liverpool and Essex, 6 per cent from Newcastle, and so on. This suggests that, if you are to keep women as near to home as possible (61 per cent of them being primary carers for children), you should recognize that the present distribution of women's prisons does not satisfy that requirement. Furthermore, the majority of women now come from urban rather than rural environments. Should not prisons be built in urban areas, where, for example, public transport facilitates visiting? If so, is it more sensible to build unmanageable monoliths like Holloway, or to build smaller houseblocks in which conditions more appropriate to educating them for living life in the twenty-first century obtain, on the lines of some of the existing probation and bail hostels? Certainly such accommodation would seem more appropriate at the end of a sentence, when the emphasis is on resettlement into the community. Those sums can be repeated for different types of prisoner.

I will now divert for a moment. One of the principal reasons why I hope that the National Health Service will assume responsibility for Prison Service healthcare is to solve the problems posed by the mentally disordered. I find it extraordinary that the Special Hospitals should send back to prison those with the most severe personality disorders, on the grounds that they are untreatable. If they cannot be treated in the hospitals with the best possible facilities, what on earth are prisons, with none, meant to do for them, and how responsible is this when the patient will return, untreated, into the community? Furthermore, medical staff often tell me that all they can do is watch mentally ill prisoners deteriorate in prison, because they lack proper facilities with which to look after them.

Now here really is an opportunity. If the NHS has to take over responsibility, what is to stop them building suitable mental health treatment accommodation on prison sites? At a stroke this would get over the problem of not wanting to house patients in Special Hospitals, and would provide prisons with suitable facilities in which to look after those who currently languish inappropriately housed. I have seen some very imaginative medium secure units, which could easily be constructed in prison grounds and which would allow prison medical centres to be used as they are meant to be – as minor injuries units with facilities for examination and consultation. I don't know who has been responsible for the design and building of prison healthcare centres over the years, but I have never seen such terrible places in my life. Too many seem to be built round a hollow square, with small rooms, inadequately lit, difficult to negotiate with a stretcher, staff intensive because of difficult vision, and so on.

Now for size. I remember much discussion about the size of army operational formations as far as command and control is concerned, the traditional number of sub-units being three, which was increased to four for balance, and, disastrously, to five for economy. I mention control, because the one factor about prisons, it seems to me, is that their bedrock is staff–prisoner relationships. That is the essence of a good or a bad prison, and is critical in terms of control. The bigger the institution, the more impersonal it becomes, which runs counter to the economic arguments about scale. Personally, I come down firmly on the side of 'small is beautiful', and have recommended, for example, that young offenders should never be held in blocks for more than 60, and that establishments should not hold more than 300 inmates. I admit that that contradicts what I said about five sub-units, but blocks are static, and I was talking about a manoeuvre formation.

I suggest that the bad need different staffing profiles to the sad or the mad. I have mentioned how I would look after the mad. The bad clearly need a staff that is heavy on custodial officers and low on rehabilitation. The sad are the reverse, and I suggest that a look at the population in this way would lead to some interesting conclusions about being able to reduce numbers in some places. However, in the interests of control, it is important that smaller numbers of staff should be able to maintain it, which comes back to design. Control is at the heart of the Victorian radial design, and I was interested recently to inspect the new prisons in the independent territories in the West Indies. They are, of course, far smaller, but they have updated the concept. A central hub forms the office to which all visitors report, and from which there is clear vision down the length of all the wings radiating off, but separated from, this hub. Each wing has an association (recreational) area nearest to the hub, so that prisoners can be observed easily. Each wing has foldaway grilles so that parts of the corridor can be shut off to house different categories of prisoner. This is all very flexible, and what is more, unlike Gosport, suitable for the climate.

Technology, of course, has a part to play in all this. In this connection, I commend the initiative of Securicor at HMP Parc, the new prison near Bridgend in Wales, where technology has been used to reduce the number of custodial staff required on duty at any one time, releasing them for work with prisoners. Staff have control in buildings designed for staff vision, and the use of electronics relieves the need for the time-expensive opening and shutting of cell doors with keys. Again this may not be suitable for all types of prisoner, but it is certainly more practical than what I found recently at HMP The Maze (in Northern Ireland), where an officer with a key stood beside each door rather than allowing staff to carry the traditional bunch of keys.

Re-designating the functions of the existing stock having been done, size of establishment minimized, and technology having been employed, what else needs to be considered? My remit is to monitor and influence the treatment and conditions of prisoners. I submit that there is nothing more significant, vital or basic than the cell in which he or she is to be confined. I have been interested to learn that, in 1839, an Act of Parliament was passed, making it the responsibility of the then Inspectors to certify all cells before they could be used for the confinement of prisoners. That responsibility passed to the Prison Commission in 1877, to the Prison Department in 1963, and then to the Prison Service, where it currently resides. At the request of the Director-General I am currently looking into this, because there is a different interpretation of how many may be confined in cells of similar size, and we are, of course, subject to UN and European, as well as national, legislation on this matter. I am amazed at the proliferation of different concepts of cell design, and am glad that, for example, the Prison Service is currently examining configurations that are safe, in that they do not present prisoners with opportunities for self-harm or suicide. However, at the same time we must consider the lifestyle of the twenty-first as opposed to the nineteenth century prisoner, and what should be provided. Integral sanitation has been installed, although I sometimes wonder whether it would not be preferable to have a pot under one's bed rather than sleep with one's head in the lavatory. I would like to see separate ablution areas, on the design of turning three cells into two with the central one used to provide each of the outer two with a basin and a lavatory, rather than the current arrangements.

Joshua Jebb also included a loom, for work, and I suppose that the current equivalent is the power point so that prisoners can plug in their TV, radio, computer or whatever, without risking life and limb by making illegal connections to the supply. However, as heavy industry, the traditional basis of work in prisons, declines in this country, I do believe that we have to ask ourselves very serious questions about what form of training is likely to help a prisoner find employment on release. Andrew Coyle has made the sad but unavoidable point that perhaps we have to prepare people for unemployment rather than employment, and to occupy him or herself in leisure time. This suggests to me that there are a number of cell-based activities which should be encouraged, in which case their design needs to take that into account.

Job training also needs to be considered in the design of prisons, and again the Prison Service is caught up in an expensive dilemma. Many of the heavy industry workshops are now largely irrelevant, because such work does not exist in the outside world. However, practical living skills are much in demand and need space designed for their teaching and learning. Education is lacking in so many prisoners that current hours are inadequate either to make good their needs or to develop what they already have. Too many educational centres have inadequate classrooms to cope with the needs. These have moved on in the educational world, and prisons could learn from them with advantage.

And then there is tackling offending behaviour, which requires a separate area, with different kinds of rooms suitable for group work. I am delighted at the increase in this work, but accept that there is so much more to be done, which needs resources of staff as well as space. However, it is critical in the fight against re-offending, and should be treated accordingly. And so back to reality.

My remit for this symposium was to consider what needs to be done, and I hope that I have laid enough trails to enable me to give you my conclusion as a basis for discussion. First, I conclude that we need to examine our penal base; in other words, to look at how and where imprisonment is conducted, in a new era in which prisons are no longer seen in isolation but as part of the criminal justice system in each and every part of the country, in which the Prison Service has to work with all other agencies inside coterminous boundaries. Furthermore, while security is of course important, because the Prison Service must keep in custody for the duration of their sentence those committed by the courts, that time must be used to tackle re-offending by the introduction and employment of regimes suitable for the task. Work done with prisoners must be designed to help them to live in the community from which they came, enabling them to maintain contact with their families.

Prisons therefore need to be given roles that enable them to satisfy the population in each part of the country, and to be of a size that allows them to be personal rather than impersonal in the all-important area of staff–prisoner relations. Provision must be made to separate both the mentally disordered and the deliberately difficult and disruptive from the remainder of the population, and the different needs of each must be treated appropriately. Work, education and offending behaviour programmes must be designed to cope with twenty-first century conditions. Cells can be used for work and not just for confinement. But none of these ideas can come to fruition unless there is suitable accommodation in which they can be delivered.

None of these ideas is new, and I hope that they have the benefit of being simple. However, the fact is that none of them can work without a suitable environment, which is where architecture comes in. I believe that it is important that architects should understand the ethos of imprisonment so that they can reflect it in their designs. I am sure that the person who designed the blocks at Woodhill knew what he or she was doing. I dread to think what the person responsible for some of the dreadful designs in the 1960s thought he or she was achieving, except responding to some formula of allowed cubic feet per person. Clearly the needs of staff were not taken into account, and the price is now being paid. Joshua Jebb certainly understood, and even set the agenda for his day. I am not suggesting that architects should necessarily do that now, but when I opened a new medium security unit the other day, and commended the design to the architect, I asked him how much contact he had had with those who would work in it, a question I also asked of staff. I was gratified to find that there had been full and regular contact throughout the whole period. I commend that approach to the Prison Service, and also suggest that they might consider adapting the phrase 'prison works' to 'let us only build prisons that can work'. They know which designs do and do not, so let them not waste money on those that don't.

In commending that to the Prison Service, may I end by also commending the administrators, academics, architects and others contributing to this symposium. I am sure that where people go from here will benefit from this opportunity for architects and penal people to share ideas and learn where each might be going. I know that penal establishments need both ideas and places where they can be implemented, and the partnership between both sets of practitioners is timely and important.

17 Prison architecture and the politics of reform

Stephen Shaw

This chapter has three main aims. First, I want to explore why the contemporary penal reform movement – unlike that of our Victorian forebears – has been so neglectful of issues of prison design and architecture. The second aim is briefly to consider the relationship (or lack of it) between form and function in the design of prison buildings. In particular, do design considerations play any part in administrators' decisions at times of rapid expansion of the prison estate? Third, I want to offer some thoughts of my own on future directions in prison policy, and the implications these have for prison size and layout.

Wilful refusal or culpable neglect?

Beginning with the issue of neglect, this is a recent – by which I mean late twentieth century – phenomenon. In the middle years of Victoria's reign, the Howard Association was very interested in the moral lessons inherent in the dimensions and structure of the penal institution. In contrast to this earlier generation of penal reformers, it is striking how little contribution campaigning and watchdog groups now make to the issues of prison design and layout. The main gate of Wormwood Scrubs is flanked by plaques of John Howard and Elizabeth Fry – a tribute that it seems improbable will be offered to the penal reformers of today.

It is now more than 17 years since I became director of the Prison Reform Trust, yet the number of times I or my colleagues have written or spoken – or been asked to write or speak – about prison architecture may be counted on the fingers of one hand. Although we may all appreciate that prisons are public buildings of great longevity, the output of the other lobbying organizations, whether in this country or abroad, reveals a similar lacuna. Casual inspection of the mainstream academic literature also suggests little interest on the part of university-based criminologists (looking up 'prison architecture' or 'prison design' in the index of any penal textbook is a fruitless exercise).

Neither has there been much journalistic interest, unless it has been a variant on the theme of penal largesse – new prisons perceived as unduly expensive and unduly solicitous of prisoners' needs (Maghaberry in Northern Ireland, which has some of the largest workshops I have ever seen, comes to mind). However, in the 1990s there was some newspaper interest in prisons that are regarded as peculiarly high-tech, of which the privately-managed Parc in South Wales is perhaps the best example. Parc is an unusual prison to look at, the architect allegedly comparing the metal-coloured cladding on the principal buildings to an American train on the prairie. It was designed as a key-free prison, although, as with similar experiments, the technology has been found wanting and keys have been reintroduced.

There have of course been things prison reformers have not liked. Twenty years ago, the focus was on decay and decrepitude. It was taken as self-evident that the Victorian prison estate was unsuited to modern penal practice. The 1979 May Committee of Inquiry (Cmnd 7673, para 6.41) recorded:

To put it baldly and without equivocation but choosing our words carefully nonetheless, we think the worst prisons are very bad indeed ... there can be no doubt that the main problem is obsolescence ... At the bottom are most of the urban Victorian local prisons ... Both Wakefield and Parkhurst, for example, require a great deal of attention if they are not, literally, to fall down. Dartmoor ... is in fact in a special category of its own: what was permissible in a convict prison for the rigours of penal servitude on the reoccupied Napoleonic site of the 1850s, is nowadays simply against nature.

This view reflected the Prison Service's own assessment of its estate. After castigating its 'out-dated capital assets' and 'obsolete buildings', a 1977 Home Office guide to the Prison Service (*Prisons and the Prisoner: The Work of the Prison Service in England and Wales*, HMSO) acknowledged that: 'It is often urged upon the [Prison] Department that the only thing to do with the Victorian inheritance is to pull it down'.

Fashions change, and with the refurbishment programme, which has ended slopping out and made all prisons lighter, cleaner and airier, Victorian galleried designs are now regarded with much greater favour and form the basis of many new prisons and houseblocks. Victorian cells are also larger than many twentieth-century cells, because to implement the separate system they had to accommodate a workbench or work activity as well as a bed.

Attention has now turned to other aspects of contemporary prison architecture. Here, for example, is Vivien Stern in her splendid polemic *A Sin Against the Future: Imprisonment in the World*:[1]

In the Caribbean Sea just off Venezuela lies the small island of Aruba with a population of 65 000. Aruba is part of the Kingdom of the Netherlands. The main industry is tourism and the island is well covered with architecturally bizarre holiday complexes. At the far end of the island, on a rather bleak piece of land on the seashore, is another architecturally bizarre building, a brand new, state of the art, top-security prison ... its security is awesome. First there is an inner wall topped with razor wire, then a gap, then an outer wall also topped with razor wire, and finally a fence fortified with an alarm system. The internal construction is also remarkable – a series of small living units built around a central area where the staff sit watching video cameras and pressing the buttons that activate the opening of all the doors ... this bizarre construction prompts a number of questions. Who decided to build a top-security prison in a country where most crime is non-violent and petty and where a long sentence is regarded as one of eight months or more? Who decided to build a prison with so little access to light and air on a tropical island? Who felt that, in a place so small that personal relationships are all-important, the right prison was one

---

1 Stern, V. (1998). *A Sin Against the Future: Imprisonment in the World*. Penguin.

controlled by electronic surveillance and high-tech gadgetry? How did such a completely Western construct end up on the beach of a South American island anyway?

This passage captures the criticisms of prison architecture that have emanated more recently from the penal reform movement – a concern that physical security may be excessive and oppressive, a suspicion of technology, and a preference for designs that encourage staff–prisoner involvement. In addition, there has been special criticism of the feature-less, claustrophobic design of top security facilities – notably the so-called Special Housing Units (SHUs) in the United States.[2]

Other targets have been dormitories (which have provided every opportunity for bullying and intimidation, and which offer prisoners little defensible space of their own), and the staff-intensive, user-unfriendly 'hospital corridor' layout of 1960s prisons like Holloway, the largest women's prison in Western Europe. Ironically, the 'new' Holloway replaced a building of the now more favoured Victorian design.

However, if we have often known what we do not like – barren, dehumanizing, stimulus-free environments in particular – we have been far less forthcoming in saying what it is we would have wished to have seen in their place. What are the reasons for this? One is clearly that the training of penal reformers hardly equips us to offer technical advice. When the Prison Service issued its report *New Directions in Prison Design* in 1985 (the report of a Home Office working party which first explained and championed so-called 'new generation' prison designs), there was some bemusement that such a glossy and well-illustrated publication could be justified. However, lack of competence has rarely proved an impediment to any campaigners worth their salt. So is there a more fundamental reason for the penal reform movement's silence? Surely it results, to some degree, from a fear on our part of being entrapped by the idea of the 'good prison'.

I am not an abolitionist myself, and in public and in private the Prison Reform Trust has lauded the improvement in performance of many penal institutions in this country. Yet I own to a certain embarrassment at the notion of a prison that works – all the more so after Michael Howard's appropriation of the phrase. This is an important contrast in approach from the Howard Association 125 years or so ago, whose inter-pretation of 'prison reform' was a prison that reformed best. This does not mean that the contemporary reform lobby is happier with a prison that fails, but it does mean that our starting point is that we have too many prisons and too many prisoners, and the sum of human happiness is unlikely to increase by adding to either of their number.

Although the argument seems now to have gone out of fashion, for many years even the 'liberal' penal reformers opposed any new prison construction on the grounds that additional capacity would drive an increase in the prison population. It would be ludicrous to suggest a simple 1:1 relationship, but I recall some statistical studies in the late 1970s suggesting that such a connection might be justified. I also recall arguing, again with a veneer of academic respectability, that no prison administration had ever succeeded in building itself out of overcrowd-ing. If that was the case – notwithstanding that, in theory, new capacity

---

2 See Chapter 11.

could be for replacement purposes rather than an addition to the stock – any interest in prison design might have appeared quixotic; worse still, it might have appeared to legitimize the construction of extra prison capacity. Quite why these arguments have gone out of vogue would repay examination. Do they no longer appear 'realistic' given the extent of the prison building programme over the last ten years? Or is the reason to be found in the demise of the radical, abolitionist perspective?

Form and function

There is one other reason why architecture has not been a first priority, or indeed a priority of any kind, for prison reformers. Quite simply, it has not been a first priority for prison administrators either, and this has been especially true at times of rapid penal expansion when cost and speed of construction become the principal considerations. Here, for example, is my colleague Stephen Nathan writing in the March 1998 issue of *Prison Privatisation Report International*:

Representatives from a private firm were in the Ukraine in February looking at two vessels that South Africa's Department of Correctional Services want to use as prison ships. Also in conjunction with the private sector, the Department is renovating empty buildings to house prisoners. Both moves are designed to ease overcrowding. An earlier proposal to hold prisoners in disused mine shafts has been abandoned.

There is not much evidence there of form following function. On the contrary, given South Africa's acute shortage of prison capacity, it seems any available space will do.

Not that there have been many signs of a strategic approach to the provision of prison accommodation in this country either. Half a dozen prisons were constructed to an identical, flawed design (the Bullingdon model) in order to save on time and expenditure. In recent years, in addition to the prison building programme itself, we have pressed into service a prison ship, converted barracks and army camps, and bought-in what are termed Ready-to-Use units (RTUs), prefabricated huts no longer required by Norwegian oil workers.

Perhaps of more long-term significance has been the erection of new houseblocks at existing prisons. Any prison of any age contains within its perimeter a hotchpotch of buildings, erected for purposes often long since forgotten. Visit any prison in Britain today that still has space for additional construction and, like as not, you will be visiting a building site.

These houseblocks are of little architectural distinction, although the speed with which they have been erected is worthy of note. However, no thought seems to have been given to the consequences for the allocation of prisoners. Most prisons with space for additional buildings are in rural areas, whereas what is most required are places in the conurbations from which the majority of prisoners are drawn. Furthermore, while the houseblocks have provided quick and cheap additional places, these have rarely been matched by sufficient additional opportunities for work, education and treatment programmes, as HM Chief Inspector of Prisons has complained in successive reports.

It would seem that little can be done to maintain aesthetic and moral qualities in prison design at times of greatest population pressure.

Indeed, at all times politicians and public seem uninterested so long as prisons are secure and basic standards of living accommodation are provided. There is little real sense of civic pride in prisons, although they are significant elements in the local economy of smaller towns, and the principle of less eligibility and a desire that prisons should present a visibly deterrent image both count against the ornate, the novel, the visually attractive.

Of course, the prison estate as a whole is a creature of history rather than of a grand penological plan. As another contributor to this volume points out, there are no fewer than 170 listed buildings in the charge of HM Prison Service.[3] Although there has been a great deal of new construction in the last 15 years – such that most prisons converted from other uses show few overt signs of their previous incarnation – some things cannot and should not be hidden. Lancaster prison occupies the site of a medieval castle, as did Oxford before its closure. Haslar at Gosport, one of the last points on the English mainland and used incongruously (or perhaps deliberately) to hold detained asylum seekers and other Immigration Act prisoners, is, like many prisons, a former barracks. It was used as a mooring site for barrage balloons during the Second World War. Dover Young Offenders' Institution (YOI) was once a fort. Kirklevington Grange was an industrial magnate's country house, and the little-known East Sutton Park women's prison has as its main building an Elizabethan manor that benefits from later Jacobean additions.

Similarly, as Rod Morgan has pointed out in the *Oxford Handbook of Criminology*:[4] 'It is a feature of penal institutions that their titles and functions change rather more frequently than their facilities and culture'. By this, Morgan means that buildings planned for one purpose are frequently converted to some other. *Albany: Birth of a Prison – End of an Era*[5] details the process at a new jail on the Isle of Wight over 20 years ago, although many of its lessons still run true. It may also be physically difficult to change facilities when functions change. One less desirable feature of the Victorian heritage is the shortage of work and other activity places on cramped sites like Brixton in South London. This shortage is the direct result of Victorian penal philosophy, with its desire to avoid contamination of prisoner by prisoner, and its consequent emphasis on activities that could be carried out in-cell. Almost the only arena for collective activity was the chapel, the physical and metaphorical heart of the Victorian penal institution.

Nor does recent prison experience lend support to a theory of architectural determinism. It may be relevant that Lancaster Farms YOI, which was at the time I first visited it the best institution for young offenders I had ever come across, had in fact been designed and built as a low security prison for adults. The buildings may or may not have helped; they certainly did not prevent the institution from becoming something rare and precious. Similarly, the prefabricated housing units (RTUs) have proved surprisingly successful, being valued by prisoners and an incentive to behave well. As in the unexpected success of the prison ship HMP Weare, the use of which has been extended for a further three years, this popularity with prisoners and contribution to

---

3 See Chapter 8, p. 81.
4 Morgan, R. (1994). *The Oxford Handbook of Criminology*. Clarendon Press.
5 King, R.D. and Elliott, K.W. (1977). *Albany: Birth of a Prison – End of an Era*. Routledge and Kegan Paul.

the Prison Service's incentives and earned privileges scheme was entirely unintended.[6]

This is not to suggest that there has been no innovation in prison design in recent years. New generation principles are reflected in a number of institutions, notably Woodhill in Milton Keynes. The cost of buildings has come down and the speed of their development has increased, and the time from deciding to build to opening the accommodation has fallen massively. In the 1970s and 1980s, under the unlamented Property Services Agency, it was commonplace for a decade to pass between deciding to build and commissioning. The current time-scale is closer to two years. There can be little doubt that private sector involvement is one important reason for these outcomes. Similarly, the involvement of private companies in designing jails they themselves will manage has been a spur to innovation. Parc in South Wales, which is run by Securicor, looks like no other prison (which is not to say the design has yet proved successful). Altcourse to the north of Liverpool, which is run by Group 4, is more conventional on the eye, but has many design features reflecting the company's experience in the other prisons it runs under contract.

Nor should anything in this short essay be taken to suggest a lack of interest on the part of penal reformers regarding the basic conditions in prison or the opportunities that they provide for purposeful activity. On the contrary, the decay and decrepitude that characterized so many prisons in England and Wales a decade ago (and which still obtain in several prisons in Scotland) was part of the deficit in 'justice' that Lord Woolf found had given legitimacy to the series of prison riots in 1990 and earlier. The European Prison Rules and our own (regrettably non-statutory) Code of Operating Standards lay down precise minimum entitlements in terms of cell size and access to natural light, work, exercise and so on. These rules and standards represent the essential starting point for all prison design.[7]

Indeed, it is the uses to which buildings are put which penal reformers regard as critical. Taking the prisons around London as an example, we can find some with no workshop places at all and others with state-of-the-art factory equipment that cannot possibly be operated cost effectively. We can find cramped sites which nevertheless maximize the use of the space available, and others with large playing fields and all-weather football pitches that are no longer used because of security fears or staff shortages.

Future directions

I wish to challenge the traditional idea of what constitutes or defines a prison. As we have seen, in practice all sorts of buildings can be converted to penal use. A prison can be a boat, a fort or a stately home (or, in a couple of American examples, a skyscraper). However, in challenging the definition of prison I intend something more fundamental: that prison

6 Cell sizes are far from uniform across the estate as a whole, although there seems to be an implicit maximum. The fact that the cells on HMP Weare are larger than normal – having room for a personal shower cubicle – explains in large part their attraction to prisoners. The cells on the seaward side of the ship are especially sought after.

7 The European Prison Rules are of course advisory only. As Stephen Livingstone and Tim Owen have rather cautiously pointed out, 'legal provisions regarding prison accommodation are somewhat thin' (Livingstone, S. and Owen, T. (1993). *Prison Law: Text and Materials*. Clarendon Press).

does not have to be thought of as a self-contained entity with its own factories, hospital, school, shops, restaurant and church. Instead, a genuinely community prison (a phrase coined by but insufficiently explained in the 1991 Woolf Report) would draw all its support services from outside. It would also encourage prisoners to find work placements or carry out community service tasks outside the prison wall. If this is a realistic model – and it certainly is for almost all women prisoners and young offenders, and for a goodly number of adult men as well – then we can begin to think of prisons as much more hostel-like in size and function. Essentially, they would be like secure residential homes – some, indeed, could operate on therapeutic community principles.

In other words, in planning new prisons we should no longer envisage a 600- or 800-place monster; one that occupies a huge site and is surrounded by a super-secure perimeter wall or walls. That vision of the prison derives from a bureaucratic imperative that jails should be multipurpose and that their function within the total estate can change over time, which necessarily suggests larger prisons with high levels of external security. We should stop thinking big and start thinking small.

It can surely be no coincidence that the best prisons in this country – those with the best staff–prisoner relationships, the best links with their local communities and the best developed regimes – tend to be small in scale. In prisons at least, small does seem to be beautiful. Building small may also be the only way of ensuring that prisoners are held close to their families and close to the community to which they will return. It makes a mockery of the idea of throughcare – of the so-called seamless sentence introduced under the 1991 Criminal Justice Act – if, as now, so many prisoners regain their freedom from prisons perhaps hundreds of miles from their home area.

It is sometimes suggested that replacing large prisons with a constellation of small ones will prove ruinously expensive. There are of course economies of scale in prisons as in everything else, but prison construction and running costs are most closely correlated with security levels, and the community prisons here foreshadowed would require a far lower general level of perimeter security. Moreover, since all prisons should be located in or close to urban areas, a general shortage of brownfield sites of sufficient acreage limits the building of traditional large prisons while allowing the construction of much smaller ones.

One of the rules governing the Prison Service as a so-called Next Steps Agency is that it has to carry out an audit of its assets. However, the value of prisons is very imperfectly captured if we are forced to assume a continuation of their current purpose. The more interesting question is what value the assets would have if they were not deployed as places of incarceration. I have always rather suspected that were the Prison Service to close Holloway, sell the site for redevelopment and use the receipts to provide places for women prisoners in secure, hostel-style accommodation, there would be money left over.[8] Assuming planning

---

8   Since first arguing this case in public, I have learned from a senior Prison Service official that an exercise on exactly this point – the sale and redevelopment value of Holloway – has in fact taken place. It turns out that the value of the site is rather less than I had imagined. However, there is a case for repeating the calculation elsewhere. One candidate might be Feltham, the largest young offenders' institution in the country, a facility that has proved notoriously difficult to manage effectively and in which the treatment of young people has frequently been woeful. Like Holloway, Feltham's very size means it inevitably draws many of its prisoners far from their home areas. It can never be a community prison.

permission, the development value of a prison like Ford would also be enormous. A serious cost–benefit analysis of the provision of smaller and less physically secure hostel-style accommodation versus the traditional model of what constitutes a prison would be welcome.

After size and security, the second criterion for the well-designed prison is the need to provide a proper balance between privacy and safety. More than anything, prison epitomizes Jean-Paul Sartre's dictum *'l'enfer c'est les autres'* (hell is other people). Prisoners need some space they can regard as their own. Amongst other things, given the 'greying' of the prison population, this means designing with the elderly prisoner in mind. Although the prison population in England and Wales is still made up predominantly of people under 30, the pattern is changing and this section of the prison population has dropped by 6.6 per cent since 1990. At the end of October 1997, there were almost 1000 prisoners over the age of 60; the number of prisoners aged 50-plus has increased by more than 1750 over the past eight years. The needs of pensioner prisoners will become increasingly important if, as seems inevitable, the number of life sentence prisoners continues to grow. Pensioner prisoners have no need of workshops or large sports areas, and are unlikely to scale the roof or the wall. On the other hand, they may have limited mobility, be intolerant of noise and make far greater demands on medical services. There are as yet few signs in Britain that the needs of elderly prisoners have been taken on board.

This balance between respect for privacy (a respect no more evident in many prisons' sanitary arrangements, with their lack of screening, than it was in the days of slopping out) and concern for safety is far from easy to achieve. Most prisoners are city-dwellers and cherish the anonymity of the city, but that anonymity also provides opportunities for criminal activity – in prison just as outside. The prison authorities owe a duty of care to both staff and prisoners; the physical environment must be one in which safety is to the fore. Designs should encourage good sightlines and, in the interests of 'dynamic security', the involvement of staff with prisoners. They should acknowledge that prisoners must have opportunities to lead a full and active life by providing sufficient places for work, education, physical education and more psychologically based programmes. They must also provide visual stimulus, not least in areas where prisoners may spend long periods of confinement (such as segregation units) and visit rooms.

There is also room for technological solutions. The installation of closed circuit television cameras in segregation units, staircases and other high-risk locations provides protection for staff and prisoners alike. It is probably no longer possible to walk from one side of central London to the other without being under CCTV observation for 80 or 90 per cent of the time, and there is little, if any, public opposition to such surveillance. Although I have been in prisons where cameras can seem oppressive, this has generally been true of those overlooking the external areas. Used discreetly but not secretly in living areas, CCTV offers real benefits in terms of safety and control in addition to its security role.

Architecture is the most public of the arts, yet prison architecture is, by definition, hidden away from the public. This is not to say that the size and shape of the prison wall has no public purpose. On the contrary, some Victorian inner-city prisons – of which Armley prison in Leeds is one of the best examples – were deliberately located to cast a long penal shadow across the slums of the new urban proletariat. The contemporary featureless concrete wall that surrounds most new prisons – such that from the outside most new British prisons look the same – may suggest, in its totalitarian brutalism, different ideological functions; exclusion, secrecy, nihilism. Indeed, insofar as one can discern a penal idea in the current architectural fashion for large, highly secure and technological institutions, it is in the prison as place of exile; what might be termed the ultimate social exclusion unit, a place of containment without moral purpose for inmates without moral worth. It is an idea captured in such films as *Escape from New York* and *Ghosts . . . of the Civil Dead*.

This notion of a prison without hope is essentially an American one, and it is most readily exemplified in prisons like the federal Supermax at Florence, Colorado. Yet importing American nostrums to the UK is unlikely to be successful, any more than British and American practices play well in Australia. This is one of the most important lessons from the past decade of penal privatization. The companies concerned may believe there is a global market in corrections, but in practice the market is highly segmented, reflecting national, historical and cultural differences. In contrast to the bleak impersonality of the American Supermax prisons, what is needed in Britain are prisons based on the minimum appropriate level of security combined with the maximum community involvement – institutions whose walls are, in the jargon, permeable, and which maximize staff–prisoner interaction; whose values are open, democratic and inclusive.

In the 1840s, Pentonville was considered to represent the acme of prison design; the ideal prison. Although generally sympathetic to new generation designs, the contemporary penal reform movement does not believe in the perfect prison. It asserts that prisons the world over are wasteful, ineffective and cruel, that we have far too many of these benighted institutions, and that many, perhaps most, prisoners could and should be subject to alternative sanctions. But just as in mental health services the fashion is away from large, isolated asylums towards smaller, locally based units of varying degrees of security, so prisons can be re-interpreted to reflect the community prison ideal. Such a shift in approach would also imply a major change in prison design. For once in the penal system, form really would follow function.

Index

Index of Prisons

(Note: except where indicated, these prisons are in England and Wales)